Nationalism, Transnationalism, and Political Islam

Mohanad Hage Ali

Nationalism, Transnationalism, and Political Islam

Hizbullah's Institutional Identity

Mohanad Hage Ali
London, UK

ISBN 978-3-319-86862-2   ISBN 978-3-319-60426-8 (eBook)
DOI 10.1007/978-3-319-60426-8

© The Editor(s) (if applicable) and The Author(s) 2018
Softcover reprint of the hardcover 1st edition 2017
This work is subject to copyright. All rights are solely and exclusively licensed by the Publisher, whether the whole or part of the material is concerned, specifically the rights of translation, reprinting, reuse of illustrations, recitation, broadcasting, reproduction on microfilms or in any other physical way, and transmission or information storage and retrieval, electronic adaptation, computer software, or by similar or dissimilar methodology now known or hereafter developed.
The use of general descriptive names, registered names, trademarks, service marks, etc. in this publication does not imply, even in the absence of a specific statement, that such names are exempt from the relevant protective laws and regulations and therefore free for general use.
The publisher, the authors and the editors are safe to assume that the advice and information in this book are believed to be true and accurate at the date of publication. Neither the publisher nor the authors or the editors give a warranty, express or implied, with respect to the material contained herein or for any errors or omissions that may have been made. The publisher remains neutral with regard to jurisdictional claims in published maps and institutional affiliations.

Cover illustration: © Wael Hamzeh

Printed on acid-free paper

This Palgrave Macmillan imprint is published by Springer Nature
The registered company is Springer International Publishing AG
The registered company address is: Gewerbestrasse 11, 6330 Cham, Switzerland

To Zena, Jad and Julia

Note on Transliteration

The transliteration of Arabic names is based on the International Journal of Middle East Studies (IJMES) simplified system. Commonly used words such as Bekaa are transliterated into Biqaʿ to conform to the IJMES system, and Q is generally used to denote the use of the Arabic *Qaf* letter. The following is a list of recurrent terms in the book:

ʿAbd al-Hussein
al-Daʿwa
ʿAli Ben Abi Taleb
ʿālim (singular), **ʿulamaʾ** (plural)
Al-Manar
ʿAshuraʾ
Hizbullah
Hussein and Husseini (Names)
Imam Husayn (Son of ʿAli)
Jabal ʿAmil, ʿAmili
Khomeini
Masraʿ
Persian (not Farsi)
Qurʾan (ic)
Sayyid
Shebʿa Farms
Shiʿi (singular) and **Shiʿa** (plural)

Umma
Walī
Wilayat al-Faqih
Zuʿama

Acknowledgements

Many people contributed, helped, and supported me in the duration of this work. My supervisors Zhand Shakibi and Steffen Hertog were very helpful and understanding throughout this process, and I am indebted to them for their effort, patience, and support. The Economic and Social Research Council's (ESRC) funding has been essential to the completion of this research; I am grateful for their support.

I want to express my appreciation to many friends and colleagues including Iavor Rangelov, Hazem Ameen, Diana Moukalled, Jamal Boughanem, Hazem Saghieh, Rafle Khoriati, Ali Ali, Navid Nekouei, Isabella Correa, Karabekir Akkoyunlu, Philip Decker, Juergen Braunstein, Pon Souvannaseng, Fabrizio Scrollini, Laura Robbins-Wright, Gustavo Bonifaz, Carolyn Armstrong, Feline Freier, Miran Norderland, Ribale Sleiman Haidar, Mansour Mirza, and, most importantly, Rose Harris.

All these people made this journey meaningful and gratifying.

Contents

1 **Introduction: The Construction of Hizbullah's Identity**   1
   1.1 *Overview*   1
   1.2 *Hizbullah and Identity Construction: Nationalism at Work*   6
   1.3 *Institutionalisation: Identity Dissemination*   11
   1.4 *Nationalism and Religion: Shi'i Nationalists?*   14
   1.5 *Conclusion*   21
   References   24

2 **The Role of Hizbullah's Institutions in the Reconstruction of Shi'i Identity**   27
   2.1 *Institutional Conventions and Rules*   28
   2.2 *Non-State Institutions*   30
   2.3 *The Invention of Tradition: A New Ashura*   31
   2.4 *Redefining Parties: The Party of God vs the Party of Satan*   33
   2.5 *Hizbullah's Organisational Structure: Ancient Islam or Leninism?*   35
   2.6 *The Role of Language, the Media, and Educational Institutions*   44
   2.7 *Al-Jarha (the Foundation of the Wounded)*   51
   2.8 *The Consultative Centre for Studies and Documentation*   56
   2.9 *Conclusion*   57
   References   63

3 The Reconstructed History of the Lebanese Shiʿa — 65
3.1 Writing Lebanese History — 69
3.2 Geography, Economy, and Classes — 73
3.3 The Myth of Shiʿi Origins — 75
3.4 Ottoman Rule: 'Direct' and 'Indirect' Phases — 79
3.5 Arab Nationalism in Jabal ʿAmil — 83
3.6 Conclusion — 88
References — 91

4 Hizbullah's Reconstruction of History — 93
4.1 Source Materials — 94
4.2 Potential Limitations — 95
4.3 Hizbullah's Historians: Inventing Continuity — 95
4.4 Making History: The 'Divine' Continuity — 123
4.5 Conclusion — 126
References — 131

5 The Supernatural in Hizbullah's Identity — 133
5.1 Supernatural Narratives as a Political Tool — 134
5.2 Islam and Supernatural Narratives — 139
5.3 Supernatural Narratives in Hizbullah's Propaganda — 149
5.4 Conclusion — 167
References — 173

6 Transnational *Wilayat Al-Faqih* — 175
6.1 The Clergy and the State — 176
6.2 Internal Shiʿi Tensions — 188
6.3 The Invention of Tradition: 'Two Images of Husayn' — 193
6.4 Transnational and National Shiʿi Tensions — 195
6.5 Conclusion — 210
References — 217

7 Conclusion — 221
References — 232

References — 233

Index — 247

List of Figures

Fig. 2.1	Hizbullah's organisational structure	39
Fig. 2.2	The executive council	40
Fig. 2.3	Regional organisation	41
Fig. 2.4	The hierarchy of the Islamic Institute for Education and Learning	55

CHAPTER 1

Introduction: The Construction of Hizbullah's Identity

1.1 Overview

In the course of Islamic organisations' history, elements of surprise are consistent. These take the form of either a military victory against a formidable foe, such as in the case of Hizbullah against Israel in its 2000 withdrawal and 2006 war, or a sweeping electoral score, as with Egypt's Muslim Brotherhood in 2011–2012 Parliamentary elections. These Islamic groups have gone mainstream, and have demonstrated an ability to effectively mobilise masses in ways that are only reminiscent of the nationalist and Marxist-Leninist era.

For Islamists themselves, this is less surprising. Their work has been generational, focusing on constructing a new identity through social services, religious rituals, education, and scout associations.

Taking Hizbullah, an Islamic Shiʻi movement, as an empirical case study, this book draws on debates in the field of nationalism studies to address the question of how this political organisation's identity is produced and embedded among Lebanese Shiʻa. This entails engaging with three related questions: how modern is Hizbullah; who produces its form of Shiʻi identity; and what are this identity's main pillars? On the basis of a review of the literature, as well as the results of discourse analysis, interpreting the findings from a series of interviews, official and unofficial party publications, and internal notes and memos, the book argues that Hizbullah seeks to embody a reconstructed Lebanese Shiʻi identity. The research has found that Hizbullah continues to deploy the many different institutions it has built over the past two decades in an attempt to replace the traditional form of Lebanese Shiʿi Islam, with its multi-polar authority structure, with another, centralised one, which revolves around the relatively novel concept of *Wilayat al-Faqih* (the 'Guardianship of the Islamic Jurists')—namely, the absolute authority of Iran's Supreme Leader over the Shiʿi 'nation'. Looking at the party's emergence through this lens will enable us to understand its success in mobilising the Shiʿi community.[1]

In examining the subject of collective identity, this book focuses specifically on the elite's role in its production, and adopts Albert Hourani's approach, which distinguishes between race and ethnicity, when defining the Shiʿi ethnic community (Harik 1972, p. 303). Ethnic community members, such as the Lebanese Shiʿa, usually share similar characteristics, such as a distinct language, religion, culture, or historical experience, and are also "conscious of [their community's] difference from other communities" (Harik 1972, p. 303). Hizbullah, an Islamic movement, does not constitute a classic case of nationalism, which is often regarded as primarily secular and ethnic, but is rather what Hourani calls a 'minority nationalism' in the Arab world (Hourani 1947, p. 36). The application of nationalism studies to an analysis of an Islamic movement such as Hizbullah is based on Ernest Gellner's contention that (political) Islam performs nationalist functions. In the contemporary Sunni–Shiʿi schism, this contention applies in the minority context. Phares Walid's work, *Lebanese Christian Nationalism: The Rise and Fall of an Ethnic Resistance* (1995), addresses Lebanon's multi-sectarian identities in a similar fashion: it equates ethnicity, religious ideology, and nationalism. Maya Shatzmiller also conflates these three concepts in her study of Egyptian Copts, *Nationalism and Minority Identities in Islamic Societies* (2005), which applies Anthony Smith's theory of "the potential for an ethnic minority revival".[2] Thus, in the following chapters, any reference to national identity refers to the Lebanese Shiʿi identity rather than to an inclusive Lebanese one.

Mona Harb and Reinoud Leenders point to this subtle differentiating element in Hizbullah's institutional activity; they refer to the "meanings disseminated on a daily basis through the party's policy networks [which] serve to mobilise the Shiʿa constituency into a 'Society of Resistance' in order to consolidate the foundation of an Islamic sphere, *al-hala al-islamiyya*" (Harb and Leenders 2005, p. 174). This 'Islamic sphere' symbolises the desired result of the consolidation of Hizbullah's reconstruction of Shiʿi identity in the Lebanese Shiʿi community. Applying Smith's and Gellner's observations on political Islam, this book contends that

Hizbullah's functions and goals, particularly in relation to its construction of a national identity and its aspiration to create a Lebanese Shiʻi 'nation', are synonymous with those of nationalism. Hizbullah is producing a new Shiʻi identity within the context of Lebanon's consociational system (in which the state encompasses different sectarian identities), setting the scene for a leading Shiʻi role, possibly similar to the Christian Maronite's dominant status prior to the country's civil war.[3] By using Hizbullah as a case study, this book aims to contribute to the debates on religion and nationalism by demonstrating that religious movements, particularly Islamist ones, can perform functions similar to nationalist groups. It rejects the contention that Hizbullah's engagement in the Lebanese political system marks a shift in its ideology; it argues rather that the party's ideological discourse remains committed to the concept of *Wilayat al-Faqih*, which is significant on a practical level in mobilising the Lebanese Shiʻa under Hizbullah leadership, using religious pretexts for the organisation's role.[4] The book maintains, moreover, that Hizbullah's increased participation in the political process is focused on protecting its military arsenal and its autonomous institutions, or what is known in contemporary Lebanese political discourse as Hizbullah's position in Lebanon as a 'state within a state'.[5] Unlike Hamas, however, Hizbullah's pan-Islamic ideology is strictly hierarchical and institutionalised.

The fieldwork for this book entailed observing the works of Hizbullah's institutions in the southern suburbs of Beirut, and interviewing directors. Given the scope of the work, the methodology linking the theoretical to the empirical is based on selective sampling. Since such research in the highly secure institutions remains largely restricted, a senior official, whom I have known for years, provided access to these institutions. However, the series of suicide bombings, which targeted the area since 19 November 2013, slowed my access. At these institutions, I interviewed directors, employees, and beneficiaries. In the southern suburbs of Beirut, I spent time at affiliated publishing houses and bookstores, searching for books and enquiring about the demand on certain publications, such as those with a special emphasis on the supernatural. The organisation's security presence in these areas was very apparent, with visible guards and plain-clothes militants on watch. During the last year of the research, I travelled to Tehran, where I tried to collect data on Hizbullah's lobbying efforts among the ruling elites. While Hizbullah's office in Northern Tehran was not accessible, I interviewed several individuals who had affirmed my observations of the organisation's lobbying efforts.

This introductory chapter reviews the major studies on Hizbullah and analyses the main approaches and debates in the field of nationalism that are pertinent to the topic in order to clarify the research question. This is based on the contention that although Hizbullah does not constitute a classic case of nationalism, the field's debates remain relevant to the party's primary function in society: that of creating a new Lebanese Shiʿi identity. This chapter highlights the limitations of the traditional ways of studying this Shiʿi organisation and argues the need to distinguish between two types of Hizbullah discourse: the political, which is targeted at a non-Shiʿi audience, and the internal, ideological discourse, whose audience comprises the party's followers and the Lebanese Shiʿa.

The second chapter looks at the institutionalisation of Hizbullah—that is, its creation of a network of institutions, which include media, education, and research, in order to organise its identity dissemination and the production of its rhetoric. The chapter demonstrates how the organisation has reproduced its identity in forms that are tailored to different audiences—for example, children in early education, scouts, university students, or the injured and the families of 'martyrs'. Although Hizbullah claims that its organisational structure is based on the 'Islamic principle' of *al-taʿbiʾa* literally translated into reserves, but implying mobilization, Marxist–Leninist influences are evident, whether in its internal general conferences or its local branches and politburo-like leading *Shura* committee. A review of both the Leninist party model and Hizbullah's structure renders these similarities apparent. For instance, the significant role publishing has in the organisation suggests Leninist influences, an assumption that is corroborated by a founding member of Hizbullah.

The third chapter provides an overview of a pre-Hizbullah construction of Lebanese Shiʿi history. The chapter argues that Muhammad Jaber Al Safa, a Lebanese Shiʿi intellectual, created historical narratives of Jabal ʿAmil, coining terms such as the 'ʿAmili people', and 'ʿAmili resistance', and, in so doing, established the foundations for Hizbullah's reconstructed historical narrative. By exploring Jaber's main historical constructions, and their relevance to Hizbullah's later narratives, myths, and symbols, the chapter complements Chap. 4's analysis of the organisation's historical narratives. Meanwhile, the fourth chapter sheds light on the constructed historical symbols in Hizbullah's narratives and/or rhetoric, and draws an analogy between the competing narratives of traditional Shiʿi historians, such as Jaber, and those of Hizbullah's intellectuals and polemicists. Both the third and fourth chapters illuminate the extent of Hizbullah's reconstruction of history, specifically the scale of invention in the organisation's historical narratives. The fourth chapter argues that these narratives are uncorroborated, and are based, for the most part, on Jaber's equally unsubstantiated 'oral sources' and narratives. In terms of the general argument of this book, these two chapters highlight the relevance of the debates in nationalism studies to an analysis of Hizbullah. The organisation, in its rhetoric and through its affiliated 'intellectual brokers', has engaged in a process that Smith, referring to nationalism, dubs 'reappropriation' or "reaching back into the ethnic past to the national present". Hizbullah's intellectuals, like nationalist intelligentsias, could be seen as "political archaeologists who aim, not to return to the past, but to recover its pristine ethos and reconstruct a modern nation in the image of the past ethnie" (Smith 1999, p. 25)

The fifth chapter examines the role of supernatural religious narratives in Hizbullah's Shi'i identity, arguing that the organisation takes a modern approach in terms of their use and in the extent of their dissemination. These narratives provide a link between Hizbullah's hierarchy and its military activity and the divine, and are intended to contribute towards building a more amenable (and credulous) base of members and followers. The chapter explores the earlier deployment of supernatural narratives—religious stories or simply 'superstitious' tales—for the purposes of political legitimacy; however, it argues that Hizbullah's use of such narratives is modern in both approach and scale.

The sixth chapter reviews the development of the *Wilayat al-Faqih* doctrine, central to Hizbullah's identity, and traces the experiences of different Shi'i groups with the same ideology. This comparative approach raises questions about the supposedly transnational nature of the organisation's identity project, as the varied experiences suggest that tensions frequently emerge between the ideology, *Wilayat al-Faqih*, and Iranian state interests, specifically when these clash with its sponsored Shi'i groups' internal politics. The case of Afghanistan's Hazara Khomeinists best illustrates the importance of these tensions in overshadowing ideology. The chapter puts Hizbullah's experience in perspective, arguing that the organisation's lobbying efforts in Iran, as well as Lebanon's specific geopolitical conditions, undermine the party's claim to embody a transnational ideology. In Iran's neighbouring states, such as Afghanistan, Iranian *realpolitik* rapidly undermines the supposed ideological transnational links when Tehran's interests are opposed to those of the local Shi'i groups.

This book aspires to contribute to the study of Islamic groups, through applying the optic of nationalism. By the same token, Hizbullah's reconstruction of identity itself highlights the high level of replicating nationalism's functions in a sectarian context. Although the research is specific to the relationship between Hizbullah and the Lebanese Shiʿi groups, the group has features that are similar to those of various other Islamic organisations, and the findings of this research could be applicable to a wider range of studies.

Two main approaches dominate the study of Hizbullah. Researchers in the field either gloss over the issue of Hizbullah's identity or argue that the party's engagement in the Lebanese political process has had a transformative effect, converting it from a transnational organisation to a nationally focused one. The origin of these approaches can be traced in the mainstream media and in US official discourse on al-Qaeda, especially in relation to the use of the 'terrorist' label, but can also be found in assumptions based on the organisation's increased participation in the political process. Studies of the organisation focused either on reinforcing the claim that Hizbullah is a terrorist label or on refuting it, also use the argument that Hizbullah's engagement in the Lebanese political system signals a shift in identity. This book argues that choosing an approach as a reaction to US policy and rhetoric, glosses over the significance of the organisation's identity project, which constitutes a continuation of colonial policies, as will be outlined in Chap. 3.

1.2 Hizbullah and Identity Construction: Nationalism at Work

This book argues that dominant approaches to the study of Hizbullah fall short of capturing the organisation's extensive work disseminating its sectarian Shiʿi identity through its centralised network of institutions; nation-building and identity construction are essential to the organisation's activities in the Shiʿi community in Lebanon. Central to this book is the metamorphosis of Lebanese Shiʿi identity since its early formation. According to Max Weiss (2010), a new sense of a collective confessional identity began to develop under twentieth-century French colonialism, a process discussed in Chap. 3. While Weiss demonstrates that it was the colonial institutionalisation of religious courts that gave birth to a Lebanese Shiʿi identity, it only manifested itself politically in the 1960s (more than two decades after the country's independence) under the leadership of Sayyid Musa Sadr, an Iranian born cleric.

Before Sadr's entry onto the scene, the political representation of the Lebanese Shiʿi was restricted to local and feudal leaders. The reason for the Shiʿi community's lack of political power—in comparison to the more established confessional communities such as the Sunnis, Druze, and Maronites—lies in Ottoman policies prior to the French Mandate in 1920. Unlike these other confessional communities, which were recognised by the Sunni Ottoman state, the Shiʿa were denied an official identity either as a community or as a distinct religious sect (El-Khazen 2000, p. 40). Lebanon's Shiʿa were "hated by the (Shiʿi) Persians as Arabs, and by Turks and Arabs as Shiʿa", observed David Urquhart, a nineteenth-century British traveller (cited in El-Khazen 2000, p. 40). As a consequence, the Shiʿi community did not develop a political agenda following the downfall of the Ottoman Empire in the same way as the Maronites and Sunnis. Local Shiʿi leaders in South Lebanon and the Biqaʿ Valley lent their support to the establishment of the new Lebanese state in 1920, and the community's identification with the state was strengthened following the recognition of Shiʿi jurisprudence (*jaʿfari*) in the community's personal affairs in 1926. This state recognition was translated into an autonomous religious status vis-à-vis the Sunni community (El-Khazen 2000, p. 41). While this new status meant the Shiʿa had a guaranteed share in the Lebanese confessionally based state system, it did not have the effect of politicising the community because it lacked the educational and social institutions of the other religious communities. The 1932 census showed that the Shiʿi had the highest illiteracy rate in Lebanon, at 83 per cent, followed by the Sunni (66 per cent), Druze (53 per cent), Greek Orthodox (53 per cent), Maronite (48 per cent), and Greek Catholic (39 per cent) communities (El-Khazen 2000, p. 65). The politicisation of the Shiʿi community only started with their urbanisation during the 1960s, largely due to the "gap that separated the traditional Shiʿi leadership from the masses on the political, social and economic levels" (El-Khazen 2000, p. 43). El-Khazen avers that "a new generation of educated and politically ambitious Shiʿa found themselves little represented by the traditional leadership in the South and the Biqaʿ" (El-Khazen 2000, p. 43). This gap paved the way for a more radical kind of politics—it was a path that led to the civil war and the rise of the Amal Movement, and, in its later stages, to Hizbullah. Compared to the other politically well-established confessional communities, the Shiʿa belatedly witnessed communal mobilisation in an era that was undergoing destabilising regional and internal changes (El-Khazen 2000, p. 45).

The growth of Shiʿi activism in the 1960s arose from the same social, economic, and political conditions as that of other radical and populist movements in the Global South (Saad-Ghorayeb 2002, p. 7). During the decade prior to this awakening of political consciousness, the Shiʿi population witnessed a period of disruptive mass urbanisation, impelled by the extreme economic deprivation of the population in South Lebanon and the western Biqaʿ Valley. Preceding the Lebanese civil war in 1975, many Shiʿa identified themselves with parties of the left, particularly the Lebanese Communist Party and the Organisation of Communist Action, whose members were predominantly Shiʿa. Their political activism had no affiliation whatsoever with Shiʿi doctrines; rather, it was governed by the secular and socio-economic contexts. This secular leaning might be explained by the fact that "communally generated mechanisms of change were obstructed partly because of the deeply-rooted and static power structure" (El-Khazen 2000, p. 43). The Lebanese political system, which was mainly dominated by the Christian and Sunni communities, did not serve the Shiʿa well: they were under-represented in parliament, the civil service, and the government. The National Pact, known as *Al-Mithaq Al-Watani*, had distributed public positions based on the 1932 census, and "this had the effect of delegitimizing the state and alienating the great majority of Shiites" (Saad-Ghorayeb 2002, p. 7). The Lebanese legal system, meanwhile, empowered the state's constituent sects by enforcing the authority of religious courts in personal affairs relating to marriage, divorce, and inheritance. However, while the 1932 census showed a Christian majority, a recent demographic study by Statistics Lebanon, a Beirut-based research firm, has concluded that Shiʿa constitute 28 per cent of the population—this is only matched by Sunni Muslims (28 per cent) and is followed by the Maronite Christians (22 per cent), Greek Orthodox (8 per cent), Druze (5 per cent), and Greek Catholics (4 per cent).[6]

Imam Sadr provided the Shiʿi community with a sectarian alternative to the secular political movements; he sought to give them an autonomous status, away from Sunni political and religious dominance (El-Khazen 2000, p. 43). Sadr established the Supreme Islamic Shiʿa Council (SISC), which became operational in 1969, and Amal or 'Harakat al-Mahromeen' ('The Movement of the Deprived') in 1974. His personal qualities and attributes provided an opportunity for sectarian mobilisation of the Lebanese Shi'a:

> The arrival of Musa Sadr as Mufti of Tyre in 1959 introduced to Shi'ite and Lebanese politics a leader who combined the attributes and skills needed to mobilize the mass of Shiites on a sectarian basis; and by doing this, to shake the Lebanese political system. He was a cleric, and profoundly Shi'ite Muslim in orientation, but he also widely read, understood the appeal of modern ideas and could handle their challenge. His unusual qualities and the timing of his arrival—at the beginning of Chehab's presidency, just after the Muslim uprising of 1958 (during which the Biqa' Shi'ites had taken up arms against the government)—combined to ensure that he immediately found his way into the Lebanese establishment. (Sayigh 2015, p. 208)

Following his disappearance in 1978, Sadr's movement gained increasing popularity amongst the Lebanese Shi'a.[7] While the civil war took its toll in terms of Shi'i radicalisation, especially after the eviction of 100,000 Shi'a from Nab'a in August 1976, the two Israeli invasions in 1978 and 1982 were the most devastating in their effect on the Shi'i civilian population: the 1982 invasion caused damage to 80 per cent of the villages in Southern Lebanon, and left 19,000 dead and 32,000 injured (Alexander and Bogdanor 2006, p. 109). Geographically located on the borders of northern Palestine, the Lebanese Shi'a bore the brunt of Israeli reprisals against the Palestinian resistance based in Lebanon. The Palestinian Liberation Organisation (PLO) played a significant role in polarising Shi'i politics by training Amal fighters, and helped turn South Lebanon into an open battlefield (El-Khazen 2000, p. 44).

After Israel's invasion, regional politics played an increasingly significant role in Shi'i politics; Iran dispatched 1,500 revolutionary guards to the Biqa' Valley to train Shi'i militants in the fight against the occupation. The Iranian efforts to export Ayatollah Khomeini's pan-Shi'i revolutionary ideology bore fruit following a schism within the Amal movement. Amal's religious members, including Hassan Nasrallah (later to be Hizbullah's secretary general), left its ranks after its leader Nabih Berri's decision to join the National Salvation Committee, which was formed by the-then Lebanese President Elias Sarkis to replace PLO fighters with the Lebanese army in West Beirut. This move was considered by Amal's ideologues to be part of a CIA plot. The split paved the way for the establishment of several smaller Shi'i movements such as Islamic Amal, led by

Hussein Moussawi, dedicated to opposing the Israeli occupation. Hizbullah's creation at first took the form of an umbrella group for these organisations. Nasrallah summarised the situation in a 1986 interview:

> The movement [Amal] had considerable political appeal ... I and many of my colleagues in Hizbullah were members of Amal before the Israeli invasion. The political issue surfaced after the disappearance of Mousa al-Sadr, due to a difference in vision, work, and other elements; but the problem remained confined to Amal and the Moslem scene until the invasion of 1982. This changed everything, and all the political movements became simple zeros in the face of the very challenging Israeli numbers. Iranian revolutionary guards arrived in the Beqa upon the orders of Imam al-Khomeini, and the faithful were of the opinion that a revolutionary and Islamist current should be established ... to have a clear Islamist political vision, and operate through a consistent ideology based on the principles and political line of Imam al-Khomeini, and according to the principle of *wilayat al-faqih* in which we believe. This is how Hizbullah came to be. (Nasrallah cited in Noe 2007, p. 26)

Wilayat al-Faqih, mentioned by Nasrallah as the basis for establishing Hizbullah, was a novel concept in Shi'i thought, formulated by Ayatollah Khomeini during his exile in Najaf in Iraq in 1970. Khomeini presented the foundations of this concept in 16 lectures, which later became his landmark book on Islamic governance, *Al-Hukumah al-Islamiyyah (The Islamic Government)*. The traditional Shi'i clergy in Iraq rejected Khomeini's concept, and copies of his book were thrown down into the wells and into the Euphrates; however, he managed to smuggle some copies into Iran (Koya 2009, p. 88). Khomeini was heavily criticised in the ensuing backlash against his ideas: according to Koya, "these people [the traditional clerics] believed conclusively that the Shah and Saddam should rule, and not an *imam* and a *mujtahid* fulfilling all the conditions. They used to say that government is no business of the *faqih*" (Koya 2009, p. 88). In *Al-Hukumah al-Islamiyyah*, Khomeini argued "the jurist-consults (*Wali Al-Faqih*) are the successors of the prophets including the Prophet of Islam (peace and blessing of Allah be on him) and all the messengers of Allah who were given the mandate of absolute leadership among their respective nations" (cited in Al-Katib 1997, p. 381). Khomeini was looking for "an institutionalised leadership" similar to "the conventional chieftaincy and other acceptable systems of government, such as the 'vicegerent' which Allah designated to David ... and also like the Prophet's designation of Ali, by Allah's instruction as ... a leader for the Ummah", and he concluded that "this is something that must inevitably be transferable and inheritable" (Al-Katib 1997, p. 381). Khomeini's frustration with the lack of much needed leadership for the political mobilisation of Shiʿi Muslims strongly influenced his theory of absolute governance. As al-Katib accurately notes, "none of the proponents of *Wilayat al-Faqih* had claimed authenticity for those narrations cited in support of this theory"; they had instead relied on "rational argument and the argument that there cannot be a government without a head or leader" (Al-Katib 1997, p. 391). This contention was grounded on the principle that Allah appointed the Prophet Muhammad and the Twelve Shiʿi Imams as the absolute rulers of their followers, and thus it was only logical that the jurist best known for certitude would be eligible to assume absolute, prophet-like leadership. This concept was introduced into mainstream Shiʿism in Iran following Khomeini's advent to power.

Hizbullah performed the same function, bringing this particular political/religious tenet into the mainstream Shiʿi faith in Lebanon, and hence establishing it as a defining concept of the Lebanese Shiʿi confessional identity. In the spirit of Khomeini's 1970 Najaf lectures, Nasrallah noted in a 2011 lecture on *Wilayat al-Faqih* that the *Faqih*, currently the Islamic Republic of Iran's Supreme Leader Ali Khamenei, "inherits the same authority bestowed upon the great Prophet and infallible Imams" (cited in Abna 2011).[8] Naʿim Qassem, Hizbullah's deputy secretary general, put forward the same argument in his 2005 book, stating "the Jurist-Theologian's authority thus represents a continuation of that of the Prophet and the infallible Imams" (Qassem 2005, p. 53). As in Iraq and Iran, however, the concept met resistance from local clergy in Lebanon, specifically the Shiʿi cleric Ayatollah Mohamad Hussein Fadlallah, who protested against the *Faqih*'s wide powers.

1.3   INSTITUTIONALISATION: IDENTITY DISSEMINATION

Despite this initial opposition, however, during the following two decades, the party expanded by creating around a dozen institutions covering a wide range of social services, while simultaneously launching a successful popular armed resistance against Israeli occupation, which culminated in the Israeli withdrawal from South Lebanon on 25 May 2000.[9] The institutions it established operate "as holistic and integrated networks which produce sets of meanings embedded in an interrelated religious and political framework" (Harb and Leenders 2005, p. 174). These networks' daily activities are aimed at mobilising the Lebanese Shiʻi community as a so-called society of resistance within a larger pool of committed followers—*al-hala al-Islamiyya* (an Islamic sphere). The wide variety of institutions and their various functions drew accusations from Hizbullah's adversaries that it was seeking to build a 'state within a state' in order to govern an autonomous Shiʻi community. Among the institutions are the following foundations: al-Shaheed (the 'martyrs'), which caters for more than 3,500 relatives of those killed in the war; al-Jareeh (the wounded); al-Muʾassasa al-Tarbawiyya, an educational institute which manages nine schools with 5,300 students; al-Qard al-Hassan (the 'good' loan), providing micro-credit for thousands of its followers; al-Imdad ('help'), which aids the poor; al-Hayaʾa al-Suhiyya (Islamic Health Committee), which runs more than 50 medical centres and three major hospitals, caring for 283,000 patients in 1995; Jihad al-Binaʾ ('the *jihad* for construction'), which specialises in rebuilding and development efforts; and a think tank called the 'Consultative Centre for Studies and Documentation' (Harb and Leenders 2005, p. 175). Some of these institutions were initially established as extensions or direct copies of Iran's post-revolution state-run institutions, such as its Imdad and Shahid foundations. However, as Chap. 2 argues, these foundations, while maintaining their connection to Iran, now create messages tailored specifically for their own beneficiaries, focusing on local manifestations of the transnational elements of Shiʻi identity, such as the doctrine of *Wilayat al-Faqih*. As such, Hizbullah's version of *Wilayat al-Faqih* has come to reside more in the party's hierarchy, the representation of the concept in Lebanon, than directly in the Iranian Supreme Leader himself.

According to its statements, the organisation's cultural policies have been focused on producing a new identity for the Shiʻi community in Lebanon. This is very clear in Hizbullah's narratives about its institutional goals. For instance, regarding the role of its educational institutes, Hizbullah states:

> The specificity of the Islamic Institute's schools is their particular spirit (*ruhiya khassa*) and their ambiance (*jaww*), which produce mobilization through all the studied topics. We want to disseminate the culture of religious commitment (*iltizam*). We insist on culture, because this is what makes identity. Resistance is not an aim, it is the result of a culture. (Hizbullah cited in Harb and Leenders 2005, p. 190)

In their speeches, the party's leaders reiterate the importance of the 'Islamic nation' and the Qurʾanic verse "you [Muslims] were the best nation evolved for mankind" (Imran, p. 110); while this verse appears to be inclusive of all those of the Muslim faith, the term in effect refers to Hizbullah's Lebanese Shiʿi supporters, whom Nasrallah called *'Ashraf Al-Nass'* ('the Most Honorable') in a 2006 speech. There are many references to the 'nation of Hizbullah' or *'Ummat Hizbullah'*, a concept discussed by the Shiʿi cleric Mohammad Hussein Fadlallah, who once claimed to be a member of Hizbullah's 'nation', although he does not have an organisational relationship with the party (Sankari 2005, p. 512).

The organisation's rhetoric on *Wilayat al-Faqih*, therefore, is intended in practice to confirm its own hierarchy's legitimacy; the continuous affirmations of the concept accentuate the party leadership's sacred authority. In a 1986 interview, Nasrallah noted "from the point of view of ideology and *Sharia*, we are required to establish God's rule over any part of this earth, regardless of the particularities and details" (cited in Noe 2007, p. 32). But Nasrallah, still a rising official in Hizbullah at the time of this quotation, acknowledges the tension between belief and practice, stating, "this can only happen if the nation adopts this ideology and safeguards it" (Noe 2007, p. 32). Although this might imply that Lebanon's diversity precludes the enforcement of *shariʿa* law, Nasrallah clarifies that "we [Hizbullah] do not believe in a multiple Islamic republic; we do believe, however, in a single Islamic world governed by a central government" (Noe 2007, p. 32). For Nasrallah, "all the borders throughout the Muslim world" are "fake and colonialist" (Noe 2007, p. 32). Despite the party's participation in the Lebanese parliament from 1992 onwards, Nasrallah's views on *Wilayat al-Faqih's* cross-border jurisdiction has remained unshaken: for example, in 1993, he declared that Hizbullah's relationship with Iran is with "the Supreme Leader who draws general policy lines not only for Hizbullah but for the nation as a whole, of which Hizbullah is only a part" (Noe 2007, p. 135). In practice, the organisation focuses on transforming Lebanese Shiʿi identity through maintaining a parallel state while participating in the national government.

Following the extreme polarisation of Lebanese politics after the assassination of the former Sunni Prime Minister Rafiq Hariri in Beirut in 2005, Hizbullah surprised many by its ability to rapidly mobilise hundreds of thousands of Shiʿi supporters. Israel's devastating 34-day war in 2006, which left 1,200 Lebanese citizens dead, the vast majority of whom were

Shiʿa, left Hizbullah's popularity among the Shiʿi community members not only intact but greatly increased.[10] The organisation indirectly, by using its affiliated publishing houses, embarked on the dissemination of supernatural narratives about the 2006 conflict, claiming a link between its fighters and divine forces.[11]

The most significant dilemma for advocates of the 'Lebanonisation' argument, however, presented itself on 7 May 2008 when, as mentioned earlier, Hizbullah's military arm took control of the capital, Beirut, after the central government moved against Hizbullah's control of the city's telephone network and airport security. The reasoning behind Hizbullah's military attack was based on protection of its 'weapons of resistance'. Nasrallah stated on the 8 May: "I had said that we will cut the hand that targets the weapons of the resistance … Today is the day to fulfill this decision" (Macleod 2008).[12] Hizbullah's military incursion came as an affirmation of the organisation's statements that its engagement in the political process serves its resistance against Israeli aggression.

1.4 Nationalism and Religion: Shiʿi Nationalists?

The predominantly secular character of European nationalism should not preclude the use of theoretical tools from the field of nationalism studies to develop a better understanding of the rise of Islamic movements—this is especially so in Lebanon, where analysis of what has been termed Christian 'ethno-nationalism' has drawn on the debates around nationalism.[13] In the Middle East, as in the West, the revolution in mass communications has aroused and stimulated ethnic consciousness, which has resulted in the emergence of nationalism, "whereby the ethnic group is called a nation and ethnic sentiment of unity is called nationalism" (Harik 1972, p. 309). In Lebanon's case, according to Harik, where ethnic loyalty has been distributed among the constituent confessional groups or 'nations', the source of legitimate authority in this communal system "was the nation—the symbol of solidarity, collective identity, and sentiment of the ethnic group" (Harik 1972, p. 309). Looking at Hizbullah through the lens of nationalism means engaging in the debate on nationalism's relationship to religion and ethnicity—Smith, for example, raises questions about the rise of fundamentalist movements in relation to nationalism, while Gellner notes that Islam performs nationalist functions. A review of these debates is crucial to underlining the relevance of the approach this book takes in its analysis of Hizbullah's constructed sectarian Shiʻi identity.

1.4.1 Definitions

From the first, nationalism has been a much-debated and often polarising concept. The primordial, perennialist, and modernist schools all have their own definitions of the concept, based on their view as to its genesis. Anthony Smith, one of the leading scholars in the field, offers a working definition, which encompasses most of the prevalent schools of thought on nationalism. According to Smith, nationalism is "an ideological movement for the attainment and maintenance of autonomy, unity, and identity on behalf of a population, some of whose members deem it to constitute an actual or potential nation" (Smith 2003, p. 24). He further states that the main ideals and goals of nationalist movements are "national autonomy, national unity, and national identity", and along with 'authenticity', these "furnish the main concepts of the language or discourse of nationalism" (Smith 2003, p. 24). The nation itself is a "named human population occupying a historic territory and sharing common myths and memories, a public culture, and common laws and customs for all members", while national identity is "the maintenance and continual reinterpretation of the pattern of values, symbols, memories, myths, and traditions that form the distinctive heritage of the nation and the identification of individuals with that heritage and its pattern" (Smith 2003, p. 245).

Hizbullah is an ideological movement that seeks the goals mentioned in Smith's definition of nationalism on behalf of the 'Islamic (Lebanese Shiʻi) nation'. The definition of national identity offered by Smith has particular importance for this book, which looks at Hizbullah's reinterpretation of Shiʻi 'values, symbols, memories, myths and traditions'. The application of the concept 'sectarian nationalism' to modern Lebanese politics (which is based on a power-sharing consociational system) offers a description of the way sectarian groups strive to acquire more power and control within the nation. As such, lacking a majority ethnic base within the overall Lebanese population, Hizbullah's goal in practice entails both taking more control within the state and achieving Shiʻi unity under its leadership, with the Shiʻi community gradually conforming to the organisation's expression of Shiʻi identity.

1.4.2 Nationalism and Religious Movements

While the relation between religion and nationalism is ambivalent due to the polarised debate over the extent of nationalism's modernity, both the modernist camp (Gellner) and the ethnosymbolists (Smith) have often adopted inclusive approaches when looking at the issue of Islamic movements and 'sectarian nationalism'. Having said this, Elie Kedourie, who produced one of the classic texts on nationalism, places himself firmly on the far side of the spectrum by insisting on the essentially secular nature of nationalism, defining it as "a modern, secular ideology that replaces the religious systems found in pre-modern, traditional societies" (Smith 2003, p. 9). Kedourie encapsulates this Eurocentric modernist argument in the opening sentence of his book, *Nationalism*: "Nationalism is a doctrine invented in Europe at the beginning of the nineteenth century" (Kedourie 1970, p. 1).

Gellner, on the other hand, while confirming the secular identity of European nationalism, allows for exceptions in the Muslim world. His contention that "[n]ationalism can serve as an instrument of industrialization" finds an exception in Islam; he concedes that Islam serves as the "functional equivalent of nationalism in a way which has not been possible for Christianity", and that his industrialisation theory therefore does not apply (Gellner 1994, p. xxv). Islamist groups, like Hizbullah, share many of the characteristics of the historical (secular) nationalist movements of the West: they delve into history for symbols and heroes, as Smith states, but are capable of the wide mobilisation of these historical resources through modern means, such as the use of mass media. The organisation's reconstruction of Lebanese Shi'i history, discussed at length in Chap. 4, bears many similarities to the activities of European nationalism's intellectual brokers.

Smith, while not a modernist, acknowledges the increasing significance of religious movements in his 2003 book, *Chosen Peoples: Sacred Sources of National Identity*, and their relevance to the study of nationalism. He first narrates the prevalent modernist arguments on the relation between religion and nationalism, and then pinpoints the often ambivalent and conflicting theories on the subject. In the conventional distinction between tradition and modernity, "religion and nationalism figure as two terms" (Smith 2003, p. 9). For the modernists, "religion and the sacred have little or no role in the study of nationalism or the analysis of nations; just as they have none in nationalist ideology or national identity itself". Smith notes that the modernists have a twofold reason for this: "[o]n the one hand, nationalism is a secular category; it is one of several post-enlightenment ideologies that oppose human autonomy to divine control, and seek salvation in human auto-emancipation"; on the other, religion is regarded by modernists as "a declining phenomenon and a residual category ... part of that 'traditional society' from which the transition to modernity began and nations later emerged" (Smith 2003, p. 10). Smith relates that for Eric Hobsbawm, John Breuilly, and Michael Mann, the state and social groups "occupy centre stage, while ethnicity and religious tradition are accorded secondary roles" (Smith 2003, p. 10). In all of these theories, nationalism is presented as "wholly recent and novel phenomena, and a secular, anthropocentric, and anticlerical modernity is always counterposed to tradition and traditional society with its emphasis on custom and religion" (Smith 2003, p. 10). However, Smith argues that Kedourie brought religion back into the nationalism debate with his work, *Nationalism in Asia and Africa*. While he sought ways to demonstrate both the adaptation and imitation of European nationalism in Africa, Kedourie conceded that nationalists in these two continents "found that they could also arouse the emotions of the masses by treating traditional prophets like Moses or Muhammad as national heroes and turning religious feasts into national festivals ... nationalism often became an ally, albeit a false one, of religion" (Smith 2003, p. 12). This acknowledgement, nevertheless, remains restricted to the use of sacred symbols by a generally secular movement. By contrast, Gellner later recognised at a much more fundamental level the capacity of Islamic organisations to perform the functions of nationalism.

However, Kedourie's description of nationalism bears many similarities to that of Islamic organisations, particularly Hizbullah. Smith describes the three main positions of Kedourie's modernist approach: the first is the 'secular replacement' view, which holds that "a secular revolutionary nationalism progressively replaces religion in the modernist epoch"; the second is the 'neotraditional' view that religion is "a possible ally and support for nationalism"; and the third sees nationalism as "a secular version of millennial political religion" (Smith 2003, p. 13). This model "depicts nationalism as a new ersatz and heterodox religion, opposed to conventional, traditional religions, yet inheriting many of their features—symbols, liturgies, rituals and messianic fervor—which now come to possess new and subversive political and national meanings" (Smith 2003, p. 13). This description is a very fitting one of Hizbullah's invention of a new set of politically charged *Ashura* rituals, as well as its reconstruction of ancient symbols and the messianic fervour associated with many of its festivals and commemorations, reinforced by the dissemination of supernatural narratives. Although Kedourie fails to acknowledge the applicability of his theory to Islamic organisations, Smith's analysis of his work highlights the link. According to Smith, these Kedourie 'models' have recently been reinforced by two further arguments: "[t]he first stems from the observation of the renaissance of 'religious nationalisms'—nationalisms that are specifically religious in form and in content—in the last decades of the twentieth century, and not just in the Islamic lands" (Smith 2003, p. 13).

Such associations between nationalism and Islamic movements have taken root in nationalism studies. Mark Juergensmeyer in *The New Cold War? Religious Nationalism Confronts the Secular State* (1993) rejects the term 'fundamentalism' due to its negative connotations in the West, and instead considers Islamists as 'religious nationalists'. He identifies a convergence between nationalist and religious movements as "increasingly religious identities and ideologies have become the basis for strident new forms of nationalism and transnationalism in a globalized, post-modern world" (Juergensmeyer in Delanty, G., & Kumar, K. 2006, p. 182). However, his observations are limited to homogeneous Muslim states and do not touch upon movements in multi-confessional or multi-sectarian contexts. For instance, he finds common elements in the statements of all fundamentalist groups in the Middle East and Asia, including criticisms of secular nationalism, including its characterisation as a 'Western intrusion' with universalist tendencies and an intolerance of religion. Gerard Delanty and Krishnan Kumar distinguish between two forms of religious nationalisms: ethnic and ideological. However, this book, taking Hizbullah as its case study, looks at religious nationalism, 'sectarian nationalism', within a multi-ethnic (confessional) context (Delanty and Kumar 2006, pp. 183–184).

1.4.3 *Ethnosymbolism*

This book aims to contribute to the ethnosymbolist–modernist debate on nationalism and the extent to which national identity is a modern construct. Smith's criticisms of Kedourie's theory on the invention of the concept of the nation were aimed at building an ethnosymbolist argument in order to "afford deeper insights into the ways in which religious and nationalist cultures underpin and reinforce each other to produce the often powerful national identities that command so much loyalty among so many people in the modern world" (Smith 2003, p. 17). Smith's approach focuses on the cultural resources of ethnic symbols, memory, myth, value, and tradition, and "their expressions in texts and artifacts—scriptures, chronicles, epics, music, architecture, painting, sculpture, crafts, and other media". Ethnosymbolism attempts to uncover what its founders call "the fundamental sacred sources of national identity and nationalism", especially as Smith considers nationalism to be a form of culture or type of belief system "whose object is the nation conceived as a sacred communion" (Smith 2003, p. 18).

Ethnosymbolism claims that nationalism draws its symbols and myths from a pre-existing sense of ethnic national consciousness. However, as outlined in later chapters, Hizbullah's reconstruction of Lebanese Shiʻi history is based on a pan-Arab nationalist reconstruction from the late nineteenth and early twentieth centuries, which was itself a result of largely uncorroborated work.[14] An example of this exercise is the book, *The Historic Roots of the Islamic Resistance in Lebanon*, written by Hizbullah activist Mohamad Kourani, and published by Dar Al-Waseela, a Hizbullah-affiliated publishing house, in 1993. This work delves deep into Lebanese history to find often uncorroborated instances of clashes or tensions between Shiʻa on the one hand, and Christians, Sunnis, and foreign forces on the other. Kourani starts by acknowledging that his account of history "suffers from the lack of references, documents and sources which were lost or burnt because of the consecutive upheavals … [T]he researcher has to analyze events and unearth it" (Kourani 1993, p. 9). Like other similar books produced by Hizbullah's publishing houses, Kourani connects Muslim resistance to the Crusaders, Mamluks, Ottomans, and the French Mandate to Hizbullah's resistance to Israeli occupation; in so doing, he constructs a history of Shiʻi suffering and of fierce opposition to injustice. The author raises controversial figures in Lebanese Shiʻi history to the status of revered symbols of resistance—for example, Sadeq Hamza, Adham Khanjar, and Mahmod Bazzi, who were previously considered bandits (Kourani 1993, p. 13). The book glosses over the role of secular resistance against Israeli occupation from the 1970s to the early 1990s, despite the fact that the Communist Party, the Organisation for Communist Action, and the Syrian Social Nationalist Party were consistently responsible for many successful operations against the Israeli Defense Force in South Lebanon, and continued to be the dominant forces resisting occupation until the late 1980s. Through his reconstruction of Lebanese Shiʻi history, Kourani grants Hizbullah pride of place as the culmination of Islamic resistance throughout the centuries, by virtue of its connection to the Shiʻi Imams and the Prophet Muhammad.

In the context of Lebanese sectarian nationalism, as Ussama Makdisi argues, the most significant element differentiating sectarian conflicts from ancient religious confrontations is the "deployment of religious heritage as a primary marker of modern political identity" (Makdisi 2000, p. 7), as will be mentioned in Chap. 3. This deployment is essentially modern, and is accentuated by the advent of print capitalism in the nineteenth and twentieth centuries, which enhanced the creation of what Benedict Anderson famously called an 'imagined community' (Anderson 1991, p. 48). While Anderson's argument is based on the primacy of language, the advent of print created different forms of 'imagined communities', which were not defined by a common language but by shared symbols, myths, set of beliefs, and the idea of a common destiny. Hizbullah is an exemplary instance of such a community: it is Lebanon's largest publisher, and runs a vast network of media outlets, including a television and radio station, a weekly newspaper, and at least one magazine for each of its institutions.

1.4.4 Islam and Nationalism in Gellner's Thought

Among the various approaches and debates in the study of Islamic fundamentalism are those belonging to the essentialist sphere, which stress the cultural and religious differences between the West and the Muslim world. Such essentialist assumptions would suggest a constructivist approach is necessary to properly understand the latter. Gellner, a social anthropologist, advocates this approach for the study of the Islamic world; nevertheless, despite this premise, his arguments support the approach of this research. Gellner contends that Islam is 'unique' among the major world civilisations or religions (Gellner 1994, p. 15); he believes that although it is by and large true that in industrial or industrialising societies religion loses much of its erstwhile hold over men and society (a widely held sociological theory), Islam remains the "only one marked exception" (Gellner 1994, p. 15). However, in the same work, he rightly acknowledges that Islamic fundamentalism and nationalism are conflated, thus highlighting the contrast between Islam and Christianity. Gellner's insight into Islam raises the question of whether the principal assumptions on the relation between religion and nationalism can be applied to Islamic societies; he clearly suggests that the debates on nationalism in the West are pertinent to Islamic organisations in the East.[15]

Gellner explains that the "puritan, revivalist or fundamentalist Islam can perform precisely the function which nationalism has performed elsewhere: provide a new self-image for people no longer able to identify with their position in village, lineage, clan or tribe" (Gellner 1994, p. 24). What makes Islam an exception is its structure. According to Gellner, Islam combines Judaism's legalism and Christianity's theocentrism, and the result is a legalistic blueprint for a social order that transcends political authority. Gellner's view of Islam is based on his observation of the Qurʾanic laws for governance and human relations; his argument is reinforced by the role religion has played in secular Arab nationalism, owing largely to the fact that the Arab peoples mainly comprised various dispersed tribes before the advent of the Prophet Muhamed.[16] The much-celebrated 'glories' of Arab nationalists mostly took place after the advent of Islam, and there have been various intellectual attempts from the nineteenth century onwards to reconcile the religion with the tenets of European modernism and nationalism.[17] Islamic fundamentalist groups have strongly criticised the European elements of secular nationalist regimes, in spite of the latter's acceptance of Islam as a state religion in many cases. These groups have, for the most part, adopted what they claim to be a return to the authentic roots of the 'Muslim nation', and present a different narrative of identity based solely on Islamic teachings. Nevertheless, Gellner's assumption that fundamentalist Islam, in creating a new identity for the masses, is performing a nationalist function is largely applicable to Hizbullah's activities. The party has mobilised previously depoliticised parts of society through preaching its revised religious ideology, and in this way has created a reconstructed Shiʿi identity. Hizbullah has sought, and continues to seek, to build a new self-image for the Lebanese Shiʿa, who—to use Gellner's words—are "no longer able to identify with their position in village, lineage, clan or tribe". In that sense, the party has succeeded in elevating their collective sense of identity, thus facilitating their mobilisation *en masse*.

1.5 Conclusion

This book proposes an alternative, albeit unconventional, way of studying the rise of Hizbullah, drawing on the arguments of nationalism to explore the main question of how the organisation's identity is produced. Answering this question requires engaging with the further questions of who produces this identity, what are its main pillars, and to what extent is it a modern construct. The studies and debates on nationalism are particularly relevant to these research questions, since Islamic movements such as Hizbullah perform similar functions to nationalist movements in terms of identity production and the mass dissemination of this collective identity through media outlets and dedicated institutions.

This book therefore breaks with the two dominant approaches in the scholarly work on Hizbullah, one focusing on the 'terrorist' label, whether supporting or opposing its use, and the other on the 'Lebanonisation' argument, which is based on the organisation's presumed shifts in ideology. The limitations of both approaches have led researchers to overlook Hizbullah's main identity project, which is directed at the Lebanese Shiʿi population. The 'terrorist' label, driven by US official rhetoric, shifts the locus of the studies of Hizbullah to either side of a narrow, polarised debate; meanwhile, the 'Lebanonisation' argument, a response to the US and mainstream approaches, overstates the significance of the organisation's participation in the political process, despite the fact that the reality suggests otherwise—Hizbullah's leader, Hassan Nasrallah, has clearly stated that the reason behind participating in the government has always been to safeguard the resistance. This approach manifests itself in the party's relatively symbolic representation in Lebanon's government (it occupies only minor cabinet positions) in contrast to their Shiʿi ally, Amal, under the leadership of Nabih Berri. Hizbullah has sacrificed much of its share in government posts to Berri and its Christian ally, General Michel Aoun, the head of Lebanon's Free Patriotic Movement.

As this chapter shows, the literature on nationalism is very relevant to an analysis of Hizbullah in particular, and to Islamic movements in general, especially those elements of nationalism pertaining to the realisation of the nation and the construction of its symbols, rituals, and myths. This purpose of this book is to contribute to the debate on nationalism through its argument that Hizbullah is a modern organisation, particularly in terms of its identity—for example, in the form it takes and the methods the party uses for its deployment and dissemination. The organisation's myriad institutions disseminate this sectarian Shiʿi identity in forms tailored to its respective audiences, thus enabling it to continue to widen its reach. A further application of the study of nationalism to the case of Hizbullah lies in its recreation of a specifically Lebanese Shiʿi history, based on earlier pan-Arab nationalist reconstructions.

Notes

1. The extent of this mobilisation was visible in the pro-Hizbullah demonstrations, numbering hundreds of thousands, which were organised following the assassination of Rafiq Hariri, Lebanon's former Sunni prime minister, on 14 February 2005.
2. This book follows Smith's definition of national identity. He describes this as "the maintenance and continual reinterpretation of the pattern of values, symbols, memories, myths, and traditions that form the distinctive heritage of the nation and the identification of individuals with that heritage and its pattern" (Smith 2003, p. 25).
3. Hizbullah's institutions explicitly state that they intend to create a new identity for the 'faithful' (Shiʿa); this is discussed later in this chapter.
4. *Wilayat al-Faqih* (the Guardianship of the Islamic Jurists) in practice means the absolute authority of Iran's Supreme Leader over the Shiʿi nation.
5. Wadah Sharara was among the first academics to refer to Hizbullah's institutions as a 'state within a state' in his landmark book, *The State of Hizbullah* (1998). Hizbullah's wide network of institutions and military activities requires a state-level political cover, which made participation in parliamentary elections in 1992 and in the government in 2005 a necessity.
6. The last official census was recorded in 1932, but since then there have been various independent statistical demographic surveys showing a consistent decline in the Christian population.
7. Sadr disappeared with his two companions, Shaykh Mohamad Yaʿcoub and Abbas Badreddine, during a visit to Libya.
8. Hassan Nasrallah in a lecture given in Beirut on 25 April 2011 (http://www.abna.ir/data.asp?lang=2&Id=238432).
9. Hizbullah and the Lebanese government still argue that since Israel did not withdraw from the Lebanese Shebʿa Farms and the southern part of the Gajar village, United Nations Security Council Resolution 425 has not been fully implemented. Nevertheless, Israel has maintained that this part of the border was under Syrian control before its acquisition in 1967. This contention remains among Hizbullah's alibis for keeping its arsenal.
10. Hizbullah's slate won about 90 per cent of Shiʿi votes in Lebanon's 2009 parliamentary elections.
11. Chapter 5 discusses this trend in the organisation's identity dissemination, reviewing its major works and publications.
12. Macleod, H. (2008). 'Lebanese declaration threatens civil war' available at https://www.theguardian.com/world/2008/may/11/lebanon (11-05-2008)
13. Phares, Walid (1995). *Lebanese Christian Nationalism: The Rise and Fall of an Ethnic Resistance*. Boulder, CO: L. Rienner. Hourani also refers to minority nationalism in the Lebanese case.

14. Many of these works' claims are based on 'oral histories', mostly uncorroborated. This is justified by the lack of documented sources due to recurrent repression.
15. Among the questions this book addresses is the following question: How modern is Hizbullah's ideology?
16. For example, the Arab Socialist Ba'ath Party has a great affinity to Islam in terms of its ideology. Its Syrian Christian founder and ideologue, Michel Aflak, converted to Islam.
17. Albert Hourani's *Arabic Thought in the Liberal Age 1789–1939* (1962) details how Arab intellectuals influenced by Western thought attempted to reconcile Islam with modernity. Among the most notable names are those of Jamaludine al-Afghani, Mohammad Abdu, Rasheed Reda, and Mustafa Lutfi el-Manfaluti.

References

Books

Alexander, E., & Bogdanor, P. (Eds.). (2006). *The Jewish Divide Over Israel Accusers and Defenders*. Piscataway: Transaction.

Al-Katib, A. (1997). *The Development of Shiite Political Thought: From Shura to Wilayat Al-Faqih*. London: Alshura Publishing House.

Anderson, B. (1991). *Imagined Communities: Reflections on the Origin and Spread of Nationalism*. London and New York: Verso.

Delanty, G., & Kumar, K. (2006). *The SAGE Handbook of Nations and Nationalism*. London and Chicago: SAGE.

El-Khazen, F. (2000). *Breakdown of the State in Lebanon: 1967–1976*. Cambridge: Harvard University Press.

Gellner, E. (1994). *Conditions of Liberty: Civil Society and Its Rivals*. London: Hamish Hamilton.

Hourani, A. (1947). *Minorities in the Arab World*. Oxford: Oxford University Press.

Hourani, A. (1962). *Arabic Thought in the Liberal Age 1789–1939*. London and New York: Oxford University Press.

Juergensmeyer, M. (1993). *The New Cold War? Religious Nationalism Confronts the Secular State*. Berkeley: University of California Press.

Kedourie, E. (1970). *Nationalism in Asia and Africa*. New York: New American Library.

Kourani, M. (1993). *Al Jozoor Al Tarikheya Lel Moqawama Al Islamiya* (The Historical Roots of the Islamic Resistance). Beirut: Dar Al Waseela.

Koya, A. (2009). *Imam Khomeini: Life, Thought and Legacy*. Selangor, Malaysia: Islamic Book Trust.

Makdisi, U. (2000). *The Culture of Sectarianism: Community, History, and Violence in Nineteenth-Century Ottoman Lebanon*. Berkeley: University of California Press.

Noe, N. (Ed.). (2007). *Voice of Hezbollah: The Statements of Sayed Hassan Nasrallah*. London: Verso.

Phares, W. (1995). *Lebanese Christian Nationalism: The Rise and Fall of an Ethnic Resistance*. Boulder, CO: L. Rienner.

Qassem, N. (2005). *Hizbullah: The Story from Within*. London: Saqi.

Saad-Ghorayeb, A. (2002). *Hizbu'llah: Politics and Religion*. London: Pluto Press.

Sankari, J. (2005). *Fadlallah: The Making of a Radical Shi'ite Leader*. London: Saqi.

Sayigh, R. (2015). *Too Many Enemies*. Beirut: Dar Al Mashriq.

Shatzmiller, M. (Ed.). (2005). *Nationalism and Minority Identities in Islamic Societies*. Montreal and Kingston: McGill-Queen's University Press.

Sharara, W. (1998). *Dawlat Hezbollah, Lubnan mujtami'an Islamiyyan*. Beirut: Dar Annahar.

Smith, A. D. (1999). *Myths and Memories of the Nation*. Oxford: Oxford University Press.

Smith, A. D. (2003). *Chosen Peoples: Sacred Sources of National Identity*. Oxford: Oxford University Press.

Weiss, M. (2010). *In the Shadow of Sectarianism*. Cambridge, MA and London, UK: Harvard University Press.

Journal Articles

Harb, M., & Leenders, R. (2005). Know Thy Enemy: Hizbullah, 'Terrorism' and the Politics of Perception. *Third World Quarterly, 26*(1) [Special Issue: The Politics of Naming: Rebels, Terrorists, Criminals, Bandits and Subversives], 173–197.

Harik, I. F. (1972). The Ethnic Revolution and Political Integration in the Middle East. *International Journal of Middle East Studies, 3*, 303–323.

CHAPTER 2

The Role of Hizbullah's Institutions in the Reconstruction of Shi'i Identity

The following chapter highlights the role that Hizbullah's institutions play in the production of a sense of sectarian identification. These various institutions mix the delivery of welfare with the promotion of religious identity, and are specifically targeted at Lebanon's Shi'i community. By illustrating the way Hizbullah uses these institutions to disseminate the idea of a collective Shi'i identity, the chapter provides further evidence in support of the contention that Islam, in this context, performs a function similar to that of nationalism. Nationalists also use institutional means to spread their picture of a unitary national community, reproducing a sense of national belonging in myriad ways in order to sustain its influence. In this regard, Hizbullah uses its different institutions to create forms of Shi'i identity that are tailored to suit specific audiences, whether they are school children, the injured, or the families of Hizbullah 'martyrs'. Through an analysis of the way Shi'i identification with Hizbullah (as manifest in its institutionalised form) is promoted, the chapter argues that this collective identity is a modern creation, which Hizbullah reinvents for its different audiences.

Unlike Iran, where the use of state-run institutions to instil a sense of collective identity is often associated with state coercion or with its mishandling of economic, social, or educational affairs (Hassan and Azadmarki 2003, p. 104), Hizbullah is able to portray its expansive welfare services as independent alternatives to weak or non-existent state institutions and services. While the Iranian state's role tends to negatively affect the dissemination of a sense of identification with the Islamic Republic among its population, Hizbullah's institutions act as auxiliary players, and the organisation's political statements criticising the Lebanese government's many failures to tackle the country's social problems resonate with the Shiʿi community. The beneficiaries of these institutions associate the hierarchical elements of its organisation, such as the authority of the *taklif* (a religious command or order), with the many benefits these services provide, which are generally perceived as acts of benevolence. This provides Hizbullah with a certain immunity from public scrutiny, as its services are external to the Lebanese citizens' social contract with and expectations of the state, and consequently they serve to enhance the organisation's efforts to reconstruct a Shiʿi identity.

2.1 Institutional Conventions and Rules

In order to establish a powerful popular social identity, an institution will diffuse certain myths, symbols, and collective memories among its target audience (Hutchinson 1994, p. 9). In Hizbullah's case, its institutions use such means to reproduce its sectarian identity among the various elements of the Shiʿi population in Lebanon.[1] Hodgson's inclusive definition of institutions as "systems of established and embedded social rules that structure social interactions" provides the framework for this research (Hodgson 2006, p. 18). According to Hodgson, institutions are structures that create "the stuff of social life", while conventions are instances of institutional rules (Hodgson 2006, p. 2). Social institutions "form an element in a more general concept, known as [the] social structure" (Hodgson 2006, p. 2). In Hizbullah's various institutions, this structure is enforced through the concept of *Wilayat al-Faqih* (the 'Guardianship of the [Islamic] Jurist'). Belief in this concept lays the ground for obedience to the *taklif sharʿi*, religious orders issued by the Iranian Supreme Leader and his representative in Hizbullah.[2] *Wilayat al-Faqih*, an Islamic theory developed by Ayatollah Khomeini to grant jurists absolute custodianship over 'believers',[3] is central to Hizbullah's identity. The Shiʿi Supreme Leader or *Wali al-Faqih* is perceived to be a representative of the hidden Twelfth Imam, Allah's emissary; the *Wali al-Faqih* is regularly referred to as *Naʾeb al-Imam*, the Twelfth Imam's 'deputy'. Although Ayatollah Ali Khamenei, the current *Wali al-Faqih*, does not leave Iran, Hizbullah's hierarchy, from the general secretary downwards, represents his authority in Lebanon. Consequently, any individual official in the organisation's hierarchy or within its constituent institutions is in theory acting in the capacity of the 'Hidden Imam'. While it is difficult to measure the true impact of such beliefs, it appears that most officials and workers in these institutions identify themselves and their work with the concept of *Wilayat al-Faqih*.[4]

Although, theoretically, Hizbullah's network portrays itself as part of a global Islamic community led by the *Walī al-Faqih*, the social structure in practice comprises the Lebanese Arabic-speaking Shiʻa. The institutions' beneficiaries interact with the Lebanese part of the *Wilayat al-Faqih* hierarchy and its localised symbols. Hizbullah's global Shiʻi status gives the organisation legitimacy, since its hierarchical structure embodies the will of the Twelfth Imam, represented by his deputy, the *Walī al-Faqih*. Hizbullah's secretary general, currently Hassan Nasrallah, also holds the title of the 'Sole Representative of Ayatollah Ali Khamenei', and as such is a direct representative of the Supreme Leader in Iran. Hizbullah's institutions (although mainly focussed on providing basic services to the Shiʻi population) operate within this context as the *Wilayat al-Faqih* hierarchy appoints the institutional heads or managers, whose commissions therefore carry religious connotations.[5] This idea of the existence of a sacred chain of command within each institution charges their daily dealings with their constituents—beneficiaries, students, or activists—with a spiritual aura, magnifying the significance of their respective identities and social roles. Psychologists Peter Berger and Thomas Luckmann capture the experience of the individual within such institutions:

> This means that the institutions that have now crystallized (for instance, the institution of paternity as it is encountered by the children) are experienced as existing over and beyond the individuals who 'happen to' embody them at the moment. In other words, the institutions are now experienced as possessing a reality of their own, a reality that confronts the individual as an external and coercive fact. … The "There we go again" now becomes "This is how things are done". A world so regarded attains a firmness in consciousness; it becomes real in an ever more massive way and it can no longer be so readily changed. (Berger and Luckmann 2011, p. 58)

Owing to the organisation's holistic, centralised structure, Hizbullah's institutions perform an organised and targeted role, building upon what Mark Tomass calls "identity-sharing groups" in the Levant, where sectarianism has been on the rise since the collapse of the Soviet Union.[6] Various institutions remould the sectarian process and work to establish a framework for identity-sharing groups, within which "members are impelled to heed informal rules" (Tomass 2012, p. 707). In Hizbullah's case, such informal institutions, where rules are made and enforced in a social setting, are tangible and targeted, rather than a natural outcome of the society's sectarian nature.

2.2 Non-State Institutions

As mentioned earlier, unlike the Islamic Republic of Iran, Hizbullah as a non-state actor is subjected less to public scrutiny and expectations; its platform is based on supporting the downtrodden of Lebanon, specifically the Shiʿi victims of state negligence and the brutality of the Israeli occupation. Hizbullah uses such policies to garner support among members of Lebanon's Shiʿi population by appealing to their sense of identification with their faith community (as embodied in the organisation) as opposed to the state.

In Iran, the endurance of the Islamic Republic could be largely attributed to the economic and social populism manifested in the expansion of its education, health, agriculture, labour, housing, welfare, and social security ministries (Abrahamian 2009 pp. 11–13). Its populist social policy managed to reduce the overall rate of illiteracy from 53 to 15 per cent, while infant mortality dropped from 104 to 25 per thousand (Abrahamian 2009, p. 13). The regime achieved advances in bridging the gap between the urban and rural populations (Abrahamian 2009, pp. 13–14). Hizbullah mirrors Iran's revolutionary populist policies and emulates its structure, which is characterised by semi-independent institutions, such as the *mostazafin* (the oppressed), martyrs, housing, Alavi, and Imam Khomeini relief foundations. These foundations account for as much as "15 per cent of [Iran's] national economy and control budgets that total as much as half of the central government" (Abrahamian 2009, p. 14). However, the advances in the social and economic spheres have had far less impact in terms of public trust in these institutions, a factor that has been attributed to their association with the Iranian state (Hassan and Azadmarki 2003, p. 104). This association with state authority also carries potential implications for the public perception of the institutions' religious claims. Hizbullah's institutions, as non-governmental actors, do not encounter these problems.[7] The grey zone in which its social institutions operate instead augments its attempt to create a sense of sectarian solidarity. The organisation's institutions cover educational, medical, social welfare, banking, and media spheres, and in so doing they have created (and continue to create on a regular basis) specific conventions that govern many aspects of their constituents' daily lives. The process is locally nuanced but centralised, despite the large number of these institutions.

2.3 The Invention of Tradition: A New *Ashura*

Hizbullah not only uses its social institutions to instill a sense of collective identity among Lebanese Shi'a, but has also adopted and transformed traditional Shi'i ceremonies. This is exemplified by its transformation of *Ashura*. This event happens every year on the tenth day of Muharram, the first month of the Muslim lunar calendar, when Shi'a around the world commemorate the death of the third imam, Husayn Ben 'Ali, a grandchild of Mohamed. Imam Husayn led a revolt against the second Umayyad caliph, Yazid ben Mu'awiya; the caliph's army killed Husayn and many of his family members at the Battle of Karbala (in southern Iraq) in 61 AH (680 AD) (referred to in Chap. 3). Following his decapitation, Husayn's head was transported to Damascus, the capital of the Umayyad dynasty.

Before 1982, according to both written accounts and interviews conducted during field work for this research, the Shi'i rituals of '*Ashura*' took a traditional, restrained, a-political form; they have since been radically transformed into a more intense, revolutionary, politically charged, and sometimes provocative sectarian display. Qassem Qassir, a founding member of Hizbullah, recalls that in the 1970s, the major '*Ashura*' festival was held in the 'Amlieh, a Shi'i educational compound in West Beirut[8]:

> It was nonpolitical. After reading the Masra' [the story of the Battle of Karbala, culminating in Imam Husayn's death and decapitation], we would simply go home. Even the latmiya [the chest beating and rhythmic chants] took the form of light slapping. (Qassir 2014)[9]

In the early twentieth century, Iranian immigrants introduced the annual ritual of the *Masra'* performance to the city of Nabatieh,[10] when an Iranian doctor, Ibrahim Mirza, successfully applied to the Ottoman Empire through the Iranian consul in Lebanon for a licence to hold the play. Up to 1919, however, Iranian families were only allowed to participate in the

Ashura performance, which was recited in *Farsi*, although later they secretly mixed with locals in the old mosque to listen to the *Masraʿ*, away from Ottoman eyes (Al-Akhbar 2008). The subsequent marches were apolitical; they were mere gatherings that took place after attending the *Masraʿ* and the theatrical performance.

However, with the Islamic Revolution in Iran in 1979, and Tehran's growing influence following the Israeli invasion of Lebanon in 1982, the *Ashura* rituals changed drastically. First, a political march or demonstration after the *Masraʿ* was introduced on a wide scale. The march is a reproduction of the demonstrations that took place in Iran in the lead up to the revolution. Known as '*Alʿasher*' ('The Ten'), these protests led to the toppling of the Shah and the return of Ayatollah Khomeini.[11] Today, Shiʿi mourners pour into the streets following the reading of the *Masraʿ*, and the march is highly political, with chants for Islamic resistance against Israel and the United States, which are equated with the killers of Imam Husayn. The Israeli and American flags are painted or placed on the ground under the feet of the demonstrators, conveying the message that the Shiʿa will never again let their 'holy leader' down, and that "humiliation is farthest from us" ("*hayhat mina al-thula*"). Marches are not restricted to Nabatieh or Beirut but encompass every Shiʿi town or centre of population in Lebanon; they even take place in towns in predominantly Sunni and Christian North Lebanon. The ritual of *latmiya* (chest-beating) has been replaced by bloodier Iraqi, Bahraini, and Iranian forms, which carry a distinct political charge. Thousands of Shiʿa perform more violent chest beatings, using metal chains and sharp objects.[12] As in certain Christian Catholic traditions, these rituals combine sadness and regret for the Imam's death, while vowing not to allow such a let-down again. While it is not possible to repeat history and make the right choices, the participants equate the choice of standing up for the Imam, with supporting his direct representatives, the 'Ulama' under the leadership of *Walī al-Faqih*. During the 1990s, the 40th day after the tenth of Muharram was established as a politicised ritual, with crowded gatherings in mosques and *hussainiyah*, featuring political speeches by Hizbullah's secretary general and the organisation's main officials in the different regions.[13] Following the 2006 conflict with Israel, the *Ashura* ritual was extended to include three extra days of mourning, including a march in honour of Husayn's female relatives, especially his sister Zaynab, who is revered by Shiʿa Muslims.[14]

2.4 Redefining Parties: The Party of God *vs* the Party of Satan

The idea of parties (or coalitions of forces)—*ahzab*—is a contentious subject in Islam. The Qur'an portrays them in both a positive and negative light, either referring to the enemies of the Prophet or, in certain instances, to Allah's followers. Hizbullah uses one of the latter verses in its logos and propaganda (number 56 of the *Al-Ma'eda Sura* [a Qur'anic chapter]): "And whosoever takes Allah, His Messenger, and those who have believed, as Protectors, then the Party of Allah will be victorious". Verse 22 in the *Sura Al-Mujadilah* in the Qur'an defines the 'Party of Allah' in distinction to the parties of non-believers or those who oppose the Prophet:

> You will not find a people who believe in Allah and the Last Day having affection for those who oppose Allah and His Messenger, even if they were their fathers or their sons or their brothers or their kindred. Those—He has decreed within their hearts faith and supported them with spirit from Him. And we will admit them to gardens beneath which rivers flow, wherein they abide eternally. Allah is pleased with them, and they are pleased with Him—those are the party of Allah. Unquestionably, the party of Allah—they are the successful.

A whole *sura*, under the title of 'Al-Ahzab' ('The Parties'), chronicles the battle between the Prophet and his enemies in Madina, the city to which he emigrated with his followers following persecution in Mecca. This *sura*, according to Hussein Abu al-Rida, head of Hizbullah's security committee, "includes all the political and spiritual dimensions of the confrontation between 'Hezb Allah' (the Party of God) and 'Hezb Al-Shaitan' (the Party of Satan)" (Abu Al-Rida 2012, p. 90).[15] A '*du'a*', a prayer attributed to Imam Husayn, also stresses the significance of belonging to the Party of Allah: "Allah, make us belong to your *Hezb* [party], your *Hezb* is the victorious [one]" (Abu Al-Rida 2012, p. 91).

According to Ayatollah Khomeini, Hizbullah is not like a modern political party but is a more inclusive phenomenon:

> Any Muslim who accepts the Islamic scales and principles, and has both precise discipline and commitment, is a member of Hizbullah. The Qur'an and Islam indicate all the laws of this party and its approach. This party differs from the current parties in the world today. (Khomeini 2011, p. 282)[16]

Contemporary political parties, Khomeini says, are established by man, while the Party of Allah (or Hizbullah), as mentioned in the Qur'an, is of divine provenance; the organisation's establishment "embodies Allah's will ... we only have one party, and it is Hizbullah". The 'precise discipline' or the 'path', in the words of Khomeini, is the belief in the *Wilayat al-Faqih* hierarchy, to which Hizbullah's leadership and structure are connected; those who have "found the path" see through the 'smokescreens' of this world and join Hizbullah on the basis of the Qur'anic verse '*Inna Hizbullah Homol Ghalibun*' ('Hizbullah is victorious') (Khomeini 2011, pp. 280–281). Based on this Qur'anic logic, Khomeini sets Hizbullah apart from any other party, which will continue to "flounder in its path until its defeat" (Khomeini 2011, p. 281). Hizbullah, in other words, is Allah's organisation in the fight between good and evil.

Hizbullah disseminates this concept of the Islamic party as a sacred mission. Shaykh Mohammad Yazbek, one of the organisation's most prominent leaders and a *shura* council member, states that movements connected with any of the prophets, from Adam to Mohamed, have all been, like Hizbullah, partisan[17]:

> It sought to change its societies and spiritual-religious reality, through either spreading the new religion or controlling the existing corrupt authority ... Martyr Mohammad Baqer Al-Sadr said in this context, when told of Imam Khomeini's victory, that Imam Khomeini realized the dream of the prophets. (Yazbek cited in Abu Al-Rida 2012, p. 106)[18]

Like Khomeini, Yazbek considers Shiʿa Islam a movement in its own right. As early as the era of the caliphs (after Mohamed's death), the party framework existed in the form of various *firaq* or religious sects, which held partisan views and beliefs (Abu Al-Rida 2012, p. 113). It was Khomeini, however, who introduced a more inclusive concept of the organisation's membership, declaring that "any Muslim who accepts the Islamic principles and balances, and has an accurate Shiʿi discipline in action and behaviour, is a member of Hizbullah" (Khomeini 2011, p. 281). Accordingly, Hizbullah's leaders argue that the party represents a continuation of those movements associated with the Prophet and the Imams as a way of enforcing its legitimacy and demonising its foes. During the ceremony of ʿAshuraʾ, as outlined previously, the party leaders equate their struggles against their foes with those of Imam Husayn.

While Hizbullah maintains that the party is an ancient Islamic concept, Abu Al-Rida acknowledges that the organisation's structure is modern, as does Qassir, who confirms that its structure was actually based on that of Marxist–Leninist parties. In the post-1982 years, during Hizbullah's establishment, Qassir was asked to bring documents detailing the internal structure and organisation of Marxist–Leninist groups to sessions discussing the party setup (Qassir 2014). However, "Hizbullah is not a narrow party in the closed organizational sense, as it launched the slogan '*Ummat* Hizbullah' [the 'Nation of Hizbullah']" to stress its ideological and political connections to Muslims throughout the world, "within the context of the Islamic *Umma*" (Qassir 2014, p. 449). For instance, while Hizbullah is widespread in many different areas, there are no membership cards, as the concept of 'belonging to the nation' has religious, not secular, criteria (Abu Al-Rida 2012, p. 450). While the lack of membership cards appears to serve as an attempt to resolve the tension between theory and practice, it leaves the dilemma of defining the relationship between members and non-members. The tension between the organisational reality of Hizbullah (with its specific membership structures and hierarchies) and its broader theological identity as the 'Party of God' persists, as is the case with other Islamic organisations. Egypt's Muslim Brotherhood, for instance, has faced a similar dilemma, with Hassan al-Banna offering a definition similar in its claim to inclusivity as that of Hizbullah. In his letter on *al-hizbiya al-siyasiya* (political partisanship), al-Banna condemns the secular party system and insists that the Brotherhood is not a political party; rather, its members are "the companions of Allah's messenger, the holders of his *raya* [banner] after him" (Amin 1981, p. 143). As with Hizbullah's self-image, al-Banna equates the role and mission of the Muslim Brotherhood with that of the Prophet and his companions—his organisation is bounded by neither geography nor time, and will not end until Allah inherits the earth (Amin 1981, p. 143). Their structure and appearance create tensions with ancient ideological claims: they employ modern political structures, and, in certain cases, even hold elections, while simultaneously claiming historical continuity from the times of Mohamed. However, in respect of the latter, Hizbullah's name, based as it is on a Qur'anic verse, puts it in an advantageous position in comparison with the Brotherhood.[19]

2.5 Hizbullah's Organisational Structure: Ancient Islam or Leninism?

Hizbullah's organisational structure has undergone some major transformations since its inception by the Iranian Revolutionary Guard following the 1982 Israeli invasion, mainly due to its increasing sophistication and the spread of its diverse state-like activities. The earlier, far looser structure, shrouded in secrecy, needed to change, especially with the establishment of the *altaʿbiʾa* (the reserves) and the Mahdi Scouts, both of which required increased oversight.[20] The last major structural change followed the Israeli withdrawal from Lebanon in 2000, when Hizbullah centralised its control over its social welfare institutions, such as the grand hospital of Alrasul al-AʿZam and Al-Imdad cultural institute, which were previously controlled by Iran-affiliated and funded clerics. The few clerics who initially opposed this move were soon co-opted (Qassir 2014).[21]

The aforementioned system of reserve brigades, *altaʿbiʾa*, mirrors that set up in Iran after the revolution. Although Khomeini and Khamenei both declared that *altaʿbiʾa* has Islamic origins, proclaiming its continuity with the movement of the Prophet and the Imams, the model bears many similarities to the Leninist concept of the revolutionary vanguard. According to this model, the party performs an organic role among the masses, helping achieve the diffusion of socialist consciousness (transformed in Khomeinist terminology to 'Islamic awakening'). As such, *altaʿbiʾa* becomes the link between the vanguard party and the masses, aimed at the successful mobilisation of Islamic awareness on a more popular level. *Altaʿbiʾa*, according to Khamenei, comprises a select group, insulated from outside influences by indoctrination and the assimilation of a set of behaviours (*Baqiatullah* 2011). The Iranian Supreme Leader, in a speech translated into Arabic by Hizbullah's main internal publication, claims the pioneer of this concept in the modern age is Imam Khomeini. His words carry the underlying message that *Altaʿbiʾa* is in fact an ancient practice, and Khomeini simply revived it.

Khamenei's words suggest he has, to a certain degree, borrowed from Lenin. *Altaʿbiʾa* education entails the teaching of a collection of behaviours, tools, and knowledge in order to establish an influential group among the larger population that can "guarantee [a] straightforward and continuous Islamic movement" (*Baqiatullah* 2011). This concept of the nation's Islamic vanguard, as outlined by Stalin later in the chapter, enmeshed in the life of the masses, is in principle similar to Leninism:

> But the Party cannot be merely a vanguard. It must at the same time be a unit of the class, be part of that class, intimately bound to it with every fibre of its being. The distinction between the vanguard and the main body of the working class, between Party members and non-Party workers, will continue as long as classes exist, as long as the proletariat continues replenishing

its ranks with newcomers from other classes, as long as the working class as a whole lacks the opportunity of raising itself to the level of the vanguard. (Stalin 1932, p. 105)

The Leninist organisation also includes a similar outlook towards indoctrinating its members through activity and theory, and in effect "severing ... ties to the outside world, maximizing ... commitment to the movement" (Selznik 1952, pp. 72–73).

The centralised structure and the role of its committees and publications within Hizbullah are, to a large extent, textbook Leninism. Publishing has always played a pivotal role in its organisational strategy, beginning with the *al-ʿAhd* and *Baqiatullah*, and later expanded into myriad institutional publications. Lenin emphasised the significance of its publications to the party's strategic aims:

> The role of a newspaper is not limited, however, merely to the spreading of ideas, merely to political education and attracting political allies. A newspaper is not only a collective propagandist and collective agitator, but also a collective organizer. In this respect it can be compared to the scaffolding erected around a building in construction, which marks the contours of the structure, facilitates communication between the builders and permits them to distribute the work and to view the common results achieved by their organized labour ... With the aid of and in connection with a newspaper there will automatically develop a permanent organization that will engage not only in local but also in regular general activities, training its members carefully to watch political events, to appraise their significance and the influence they exercise upon various strata of the population, and to devise suitable means by which the revolutionary Party could influence these events. (Lenin 1953)

Lenin called, in the first place, for a national publication; he considered the existence of a large number of publications a luxury that the party could only afford when it was firmly established. Since the Israeli withdrawal, Hizbullah has entered such an established phase, so each of the organisation's individual institutions currently publishes its own magazine.

In line with its close adherence to Lenin's idea of the role of the organisation, Hizbullah's structure bears many similarities to that of the Leninist party. The secretary general is the party's leader and the senior representative of the *Walī al-Faqih* (the Supreme Leader in Iran), and although nominally elected by the seven members of the *shura* council, it is generally accepted that this appointment lies with the *Walī al-Faqih*. The secretary general's deputy, currently Naʿim Qassem, plays a political role, in addition to being the organisation's interim leader in case of the former's death. Hizbullah's firm organisational structure and ability to avert major splits have marked it out as a singular phenomenon in Lebanon, where the leadership in all the other major political parties face constant challenges. The organisation's mechanisms of change, through the election of officials and its practice of collective decision-making, help contain internal differences, but even more important than these, it appears, is its commitment to *Wilayat al-Faqih*. Unlike other parties, Abu Al-Rida argues, "the steel[y] commitment to the concept of *Wilayat al-Faqih*, and its implementation on the level of Party intra-relations inside Hizbullah, prevents this conflict, and nearly eliminates it" (Abu Al-Rida 2012, p. 503). This faith in the absolute leadership, while theoretically significant in augmenting the party's hierarchy, is complemented by its general conferences, similar to those in the Communist Party, which provide Hizbullah with a necessary internal mechanism through which to ensure cohesion and resolve differences. In the words of Naiʿm Kassem:

> General conferences in the party are for securing stability in the leadership, harmony in intellectual, ideological and organizational vision. The amendments in the organizational, political or intellectual body, during general conferences, are for ensuring this body's cohesion. (Qassem 2005, p. 503)

Since 1989, internal party elections have occurred every two years, although this period is extended at times when the security situation is heightened. Hizbullah's membership is based on faith in and commitment to the principle of *Wilayat al-Faqih*, which manifests itself in the sanctity of the hierarchy's commands or *taklif sharʿi*; under this system, elections serve an internal purpose. As Abu Al-Rida explains, the democratic process within Hizbullah does not mirror that known in liberal democracies, as these sorts of practices would contradict the party's intellectual and religious foundations (Abu Al-Rida 2012, p. 464). Hizbullah's 'democracy' therefore merely creates space for members at the lower levels of its organisational hierarchy, especially its mid-level leaders, to "discuss its problems and obstacles in closed and limited scope", meaning that their participation in decision-making is limited to making 'suggestions' (Abu Al-Rida 2012, p. 464). Only the leadership connected to the *Walī al-Faqih* has the final say on whether to take these suggestions into consideration or not. For Hizbullah, the *Walī al-Faqih* is in practice synonymous with its leader, Hassan Nasrallah, as the connection to the Iranian Supreme Leader is limited to those in the party's upper echelons. Nasrallah's political associates carry out his will within the party's hierarchy—for example, ensuring the 'election' of his preferred candidates to important positions.

The party's limited democratic process is also used as a mechanism through which to change its mid-level leadership, thus containing any frustrations that might arise within the organisation (Abu Al-Rida 2012, p. 462). The top leadership, however, remains at heart a reflection of the *Wilayat al-Faqih* doctrine, regardless of changes at its lower levels, and the whole party is based on this religious and ideological belief—this is a critical limitation in electoral terms, as it places severe limitations on its members' input into decision-making. The organisation's mid- and lower levels, nevertheless, are able to play a role in the implementation of its policies and decisions. The *shura* council has seven members, and includes the secretary general, his deputy, and the leaders of Hizbullah's five major councils (see Fig. 2.1). The secretary general leads the council, which votes on major policies. Owing to the organisation's strong commitment to the principle of *walī al-Faqih*, the secretary general plays a crucial role in relaying the Iranian leader's general policy guidelines to the Hizbullah leadership. The secretary general's channels to the Iranian Supreme Leader are numerous, from messages from various representatives and emissaries to regular visits to Iran to meet with Khamenei; the latter visits are viewed as highly significant, as they usually occur before major policy shifts are announced at the general conference.[22]

The position of deputy secretary general was introduced in 1991,[23] and involves overseeing Hizbullah's activities in Lebanon's national parliament (since 1992) and government (since 2005). In the case of the secretary general's absence, the deputy is tasked with taking over the organisation's

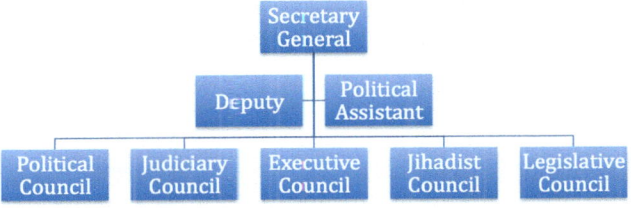

Fig. 2.1 Hizbullah's organisational structure

leadership (Abu Al-Rida 2012, p. 470). He also oversees the implementation of policies, alongside the heads of both the legislative and political councils. Current and former party cadres have stressed in interviews that only a cleric would have the authority to ensure that Hizbullah's legislative and ministerial work conforms to Islamic law, as delivered in the Supreme Leader's *fatwas* (Islamic judgements on different aspects of daily life), suggesting that a form of overall checks and balances exists. Apart from this general oversight, however, the two specialist councils are otherwise free to run their day-to-day affairs.

2.5.1 The Executive Council and the Party Branches (Qeta')

The executive council remains the most significant body in the organisation; lying at the heart of the hierarchy, it oversees Hizbullah's institutions and regional leaders, and decides on party internal procedures. Executive council members play a vital role at different levels of the party, especially in relation to devising new internal procedures. A board of directors runs every institution, each of which is represented on the executive council to ensure that any decisions take their respective needs and interests into consideration (Fig. 2.2). The main institutions are al-Shahid (the Martyrs' Foundation), al-Jareeh (the Foundation of the Wounded), Bayt al-Mal (the party's major financial institution or bank), al-Wahda al-Thaqafiya al-Markaziya (the Central Cultural Unit), al-Majmuʿa al-Lubnaniya Lil Iʿlam (Al-Manar Television and Al-Nur Radio), al-Mahdi Scouts, al-Mahdi schools; al-Hayʾa al-Suhiya (Hizbullah's health institute), and Jihad al-Bina' (its main construction company).

The executive council also oversees the party's most populous body: the five major geographic branches that include tens of thousands of members. These branches comprise the first and second Southern regions, the Beirut region, the Biqaʿ region, and the Northern region (Abu Al-Rida 2012, p. 479). Each region (or *qetaʿ*) comprises several if not all of these branches (or *shoʿab*), according to the significance of the area concerned,

Fig. 2.2 The executive council

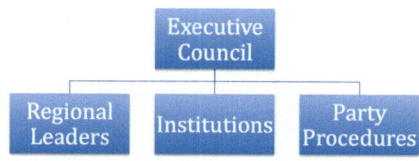

and the number of members varies from dozens to thousands, depending on the party's popularity and the extent of the Shi'i population in that region.

The region, *qeta'*, is an institution by its own right,[24] a fact best exemplified by the description of the West Beirut regional headquarters in Noueiry (visited during fieldwork for this book). The building itself holds many different offices and departments, focused for the most part on the delivery of social services and religious and ideological education, while military and security affairs are usually conducted in secret.[25] The regions serve as human reservoirs for the organisation's specialist institutions, especially the military (known as the *jihadi*). Lower-ranking members mostly work part-time in the party's vast network, and are recruited for full-time service as and when required. Participation in military and security missions is rewarded financially according to the amount of time involved. This category of members, the largest in number, is known as the *al-ta'bi'a*, that is, the 'reserves' (mobilisation forces).

2.5.2 Al-Ta'bi'a (the Mobilisation Forces)

Following the model of the Islamic Republic's organisation of reserves or mobilisation forces, *sazman-e basij-e mostazafin* (the Organisation for Mobilisation of the Oppressed), Hizbullah's regional branches have built a large network of militarily trained followers with various specialties. Just like the *basij* who fought alongside the regular Iranian forces in the Iran–Iraq War, this network of reserves serves in times of conflict, providing local and logistical support for the organisation's specialist military personnel.[26] The main unit of the *alta'bi'a* is called the *shu'ba*, which, although playing various local roles, from recruitment (*istiqtab*) to social relations, is basically a brigade. Within each *shu'ba*, there are smaller groups, *faseel*, which are in turn composed of *majmu'a* (see Fig. 2.3). In their regular meetings, the smaller units, the *majmu'a* and *faseel*, always begin their discussions with a Qur'anic verse and a saying of the *Walī al-Faqih*, the Supreme Leader (Abu Al-Rida 2012, p. 479).[27]

Fig. 2.3 Regional organisation

In its educational institutions, Hizbullah's branches are part of *altaʿbiʾa altarbawiya*, the 'educational mobilisation forces', which perform a similar role to that of the general *altaʿbiʾa*.[28] Student members are given military training and receive religious and ideological education, while performing logistical support tasks. In times of conflict, they are called on for service in the organisation's military branch.

The judicial council, meanwhile, resolves disputes within the organisation and among its followers; its current chief, Mohammad Yazbek, carries the title of 'Legal Representative of Imam Khamenei'. The political council supervises the policy messages, both defining and disseminating them, and oversees legislation and Hizbullah's parliamentary and governmental activities. There is a degree of overlap between the powers of the political and legislative councils, but the former maintains seniority due to its inclusive authority.[29]

2.5.3　Al-Wehda Al-Thaqafiya Al-Markaziya (Central Cultural Unit)

Hizbullah's institutions use their daily interactions with their beneficiaries to relay a single, coherent message, through mission statements, publications targeted at specific constituencies and religious/political training sessions, as well as rituals and traditional ceremonies. The Central Cultural Unit (CCU) oversees this comprehensive process, contributing to and guiding it by means of its numerous publications. Hizbullah, though at heart a military and security organisation, is by far Lebanon's largest publisher: its magazine *Baqiatullah*, according to its editor, has a print-run of 30,000, more than any other periodical in the country. Each of its institutions has at least one publication; for instance, the Mahdi Scouts, which has tens of thousands of members, publishes the following magazines: *Mehdi, Tasneem,* and *Murshidat al-Mahdi*. The first two target different age groups within the militaristic institution, while the third is for their female branch, Al-Murshidat. The accrual of publications began in the 1990s, and then accelerated after the Israeli withdrawal in 2000.[30]

The institutions' beneficiaries and members, who range from child scouts to the families of 'martyrs', have different interests, which the respective specialist institutions endeavour to harness to Hizbullah's cause. However, to ensure coherence, the CCU oversees and produces most of the ideological and religious materials, and provides trained clerics for each of these institutions.[31] For example, in the case of the female scouts, their magazine's section on *Wilayat al-Faqih*, entitled 'The Solution is with the Leader', explains Ayatollah Ali Khamenei's *fatwas* in the form of a dialogue between a mother and her daughter (*Murshidat al-Mahdi* 2013, p. 24).[32] The magazine's numerous contributors and its letters' section convey a sense of spontaneous interaction with its young female readers.[33]

The CCU (visited during fieldwork for this research) is situated in a large building, which houses its magazine department, various coordination offices, and publishing enterprise.[34] The unit maintains a strict religious hierarchy and a tightly run bureaucracy, whose centralising tendencies lead to many complaints lower down in the party's ranks.[35] The bureaucracy stems from its stringent supervisory code, which ensures that the major themes of *Wilayat al-Faqih* and resistance are emphasised and reproduced to suit its different beneficiaries. The unit's clerics vet all cultural or ideological activities, from the teaching of religion at Hizbullah's schools to the religious indoctrination of its military and security branches. The process of oversight is either initiated by the CCU or is activated by an institution seeking the unit's approval on a particular matter. Strictly, none of Hizbullah's institutions can publish religious propaganda or deliver lectures unless approved by the CCU; even the Mehdi schools, a branch of Hizbullah's educational network, and the Mahdi Scouts seek the CCU's approval when it comes to their religious and ideological publications and training.[36]

The CCU, apart from its role of oversight of the various institutional publications and educational materials, also produces periodicals and publications on Islamic studies. Qassir has commented on this centralised process of identity dissemination:

> Hizbullah and its cultural, religious, research, educational and party institutions constitute the largest pot of cultural consciousness in Beirut's Southern Suburbs. The Central Cultural Unit undertakes the most significant role in this through a number of departments and watchdogs, all of which are overseen by Sheikh Akram Barakat, the cultural assistant of Hizbullah's Executive Council President. The Unit includes another important institution, the al-Ma'aref, which has published hundreds of books and studies on ideological education, in addition to the Baqiyatullah Magazine. The latter enjoys a compulsory distribution among all party officials and members; it is similar in that fashion to the Lebanese Army and Security Forces' Magazines. (Qassir 2010)

The centralisation of Hizbullah's cultural message throughout its vast array of institutions emphasises the significance to the party, of building and maintaining a mass identity. The message of resistance, or *jihad*, and commitment to the concept of *Wilayat al-Faqih* dominate all Hizbullah's different forms of discourse, both directly and indirectly, and are manifested in the organisation's successful mobilisation of the Lebanese Shi'i community during times of conflict. Its reaction to the destruction of South Lebanon and Beirut's southern suburbs surprised many by its force and resilience.

The CCU has subsumed into a single institution the roles previously played by several of the organisation's different bodies. A member of Hizbullah's executive council has described the motivation behind creating the CCU in these terms: "Several bodies were in charge of the cultural and ideological policies, leading sometimes to contradiction and deviation in ideology and beliefs. Certain dangerous spiritual trends emerged, pressuring the leadership to establish the Central Cultural Unit".[37] A further concern for Hizbullah was the decentralised Shi'i tradition of *taqlid*, whereby the faithful choose which senior cleric will issue *fatwas*. The party has sought since 2000 to promote Khamenei as the sole *marje'* (authority) for *taqlid* among its followers, despite many objections about his religious qualifications for the role.[38]

2.6 The Role of Language, the Media, and Educational Institutions

According to Smith, "[t]he need for mass education is what gives nations their large scale, just as modern societies' requirement for mass literacy turns language into their effective boundary marker" (Smith 2009, p. 82). Language was central to Benedict Anderson's seminal theory on nationalism and his idea of nations as 'imagined communities'; they are "bounded print communities and the dissemination of literature through 'print capitalism' makes it imperative to standardise the languages disseminated by printed books and, later, newspapers" (Anderson cited in Smith 2009, p. 82).[39] The role of such media is pivotal as they communicate, in the case of nationalist publications, a sense of national identity, and produce various forms of this identity to suit different audiences and contexts. Hizbullah's educational and media institutions have an identical function in terms of identity production among different members of Lebanon's Shi'i community.

Hizbullah's network of educational and media institutions covers a large portion of the Shiʿi community, which, according to a 2010 United Nations estimate, comprises around 30 per cent of Lebanon's population of 4.3 million.[40] The organisation's institutions have beneficiaries in every Shiʿi region, from small towns in the north to the Shiʿi heartlands of the northern Biqaʿ valley, South Lebanon, and the southern suburbs of Beirut. This wide reach has implications for the way the Shiʿi population in the various regions identifies with the organisation and the concepts that form its two central pillars: *Wilayat al-Faqih* and resistance. Hizbullah has managed to penetrate various levels of society—for instance, many Shiʿi butchers in Nabatieh and parts of Beirut's southern suburbs are made aware of the *fatwas* pronounced by the 'leader' on meat, and for the most part identify with them as a form of expert Shiʿi knowledge. The magnitude of the mass indoctrination effort can be best understood by the activities of Mahdi Scouts. These scouts exist in nearly every major Shiʿi centre, and have launched a mobile library project which organises trips to smaller population centres in the South, Biqaʿ, Mount Lebanon, and North Lebanon regions; equipped with laptops and a collection of Islamic books, the library is a useful tool for attracting new members. To complement Hizbullah's educational and media work, it has built facilities to host various recreational activities—for example, a major scouts centre, Imam Khomeini's Scout City, encompasses a sports centre, training facilities, a religious study centre, and 26.000 square metres of green space.

The organisation's message, however, is most effectively and widely disseminated through its publications. *Baqiatullah*[41] is Hizbullah's main journal, distributed among its members and institutional employees; it is also sold in shops and bookstores throughout the different parts of Shiʿi Lebanon (Musawi 2012). Given its wide circulation, it mainly concentrates on interpreting different facets of the Shiʿi faith and repackaging the foundational concepts of Hizbullah identity—*Wilayat al-Faqih* and resistance—for its different readerships. *Baqiatullah* is thus basically composed of four sections: one focuses on the *Walī al-Faqih*, Ayatollah Ali Khamenei; one on *jihad* and martyrdom; and the other sections revolve around these themes. *Wilayat al-Faqih*, a significant part of Hizbullah's identity, is disseminated in different contexts to suit its respective audiences, whether in *Baqiatullah* or its myriad other publications. *Baqiatullah*, however, remains the most significant publication as it targets party members, and is not only the most popular journal within the organisation itself but also the largest nationwide in terms of circulation (30,000, according to its editor).[42] On its eighth anniversary, an op-ed discussed the many meanings of its name, *Baqiatullah*, focusing on the most significant for Hizbullah ideology, that pertaining to Imam Mehdi, the 'Saviour and Imam' (*Baqiatullah* 1998, pp. 5–6). "Our policy was to embark on Imam Khomeini's ship to pave a way amid loss and arrogance" (*Baqiatullah* 1998, p. 7). The editorial highlights Khomeini's teachings, stating in bold text that "the Imam taught us that the *Walī Al Amr* [Iran's Supreme Leader or *Walī al-Faqih*] is Hojatollah ['Allah's proof']", meaning Allah's representative on Earth.[43] The editorial then quickly moved on to the second pillar of Hizbullah identity, also connected to the leader's message and guidance: "The Imam taught us that Jihad and Martyrdom are eternal glory" (*Baqiatullah* 1998, p. 7).

These two elements are reproduced in various contexts within the same magazine. Sayyid Hashem Saffieddine, the head of Hizbullah's executive branch, argues in *Baqiatullah* that in Islam, the leader or *Walī al-Faqih* is a representative of the infallible Hidden Imam (*Baqiatullah* 1998, p. 18). The absence of the Twelfth Imam, known as *Al-Ghaibah Al Kubra*, is 'exceptional' in its nature, requiring exceptional rules: "[W]hat we understand from the Prophet's clarifications of the Infallible Imam's status and role is the referral in all matters to the *Al Walī*, the leader and enlightener" (*Baqiatullah* 1998, p. 18). *Baqiatullah*'s journalists, while emphasising the role that strife, sacrifice, and martyrdom play in Shiʿa Islam, also provide promises of global domination under the leadership of the Hidden Imam and his deputy, the Islamic Republic's Supreme Leader. "[The] scrolls [predict that] the Twelfth Imam's state's political influence will reach the entire world, all societies and regimes in the East and West; all humanity will be the subject of one leader, under one Central Government, where a single socio-political regime exits, and that is the Islamic regime" (Daʿmoush in *Baqiatullah* 1998, p. 27). Such statements, while similar to those found in Iran, serve a local purpose as the members of Hizbullah's hierarchy portray themselves as representatives of the *Walī al-Faqih*.

2.6.1 *The 'Nation's Leader'*

The transnational authority of the *Walī al-Faqih* is discussed directly and indirectly, with indirect discussion taking different forms. Direct articles explain, in the language of Islamic jurisprudence, why the *Walī al-Faqih* has transnational authority outside the borders of the Islamic Republic. Taking one article by way of example, Ayatollah Mesbah Yazdi, a conservative cleric in Iran, concludes his detailed legal argument by declaring that:

> The Shiʿa who were deprived of the government of the Imams of the Prophet's household, on one hand, and rejected the legitimacy of the current governments, on the other, have lived in difficult conditions; they are ordered according to certain narratives, like Omar Ben Hanzala and Mashoura Bent Khadija, to refer in their governmental needs, especially the judiciary ones, to the *Faqihs* [Islamic jurists]. (Yazdi in *Baqiatullah* 2000, pp. 15–16)[44]

Yazdi then reiterates the common themes of Hizbullah's *Walī al-Faqih* arguments: "opposition [to] these [jurists] is as grave as opposing the Infallible Imam, a type of polytheism/apostasy" (Yazdi 2000, p. 16). Sheikh Khalil Rizk, a Hizbullah official and ideologue, also writes in a similar vein, with direct references to the connection between the Hizbullah's leader and the 'Infallible Imam', stating that "the jurisdiction and governance of the *Faqih* is similar to that of the Infallible, meaning that his legal orders are applicable to all" (Rizk in *Baqiatullah* 1999, p. 34).[45]

The leader's importance lies in expanding the party's role. The question that concerns many of these ideologues is whether this role is similar to that of other political parties. Sheikh Shafic Jradi, a Hizbullah official, returns to the theme that was discussed earlier in this chapter by emphasising that the organisation's name is itself derived from the *Qurʾan*, which differentiates between the Hezb Al Shaitan (the Party of the Devil) and Hizbullah (the Party of Allah) (Jradi in *Baqiatullah* 2000, p. 19).[46] The party is not the *ummah*, the nation, but rather "an organ of the body", which is led by the *Walī Faqih*; in that sense, it embodies the Leninist concept of the vanguard, an organisation leading the masses towards its Islamist goals. However, it is the 'leader of the nation', the representative of divine authority, who gives the party its purpose. "Hizbullah", Jradi continues, "is a single member in a national movement, led by the Imam of the *Ummah*. From him, it takes legitimacy, meaning and belonging" (Jradi in *Baqiatullah* 2000, p. 21).

2.6.2 Sacrifice, Jihad, and Martyrdom

The glory promised to the Imam's followers, who are by default the followers of the 'nation's leader', has a price, as *Baqiatullah* notes. The theme of the ultimate sacrifice, martyrdom during resistance, is a recurrent one in nationalism, where "the ideal of public sacrifice could inspire in successive generations a desire to emulate their ancestors and repair or strengthen the bonds of political solidarity" (Smith 2009, p. 97). The ideal of a national destiny, as Smith terms it, "requires ceaseless striving and sacrifice on behalf of the community" (ibid, p. 97). In Hizbullah's case, sacrifice is part of its identity, as the Imam's followers are the *mostazafin*, the oppressed, who are "distinguished as a movement to change society" (Khatun in *Baqiatullah* 1998, p. 31). According to a *Baqiatullah* article, they "did not become oppressed willingly, but as a result of their refusal to give in to the strong, so the latter tried by means of force to oppress and defeat them" (Khatun in *Baqiatullah* 1998, p. 31).

2.6.3 The 'Sacred Homeland'

In every edition of *Baqiatullah*, there are stories of Hizbullah's 'martyrs', some of whom were killed during the 1980s, in the party's early years; these articles sanctify the homeland through connecting it to faith and resistance. In its December 1998 edition, when South Lebanon was still under Israeli occupation, an article entitled "Martyr ʿAdel Hussein Al Zein" namechecks those regions associated with resistance in South Lebanon:

> In every morning, hope renews, and with the morning's dream comes hope, so that the dream resides in every Human's memory ... and with this dream, we embark on the road to Safi and Sojod, Alrafeeʿ Mountain and Mleekh. There, where the heroic Mujahideen are, we learn the meaning of eternal life. (*Baqiatullah* 1998, p. 100)

The Safi Mountain became a symbol of Hizbullah's resistance to the occupation; its sacred nature was constructed during the 1990s by means of songs and stories of holy visions during the conflict with the Israeli army.[47] The argument for the sanctity of South Lebanon, referred to in Hizbullah's discourse by its religious name, Jabal ʿAmil, draws on the existence of shrines in the area.[48] One of these, in the village of Al-Sarafand, is claimed to be the grave of Abu Dhar al-Ghifari (referred to in Chap. 3), the most revered companion of the Prophet and Imam ʿAli in Shiʿi narratives.[49] The al-Maʿaref Association, which publishes *Baqiatullah* and operates within the CCU, comments: "The hills of Jabal ʿAmil were honored to carry the name of Abu Dhar... he was attached to this good land".[50] In Shiʿi doctrines, Abu Dhar bears special significance as a "true" companion to both the Prophet Mohammad and Imam ʿAli Ben Abi

Talib, and as a rebel against the rule of Muʿawiya Ben Abi Sufian, the first Umayyad Caliph.

The process of sanctifying homelands, Smith argues, mainly relies on the "presence and activities of saints, prophets and sages" (Smith 2009, p. 97). He notes:

> St Gregory's missions to the various provinces of the kingdom of Armenia endowed them with a novel sanctity, binding them together as a union of Christians. Similar functions were performed by St Patrick in his missions across Ireland and St David in Wales, as well as by the shrines of the Virgin of Yasna Gora in Poland, and of the Virgin of Guadelupe in Mexico. Of course, many of the saints were more localised—St Cuthbert in Northumbria, St Genevieve in Paris, SS Boris and Gleb in Kiev—but some of them became patron saints of dynasties and, in the course of generations, of delocalised territories and their populations. (Smith 2009, p. 97)

The Safi Mountain's religious significance is reiterated in the various narratives glorifying Hizbullah 'martyrs'. In the story of Hussein and Mohamad Ahmad Salhab, two brothers who died fighting in South Lebanon, a *Baqiatullah* journalist recounts that they both grew up in Brital, a Shiʿi town in the Biqaʿ valley, "which was, since the earliest phases of Jihad, a martyrs' [breeding ground] for the Islamic Resistance" (*Baqiatullah* 2000, p. 80).[51] The two men decided at an early age, the article goes on, to go south to join the holy fight against Israeli occupation. The author uses the word '*tayamum*'—the exceptional use of soil for ablutions, in the absence of water, in preparation for prayer—to describe the brothers' decision to join the fight in Jabal ʿAmil (*Baqiatullah* 2000, pp. 80–81), and establishes the recurrent link with the legendary Safi Mountain in South Lebanon: "[T]hey sought sanctuary in Safi Mountain's frost and complex tracks, receiving warmth from each other's breath" (*Baqiatullah* 2000, p. 81).

As in nationalism, an integral part of the nation's significance, especially in a Shiʿi religious context, lies in its perceived historical continuity. The history of Jabal ʿAmil, in Hizbullah's narrative, is one of a continuous Islamic struggle, with martyrdom and leadership as its basic defining tenets. sayyid Ali Al-Musawi, *Baqiatullah*'s editor in chief, claims in an interview conducted for this research:

> Around the year 900 Hegira [1500 AD], Jabal ʿAmil witnessed some kind of movement with what is known as the First and Second Martyrs. Studies

on the history of Shiʿa in Lebanon and Jabal ʿAmil in that period showed that the First Martyr was able to gather all the Shiʿi people in a specific frame and started [wielding] his authority. Some said that his murder was not just the result of a confessional disagreement because he was Shiʿa and the Ottomans Sunni. The Ottoman authorities decided [to eliminate him] because he was leading an on-the-ground political and administrative movement through the collection of *zakat* (a Muslim tax), and other ... measures. Since then, the Shiʿi presence was established in Lebanon in general, and in Jabal ʿAmil specifically, where a group of Shiʿi people imposed themselves as an entity [with] its own personality, existence and independence. (Musawi 2012)

Musawi, a cleric, emphasises in his narrative of Jabal ʿAmil's history, the leading role played by a single Shiʿi *aʾlem* (cleric) in every phase, lending more legitimacy to the current adherence to the *Wilayat al-Faqih* doctrine. Through this approach, Musawi represents *Wilayat al-Faqih* as a continuation of the historical authority of imams as leaders since Mohamed's death.

The underlying references to the sanctity of the homeland are also modern, as the fallen soldiers of Hizbullah have further contributed to the more ancient religious history, most of which is constructed.[52] This is evident in *Baqiatullah*'s 1999 story of the 'martyrs' and friends Samer Shehab and Ali Kashmar. The former died during combat in 1995, while the latter launched a successful suicide attack against an Israeli force in 1996. The article describes their close relationship, describing how Kashmar "rarely returned home" following his friend's 'martyrdom'; it draws on religious symbols to describe his decision to commit to fighting till death, comparing *jihad* with prayer (*Baqiatullah* 1999, p. 75). The locations of both men's deaths are described in detail in order to link their sacrifice to the sanctity of the homeland: "He blew himself up in a martyrdom operation in the Udaiseh-Rob Thlatheen triangle, his body scattered to embrace the soil of the South, may the wind carry from the soil of Yuhmor-Shkeef some of Samer's body perfume, so that ... Ali meets his beloved Samer Bechara [another martyr]" (*Baqiatullah* 1999, p. 75).

While Hizbullah's presence and popularity currently thrives in both South Lebanon (Jabal ʿAmil) and the eastern Biqaʿ valley, the idea of the 'sacred homeland' includes the latter in public discourse but puts the emphasis on the former.[53] Musawi, however, whose descendants were from the northern Biqaʿ valley, is more inclusive and includes his home region in the narratives. In the aforementioned interview, Musawi states that Malek Al Ashtar, Imam Ali's faithful and revered companion, was buried in the Baalbek region (Musawi 2012).[54]

2.7 AL-JARHA (THE FOUNDATION OF THE WOUNDED)

In keeping with this concept of the sacred duty of resistance, Hizbullah's Al-Jarha Foundation, registered as a charity since 1992, cares for 8,000 injured fighters and their families.[55] Its network of services includes three rehabilitation centres in South Lebanon, the Biqaʿ valley and Beirut, Al-ʿAbbass physiotherapy and prosthetic centres, and the Jwaya and Al-Furdaws care centres.[56] The Hizbullah's Al-Jarha Foundation assists the families of the wounded during their care and rehabilitation, and organises events, educational sessions, and courses. As a result, some of the wounded, according to the head of the foundation, have re-joined Hizbullah's forces (Kheshman 2012). In addition to courses, the foundation distributes a magazine to its beneficiaries. While its narratives conform to Hizbullah's basic themes, the focus is more specific, emphasising the significance of injured figures in Shiʿi versions of Islamic history, such as Imam Husayn's brother, Abul Fadl Al Abbass, who lost his hands during combat but continued to fight until he was killed. The foundation named two of its care centres after Al Abbass, while his sacrifices are recurrent themes inside the foundation's buildings and in its dealings with beneficiaries. The *Wālī Al Faqih* Ali Khamenei was also injured in a 1981 bombing, and his right arm paralysed, a connection that the foundation frequently highlights in its publication and educational sessions. Ayatollah Khamenei's *fatwas* concerning the day-to-day lives of the disabled are repeated to the foundation's beneficiaries, and his photograph is edited to display an aura of light, implying spirituality.[57] Kheshman, an al-Jareeh foundation leader, provides the following interpretation of the 'special' connection the injured have to the Islamic Republic's Supreme Leader:

> There is a special relation that connects us, the wounded, with the leader Khamenei. Sayyid Khamenei said that like us, he was wounded and injured, and his hand was paralysed during the attempt to kill him when a recorder exploded. He was injured and his right hand is handicapped for good. Sayyid Khamenei is a jihadi and a militant, in addition to being a religious ideologue, missionary, jurist and cultural reference. He was among the peo-

ple who gathered in the squares [during the revolution] and confronted the regime, and he represented Imam Khomeini for a long time in the Higher Council for Defence. He was at the frontline, wore military uniform, carried weapons, and participated in battle. All the constituents of his personality are models. We are a jihadi and believing young generation and look up to our models. (Kheshman 2012)

The foundation's main work, however, focuses on helping the injured cope in their daily lives through learning new skills and attaining a measure of independence, so that they are no longer financially dependent on the organisation and physically dependent on their families (Kheshman 2012). The education and training the foundation provides encompasses family carers, helping them to improve their injured relative's quality of life and enhancing the care within the family. Its monthly magazine, *Sada Al Jirah* (the *Echo of Wounds*), is generally focussed on its regional activities and inspirational stories of wounded fighters who have been enabled to actively pursue their dreams (*Sada Al Jirah* 2012).[58] In one example, the magazine profiles Ibrahim Roumani, a Hizbullah scout, who was wounded during a field trip; he was a talented painter until paralysed from the neck down. The foundation encouraged him to resume painting using his mouth to hold the brush, and he gradually improved his technique until "he now dreams of organising his own show" (*Sada Al Jirah* 2012, p. 15). The publication also includes a section for profiling those who have been wounded, emphasising the central theme of sacrifice and perseverance in the face of injury and pain. The role of the CCU in unifying the various stories in the magazine is evident: the profiles of the 'martyrs' in *Baqiatullah* and those of the wounded in *Sada Al Jirah* carry the same underlying message—that of faith in Hizbullah ideology and resistance or *jihad*. In an obituary for Ahmad Al Kheshen, a wounded Hizbullah fighter who died aged 42, due to deteriorating health, the magazine stressed the he "continued his *Jihadi* duties until he passed away of an incurable disease" (*Sada Al Jirah* 2012, p. 7). The al-Jareeh Foundation also organises trips to the Biqa' valley to visit the graves of Khawla, Imam Husayn's daughter, and Syed Abbas Al-Musawi, the former secretary general of Hizbullah, assassinated in an Israeli air raid (*Sada Al Jirah* 2012, p. 7).

The foundation also organises monthly workshops for the sons and daughters of the wounded to educate them on time management and study skills, while running awareness sessions on the rights of the disabled under Islamic and Lebanese Law. On Mother's Day, it honours a number of mothers and wives of the wounded, citing their sacrifices for the cause (*Sada Al Jirah* 2012, p. 10). The foundation's president, who was also wounded during combat, describes its activities in a nutshell, revealing the focus on religious education[59]:

> We try to provide guidance and education for the family members in day to day issues, like organising the family's daily life, how to rationalise spending. As you know, a lot of people face economic crises and challenges despite the assistance and aid we provide them, and despite their jobs and earnings. We still have to emphasise guiding the family, teaching the parents how to raise the children and care for them, how to follow up their children's behavioural, pedagogic, and educational affairs. We are also involved in the religious education of these families, which is part of the general and educational programme of the resistance and Hizbullah in Lebanon. These brothers and sisters participate in our programme. There isn't a specific programme set by the institution for them; as I said, the institution assists, it is not there to replace the family. It has always been there to assist and help the family. The family is the reference and roots. This is why we do not see or encounter important psychological problems or crises. Everybody suffers from the war, which leaves its effects on their personality. All soldiers in the different armies of the world, throughout history, suffer from injuries, wounds, disabilities ... What matters the most is the family's embrace, its presence around the person in need, the availability of independent housing for him, and having a life that he can share and develop. We have several plans that allow the wounded or disabled person to live his life normally, away from any pressures. We focus on the fun part, and we help the person to develop his abilities through vocational and professional training, and art and crafts. We also focus on sports and have special places for sports training and have our own sports teams. We have a website that reflects our reality, as well as our own magazine where we publish our activities and programmes. It is a big organization. (Kheshman 2012)

The foundation's financial and medical assistance gives the organisation leverage with families, especially as the sons and daughters of the wounded are educated in Hizbullah's network of schools, which are free of charge for children of full-time members, 'martyrs', and those who have been wounded.

2.7.1 Al Mu'assasa Al Islamiya Lil Tarbiya Wal Ta'leem: Al Mahdi Schools

The Islamic Institute for Education and Learning, Hizbullah's educational arm, controls 14 schools, boasting a capacity of 21,356.[60] The network covers South Lebanon, the Biqaʿ valley, the southern suburbs of Beirut, and Qom in Iran, where it caters for the sons of Lebanese students at the religious school in Qom. The pupils are taught about *Wilayat al-Faqih* and resistance from an early age in a range of material and contexts, from religious classes to bedtime stories. *Aldar Al Islamiya* (the Islamic Publishing House), a Hizbullah-affiliated private institution, provides such stories to schools and bookstores operating in Shiʿi neighbourhoods under the party's control. Series of these bedtime stories, aimed at children in elementary classes, carry themes of resistance and loyalty, often in dramatic settings. In the storybooks, *The Precious Freedom*, *The Mothers' Sacrifices*, and *The Consequences of Treachery*, the same themes appear in different forms and places, showing the child a world of 'resistors and traitors' (Fig. 2.4).

The school network caters for both girls and boys, and plays on gender to disseminate the same message in different forms. For instance, parallel to the bedtime stories, a series called 'Fatema', published by *Dar Al Walaa*, another Hizbullah-affiliated publishing house,[61] is aimed at girls in elementary school. The essence of the stories is that Fatema enthusiastically asks her parents about religion, *jihad*, and *Wilayat al-Faqih*. In *Fatema Loves Jihad* (2010), she questions her mother on the importance of *jihad*, begging for stories about the 'heroic resistance' to the Israeli occupation.[62] *Fatema Follows Welat Allah* tackles the girl's curiosity regarding *Wilayat al-Faqih*, depicting her as a good student and praiseworthy daughter for understanding the significance of the concept. The story, full of cartoon sketches of the *Wālī al-Faqih* and the faces of the Infallible Imams emanating a holy radiance, ends with a mission statement: "Fatema felt that her heart adores Allah's *Walis*, she pledged to remain forever obedient to Allah, his Prophet and his household".[63]

2.7 AL-JARḤA (THE FOUNDATION OF THE WOUNDED) 55

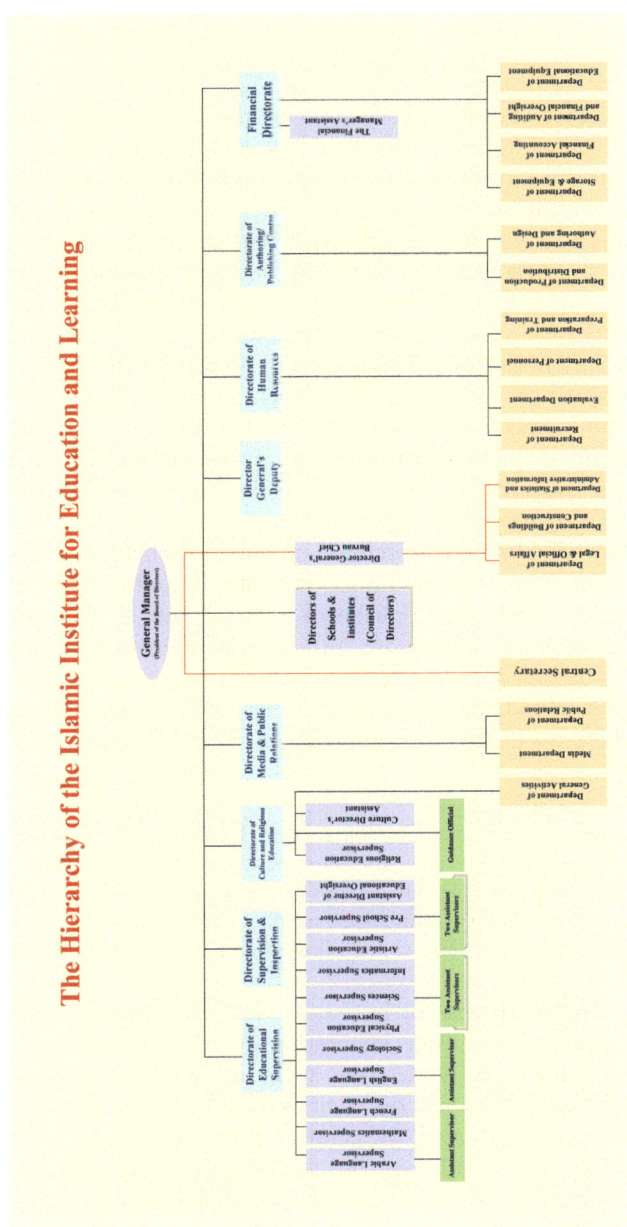

Fig. 2.4 The hierarchy of the Islamic Institute for Education and Learning

2.8 The Consultative Centre for Studies and Documentation

The level of higher education is covered by the Consultative Centre for Studies and Documentation, Hizbullah's think tank, which hosts academics and helps justify and/or devise the organisation's internal and external policies. The institution publishes academic books, treatises, and policy recommendations conforming to the party's ideology. Its sizeable library, located in the southern suburbs of Beirut, and its academic experts offer their services to Hizbullah supporters and members from a different class—educated professionals. The organisation, which was first introduced to the Shiʿi population in Lebanon as a party of the downtrodden and oppressed, has since expanded its reach to the middle classes. The centre's academic experts and librarians provide advice on economic, legal, and urban matters, thus refuting the widespread secular argument that religious ideologies are incompatible with day-to-day affairs, which are better addressed by secular professionals.[64]

At the institute's library, researchers—mainly university students—pursue their studies, either attempting to vindicate Hizbullah's ideologically oriented economic and social policies or explain them in their academic projects or coursework.[65] They are more eloquent in their defence and explanation of the party's identity, specifically concerning the concept of *jihad* or resistance and the more controversial *Wilayat al-Faqih*. One of the centre's directors explains the importance of Imam Khamenei's annual *Eid* and *Hajj* messages:

> These messages are the main reference that I follow. These words are immortal; they are not just any words or messages, they come from Walī al-Faqih. He is not infallible but he rises above a lot of things and comes close enough to infallibility. Thus, these messages are neither a religion nor a Sharia, but they are teachings to be followed and learnt. (Qassem 2012)[66]

The centre publishes dozens of books, as well as providing Hizbullah's MPs with necessary policy advice, suggesting laws that will serve the party's interests and conform to its ideology, while its academic experts advise Hizbullah's graduate students on their research.[67] In a similar way to Hizbullah's welfare institutions, the centre's library and offices are open to students, providing them with free consultations, simultaneously taking the opportunity to showcase their large collection of ideological propaganda.

2.9 Conclusion

This chapter shows that the organisation's institutions play a significant role in the dissemination of Hizbullah's identity among different strata of Lebanese Shi'i Muslims. While providing basic welfare services and distributing publications tailored to their beneficiaries' interests, they also organise ideological training and interact with them at the level of their daily lives. Despite Hizbullah's insistence on its continuity with the earliest forms of Islamic organisation, the party's internal structure bears a marked resemblance to, and is in fact modelled on, Lenin's idea of the party as the vanguard in theory and practice. The historical experience of Shi'a commitment to communism and Hizbullah's understanding of how a successful Marxist–Leninist organisation functions were equal factors in its decision to adopt this model. As the organisation has expanded its institutions and structure, and widened its reach, Hizbullah has increased its centralisation in order to control the dissemination of a sectarian Shi'i identity, based on the concepts of Islamic resistance or *jihad* and *Wilayat al-Faqih*.

The vast network of institutions (concerned with, for example, welfare, religious rituals, different levels of education, scout troupes, and cultural events) and the party's expansive geographic structures has extended its reach in the Shi'i community. At a scale comparable to the promotion of nationalist identity through state institutions and governmental frameworks, Hizbullah continues to work on transforming Lebanese Shi'i identity. Hizbullah's ideology, although centralised under the control of the CCU to ensure coherence, is tailored to different audiences by the party's specialist institutions. The process of disseminating a sense of Shi'i identity, as channelled through Hizbullah, occurs on different levels, either indirectly through its publications or directly through its operatives and institutions, which provide specifically targeted education for the different strata of Shi'i society. These institutions, whether educational or service-based, are responsible for the party's expansive reach, geographically and socially. Contrary to the 'Lebanonisation' argument currently dominant in studies of Hizbullah, the organisation's transnational identity and ties have become entrenched at the level of its institutions and among its constituents, the Shi'i community in Lebanon. The contention that Hizbullah's increased participation in Lebanon's political process has had a significant impact on the organisation glosses over a simultaneous increase in the strength of its commitment to the doctrine of *Wilayat al-Faqih*. Hizbullah has not ceased to remould the identity of Lebanon's Shi'i community based on the twin pillars of resistance and *Wilayat al-Faqih*.

Notes

1. Institutions are significant in embodying and manifesting identity. For instance, Hizbullah's sanctification of 'resistance', as embodied in a collection of institutions, helps disseminate its idea of Shi'i identity in society. Hizbullah's supporters today identify with the idea of Islamic resistance.
2. *Taklif shar'i* literally means 'legal commissioning', with 'legal' here pertaining to Islamic law.
3. Khomeini's *Wilayat al-Faqih* theory, crystallised during his years of exile in Najaf, was later published in his landmark book *The Islamic Government*.
4. During my visits to a number of Hizbullah institutions and interviews with officials there, the issue of *Wilayat al-Faqih* surfaced in different contexts. For instance, when discussing an institution's performance, the explanation for welcoming 'unexpected results' would be that they were the blessings of *Wilayat al-Faqih*. There is a general belief in the hierarchy's ability to bring about inexplicable and unexpected outcomes.
5. A Hizbullah member who enrolled in religious training at the Imam Jawad clerical school, a *hawza* that is considered to be one of the organisation's main clerical institutions, said that after lectures, the teacher often discussed stories about the way light emanated from both Imam Khomeini and Khamenei's office during important meetings. When asked repeatedly whether he believed this indicated they were meeting with the 'Hidden Imam', the teacher nodded. Such teachings, though mostly less direct, suggest that orders from the *Wali al-Faqih* emanate from the 'Hidden Imam' himself. This has been suggested in Hizbullah leaders' statements and speeches to the organisation's followers.
6. This is similar to the rise of ethnic identities and nationalism in former communist countries, where 'sectarian nationalism' has gained momentum following the fall of the Soviet Union.
7. In the organisation's discourse, the government is blamed for the lack of services in the various areas, and therefore Hizbullah's services are seen as compensating for this lack. In the post-war political system, up until recently, the Amal movement assumed the responsibility of representing the Shi'a in Lebanon.
8. The 'Amlieh compound was the major Shi'i centre in Beirut before the Lebanese Civil War. For many decades, two central *'Ashura'* gatherings were held in 'Amlieh and in the southern city of Nabatieh.

9. The *Masraʿ* is the day of Imam Husayn's death in the battle of Karbala. The day is also called *ʿAshura* or *al-ʿasher*, meaning the tenth day, as the rituals start from the night of the first day of the holy month of Muharram in the Muslim lunar calendar.
10. Iranian Shiʿi immigrants during the Safavid era played a significant role in providing medical care for the local population, based on religious ties.
11. These protests are chronicled in Hizbullah's historical and educational literature as a major event in Islamic history and 'awakening' (*al-sahwa*).
12. In South Lebanon, the city of Nabatieh became a major destination for the commemoration of *ʿAshura*, during which participants, in their hundreds, use sharp objects to increase the blood flow.
13. *Hussainiyahs* are Shiʿi religious centres where rituals and public functions are held.
14. Imam Hussein's female relatives marched from Karbala in Iraq to Syria as *sabaya*, the special Islamic status for the women relatives of non-Muslim enemy combatants. Shiʿi narratives emphasise the irony that the female members of the Prophet's household, including his grandchild Zaynab, were treated as non-Muslims under Yazid, the Umayyed caliph.
15. Abu Al-Rida heads the powerful security committee, known as *al-lijna al-amniya*, which coordinates the organisation's security and military branches with the various other actors in Lebanon, including the government security apparatuses and army. His PhD dissertation at the Lebanese University discusses the organisation's educational approach from a Hizbullah perspective. Al-Rida has also undertaken several mediation roles, some of which were political, and is usually known in the local media by his *jihadist* pseudonym, Hajj Sajed.
16. This book, published in 2011, is a collection of Khomeini's short statements.
17. Yazbek is currently the head of the Judicial Council, and Khamenei's legal representative.
18. Mohammad Baqer Al-Sadr was a leading Iraqi cleric who wrote prolifically in defence of Islamic concepts and ideology, while criticising the 'failings' of both liberal and Marxist ideologies. He is most known for his two books, *Iqtisaduna* (*Our Economy*) and *Falsafatuna* (*Our Philosophy*). In 1981, Saddam Hussein's regime executed Al-Sadr and his sister Bint al Huda.
19. There is a degree of word play and manoeuvring in Hizbullah's discourse with its members and followers. This is clear when it discusses the verses on 'Hizb Allah'; the connection between the actual party and the party described in the verse is left ambiguous.
20. The major challenge to Hizbullah's unity came in 1997, when its former secretary general Sheikh Sobhi al-Tofaili (1989–1991) declared "the revo-

lution of the hungry" (*thawrat al jiya'*), splitting the party's base in the northern Biqaʿ valley. Tofaili's dissent resulted in a fight with Hizbullah's remaining loyalists. According to Hizbullah officials interviewed during my fieldwork, Tofaili's rebellion highlighted the significance of *Wilayat al-Faqih*, leading to a restructuring of the organisation, in order to deprive any single leader of the ability to split the party's base in future.

21. The organisation's post-2000 control over these affiliated institutions has been corroborated by various sources. Qassim says that a Hizbullah-affiliated Iranian cleric, who ran one of these social welfare networks in the southern suburbs of Beirut, was coerced by party militants into signing after his initial refusal.
22. In interviews with Hizbullah members and officials during my fieldwork, they reiterated the role of *tawjeehat al kaed*, the leader's guidance, as relayed by senior figures at Hizbullah meetings. These messages of guidance lead or control the discussions within the meeting, limiting any major differences in opinion. They often restrict debates to discussion on methods of implementation. For instance, the Iranian leader approved in a *fatwa* the organisation's participation in government in 2005, leaving the details of its participation—the number of ministers or ministries—to the party leaders to decide.
23. The assassination of Abbass Al-Musawi, Hizbullah's secretary general, in 1992, increased the deputy position's importance.
24. The *qetaʿat* or regions, and the role they play in Hizbullah's general hierarchical structure, are very similar to Marxist-Leninist organisations' local branches. For instance, the South Vietnam Communist Party's branches in regions and towns have the same sort of features.
25. The military and security branches remain secretive, often changing their locations.
26. The Jihadi Council oversees Hizbullah's specialist military forces, which tap the branches for extra support and recruitment.
27. The pictures and sayings of both ayatollahs, Khamenei and Khomeini, are hung nearly in every office and building I visited during the fieldwork for this research. Their presence and their resonant message of *Wilayat al-Faqih* carry an underlying organisational purpose, equating obedience with faith.
28. Certain branches of the educational reserves, such as that of the Faculty of Sciences in Hadath in the southern suburbs of Beirut, have played a significant role in supplying the party with specialist cadres, many of whom have since lost their lives.
29. The same figure often led both the political and legislative councils.
30. Islamist publishers opened in the southern suburbs of Beirut, some of which were run by Iranian immigrants, such as the Alma'aref al-Islamiya publishing house.

31. Al-Jareeh was distinct in character, especially in regards to its *Welayat al-Faqih* message. The institution's publications and programmes have an interest in Abu al-Fadl al-Abbass, Imam Hussein's half-brother, who lost his hands in the symbolic battle of Karbala. On the *Welayat al-Faqih* level, there is a strong or special relationship with Khamenei, the Supreme Leader, who was injured in a bombing that left him with an amputated arm.
32. *Murshidat al-Mahdi*, 21st edition, July 2013.
33. In the long version of Lenin's aforementioned statement on the significance of party newspapers, he speaks of the publication's role in establishing a network of agents who distribute the paper and also contribute to it. Beyond its role as a propaganda tool, therefore, it has an important organisational one.
34. The offices are in an unusually large multi-story building in the crowded Ma'moura area in the southern suburbs of Beirut. The building's circular interior encompasses various offices, housing the bureaucracy. Symbols and posters signifying the importance of *Welayat al-Faqih* and resistance are very visible and appear to dominate every office.
35. The complaints were partly due to slow and bureaucratic processes, as the organisation became increasingly centralised. Many publications, at least one for each Hizbullah institution, overstretched the CCU's resources.
36. Interview with a member of Hizbullah's executive branch, Beirut, 6 November 2014.
37. Interview, Beirut, 6 November 2014. (The interlocutor asked to remain anonymous).
38. Mohammad Hussein Fadlulah, a Lebanese cleric turned *marje'*, challenged Hizbullah's authority through a *fatwa* on the limits of *Welayat al-Faqih*. The *fatwa* resulted in clashes with the cleric's followers, while he was bombarded with criticism for his reformist ideas.
39. The *Welayat al-Faqih* doctrine has created an 'imagined community' and a leader who, unlike in Iran, is not associated with or accountable for government failures.
40. See: http://www.escwa.un.org/popin/members/lebanon.pdf
41. The name *Baqiatullah* means, literally, the 'remains of Allah' or 'that which Allah has left behind', a Shi'i reference to Imam Mehdi, known as the 'Saviour' and Twelfth Shi'i Imam. According to the Shi'i narratives, the imam entered a long phase of absence in the tenth century, and will return near the end of time to "fill the earth with justice". 'Limaza Baqiatullah?' ['Why Baqiatullah?'], *Baqiatullah*, 8 December 1998, p. 5.
42. While the number could not be corroborated independently, the magazine's wide dissemination in the country, and its presence in various insti-

tutions and offices visited during my fieldwork, suggest that it does have a wide circulation.
43. Ayatollah Khamenei's international communications in the Iranian media and on his own website refer to him as *Walī Amr Al Moslimeen* (The Guardian of Muslims), to emphasise the reach of his authority over non-Iranian Muslims as well.
44. 'Salaheyat Walī Al Faqih Kharej Hodood al-Watan' ['The authority of the walī al-faqih outside the borders of the state'], *Baqiatullah*, February 2000, pp. 10–16.
45. Rizk, Khalil. Fee Thel Al Welaya Wefkan Lee Ru'yat Al Imam Al Marja'ia (In the presence of leadership according to the view of the reference Imam), December 1999. Shiʿa believe that their 12 imams are infallible; their actions and sayings point to the 'righteous direction'.
46. Hizbullah, Thaqafat Al Intimaa Wa Maham Al Istinhad [The Culture of Belonging, and the Mission of Awakening], February 2000, pp. 18–21.
47. The Safi Mountain in South Lebanon was equipped with underground tunnels and installations, paving the way for the rise of a mythology about the land's endurance against Israeli attacks and bombings.
48. The Lebanese government officially uses the name South Lebanon when describing the region, while Hizbullah employs the historic name of Jabal 'Amil in its literature and public discourse.
49. In Shiʿi narratives, only four of the Prophet's entourage, the *sahaba*, are revered: Abu Dhar, Salman Al Farsi, Ammar Ben Yasser, and Almoqdad Ben Aswad.
50. See: http://www.almaaref.org/maarefdetails.php?number=&bb=&cid=118&subcatid=426&id=1463&supcat=7&searchstring=%CC%C8%E1%20%DA%C7%E3%E1
51. 'MAA Al Shuhada Hussein wa Mohamad Salham', *Baqiatullah*, February 2000, pp. 78–85.
52. Chapters 3 and 4 demonstrate the disparity between academic history and Hizbullah's popular narratives. Much of the latter's claims concerning the region's religious and sacred history is constructed.
53. Within Hizbullah, as in Lebanon itself, there are tensions between the southern and Biqaʿ branches, with claims that the latter is under-represented in the party's leadership. Hassan Nasrallah, Hizbullah's secretary general, and his deputy Naim Qassem are both from South Lebanon.
54. Imam Ali Ben Abi Taleb, the Prophet Mohamed's cousin and First Shiʿi Imam, had four faithful companions, among them are Abu Dhar and Salman the Farsi.
55. Interview with Imad Kheshman, 2012.
56. The two million-dollar Alfurdos Centre is the largest of its kind in the country; it includes swimming pools, football grounds, and basketball courts, in addition to a library for the disabled. (http://www.aljarha.net/essaydetails.php?eid=11&cid=304).

57. See: http://www.aljarha.net/essaydetails.php?eid=42&cid=356
58. Sada Al Jirah [Echo of the Wounds], May 2012.
59. Although established in the 1980s, the foundation drew on experiences from its mother institution, Iran's Mostazafan Foundation, allowing it to expand in spite of its lack of experience and smaller resources.
60. The Mahdi schools website, http://www.almahdischools.org/newsite/index.php, states only the capacity, while Hizbullah members generally complain of overcrowding, suggesting there is a greater number of pupils than there are places.
61. Fatema is the Prophet's daughter, Imam Ali's wife, and Imam Hussein's mother.
62. Safwan, Moussa (2010) *Fateman Tohebo Al Jihad* [*Fatema loves Jihad*]. Beirut: Dar Al Walaa.
63. Safwan, Moussa (2010) Fatema Towali Awliaa Allah [Fatema follows Welat Allah]. Beirut: Dar Al Walaa.
64. From fieldwork at the centre, undertaken in September 2010 and August 2012.
65. See note 63.
66. Interview with Dr. Mohamad Qassem at the Consultative Centre for Studies and Documentation, Beirut, August 2012.
67. See note 65.

References

Books

Abu al-Rida, H. (2012). *Al-Tarbiya al-Hizbiya: Hizbullah Namuzajan* (Party Education: Hizbullah as a Case Study). Beirut: Dar Al-Amir.

Amin, S. (1981). *al-Daʿwah al-Islamiyah Faridah Sharʿiyah Wadarurah Bashariyah* (The Islamic Call Is a Legal Obligation and a Human Need). Port Saʿid: Dar al-Tawziʿ wa al-Nashr al-Islamiya.

Berger, P., & Luckmann, T. (2011). *The Social Construction of Reality: A Treatise in the Sociology of Knowledge*. New York: Open Road Media.

Hutchinson, J. (1994). *Modern Nationalism*. London: Fontana Press.

Khomeini, R. (2011). *Al-Kalimaat al-Qisar Lil Imam Al-Khomeini* (Imam Khomeini's Short Sayings). Beirut: Markaz Noon.

Lenin, V. I. (1953). *Works* (Vol. 5). Moscow: Foreign Languages Publishing House.

Qassem, N. (2005). *Hizbullah: The Story from Within*. London: Saqi.

Selznik, P. I. (1952). *The Organizational Weapon: A Study of Bolshevik Strategy and Tactics*. New York: McGraw-Hill Company.

Smith, A. (2009). *Ethno-symbolism and Nationalism: A Cultural Approach*. London: Routledge.

Stalin, J. (1932). *Foundations of Leninism*. New York: International Publishers.

Journal Articles

Abrahamian, E. (2009, Spring). *Why the Islamic Republic Has Survived?* Middle East Report No. 250, The Islamic Revolution at 30, pp. 10–16.

Hassan, R., & Azadmarki, T. (2003, Spring). Institutional Configurations and Trust in Religious Institutions in Muslim Societies. *Islamic Studies, 42*(1), 97–106.

Hodgson, G. (2006). What Are Institutions? *Journal of Economic Issues, 40*, 1–25.

Jaber, K. (2008). 'Ashura' al-Nabatieh Hadath Sanawy Yastaqteb al-Alaf ('Ashura' in Nabatieh, an Annual Event that attracts Thousands). Al-Akhbar, 15 January. Retrieved June 5, 2011, from http://www.al-akhbar.com/node/126136

Qassir, Q. (2010). Man Yasna' al-'Aql al-Shi'i Fee al-Dahiya Al-Janubiya (Who Creates the Shi'i mind in the Southern Suburbs?). Islam Times, 29 October. Retrieved June 5, 2012, from https://goo.gl/yhhTVB

Tomass, M. (2012). Religious Identity, Informal Institutions, and the Nation-States of the Near East. *Journal of Economic Issues, 46*(3), 705–728.

Magazines[1]

Baqiatullah Magazine, December 1998, 87
Baqiatullah Magazine, September 1999, 96
Baqiatullah Magazine, February 2000, 101
Baqiatullah Magazine, December 2011
Murshidat al-Mahdi, July 2013, 21
Sada Al-Jirah Magazine, May 2012, 35

Interviews

Kheshman, I. (2012). Interview by Mohanad Hage Ali. Al-Jareeh Foundation's Central Office, Bir El-'Abed, Southern Suburbs of Beirut, 15 January 2012.

Mohamad Qassem, interview by Mohanad Hage Ali, The Consultative Center for Study and Documentation, Haret Hreik, Southern Suburbs of Beirut, August 21, 2012.

Qassem Qassir, interview by Mohanad Hage Ali, Southern Suburbs of Beirut, July 28, 2012.

Sayyid Ali al-Musawi, interview by Mohanad Hage Ali, Central Cultural Unit, al-Ma'moura, Southern Suburbs of Beirut, May 20, 2012.

---

[1] Hizbullah magazines feature articles without a Byline, especially in the sections discussed in this book.

CHAPTER 3

The Reconstructed History of the Lebanese Shi'a

This chapter examines the 'dispersed identity' of the Lebanese Shi'a in the period preceding the emergence of Hizbullah and explores earlier attempts to remodel their history and establish a collective sectarian consciousness. Although Shi'i society in Lebanon was historically dominated by local and tribal elements, Arab nationalists and Shi'i clerics in the late nineteenth and early twentieth centuries began to reconstruct its history as a story of proto-national cohesion, and their Shi'a-focused history laid the foundations for Hizbullah's later historical narrative. This chapter argues that the main themes of Hizbullah's reconstructed history—the historic symbols, the leadership of the *ulama* (the Shi'i religious scholars), and the centrality of resistance to Shi'i identity—can already be found scattered throughout the early histories (although there are various discrepancies between these versions). These earlier historical works, especially that of Mohamad Jaber Al Safa (1875–1945), were among the first attempts to establish a Shi'i version of what Makdisi calls Lebanon's 'sectarian nationalism'. However, while it is true that certain practices specific to the Shi'a did exist, and occasional clashes did take place, this chapter demonstrates they were not the predominant factors in Shi'i history or sense of identity that *Hizbullah's* later narrative claims.

The earlier nationalist narrative recast the movements of the Shi'a population from the north of Lebanon to the south and the eastern Biqa' Valley during the era of the Mamluks and the Crusades as series of catastrophic events in a continuous cycle of repression. This interpretation of Shi'i history was used to justify the demand for a form of federal rule in the region within a larger pan-Arab state structure. Jaber's historical narrative chronicles the story of Shiʿi resistance in South Lebanon, especially during the late Ottoman era when the region was stripped of its informal semi-autonomous status, igniting clashes with the Shiʿi feudal landowners. The subsequent (short) period of French colonial rule witnessed a transformation in Shiʿi politics, fostering the wider appeal of Arab nationalism under the Sunni leadership of Reda Bey al-Solh, who challenged the power of the feudal families, particularly that of the al-Assʿad clan. This chapter demonstrates that the basis for Hizbullah's reconstruction of the historical record lies in the modern era and is the result of a combination of elements, including the Ottoman reforms and the sectarian policies of the French colonialists. As such, Hizbullah's narrative is not purely of its own making but is rooted in an earlier historical narrative constructed in the twentieth century, which it further reworked to affirm the idea that the aspiration for a Shiʿi nation has existed in Lebanon since time immemorial.

Theoretical Framework

At the heart of many of the debates in the study of nationalism lies the contested relationship between modern nations and pre-modern ethnic communities. Generally, the claim that the foundations of an existing nation, or a community's aspiration to nationhood, lie in its ancient past is an effective political tool: the assertion of historical continuity provides the idea of the nation with legitimacy. This is particularly so in Hizbullah's case. Yet, the major sources of Hizbullah's history of the Shiʿa date from the political debates that took place in the last years of the Ottoman Empire and during the subsequent colonial conquests in the Levant in the late nineteenth and early twentieth centuries. Indeed, historical evidence of a common sectarian Shiʿi identity in earlier times is both scanty and incoherent. Sectarianism in Lebanon, both as an identity and a form of political association, was fundamentally a modern phenomenon, a product of Ottoman and French policies. In his study of sectarian violence in Mount Lebanon, Makdisi distinguishes between the ancient and medieval religious 'confrontations' in Europe (and elsewhere) and modern sectarianism, which he describes "as the deployment of religious heritage as a primary marker of modern political identity" (Makdisi 2000, p. 7). But although Makdisi clearly contends that sectarianism, or sectarian nationalism, is a modern phenomenon, this does not necessarily presuppose that its claims to historical validity are a complete invention. This raises the question of whether sectarian history is constructed out of pre-existing cultural materials, as ethnosymbolists argue, or is a wholly modern creation.

The ethnosymbolist argument that nationalist histories draw on a community's historic symbols is based on a distinction between the concept of the nation as a "historical form" and as an "analytic category of community" (Smith 2009)—a distinction that is very similar to that made by Makdisi. Smith notes:

> Methodologically, we need to distinguish the concept of nation as an analytic category of community from its use in describing and enumerating the features of particular kinds and cases of the nation as an historical form. While the definition of the nation as a sociological category must be free of temporal restriction, to be of analytical use, and must therefore be transhistorical and cross-cultural, concrete cases of nations (or kinds of nations) need to be seen as historical forms of community which can be described and classified according to period, area or social and political context. (Smith 2009, p. 30)

The Shiʿi sectarian or nationalist identity may be modern, but Jaber lifted a plethora of far earlier events and symbols out of their original context to use in his history, and these were later remoulded to fit Hizbullah's narrative.

Until the early twentieth century, the feudal landowning families dominated the history of the Shiʿa peoples of Jabal ʿAmil (the historic name for South Lebanon), with their internecine feuds and turbulent relationship with the Ottoman administration:

> The early history of the Ottoman rule in these parts of Syria was characterised by a series of rebellions, internecine fighting between the ethnic/tribal chiefs and local rulers, alliances and counter-alliances with the Ottoman authorities against the other/s, and frequent invitations to European powers seeking a foothold in the eastern Mediterranean to intervene in the various conflicts. (Traboulsi 2007, p. 5)

The Shiʿi Harfoush and al-Sagheer feudal clans dominated Bʿalbak and Jabal ʿAmil, respectively, and their relations with Constantinople were based on their coercive collection of taxes from the peasantry on behalf of the Ottomans. Jaber glosses over this peasant–feudal dichotomy in his construction of Shiʿi history and portrays the ʿAmili Shiʿa as a cohesive 'nation'. However, as Weiss (2010) argues, a sense of collective sectarian sentiment among the Shiʿi population did not emerge until the institutionalisation of religious courts under the French Mandate. Thus, while the existence of actual historical figures and the occurrence of certain events cannot be contested, historians and other scholars have sometimes been guilty of taking them out of their historical context, redefining them or magnifying their importance, according to their specific political or nationalist agendas. Smith explains this process using Iranian and Slavic examples:

> In this model, elites, and particularly intellectuals, hark back to heroic exempla from earlier periods in the nation's history or from cognate ethnic pasts. So Slavophiles yearned for the restoration of 'authentic' Old Russia before Peter the Great's westernising reforms, and sought to regain that sense of national communion that his modernising bureaucratic regime had destroyed, at least in the cities. In similar manner, various Arab intellectuals, notably Rashid Rida and Muhammad Abdu in early twentieth-century Egypt, harked back to a pristine Islam in the Age of the Companions of the Prophet, as the authentic realisation of the Arab genius. In neighbouring Iran, a similar official re-appropriation of the glorious ethnic past was evident. First, the Pahlavis aimed to restore the grandeur of the 'Aryan' Achaemenid Empire, culminating in 1975 in a grandiose display of the Shah's might at the ruins of Darius' palace at Persepolis. Then, just a few years later, his enemies, the Shi'ite mullahs, who had helped to overthrow his regime, turned back to the golden age of Ali and Husain in the seventh century, and commemorated the latter's martyrdom with dramatic re-enactments. In each case, we see a significant ethnic past being 'rediscovered' as the golden age and reappropriated (and often manipulated) for modern political ends. (Smith 2009, p. 30)

This process of reappropriating an ethnic past in Lebanon started in the early twentieth century as the Shi'i elites sought to document the region's history and discuss its future. However, the idea of nationalism that arose during the last years of the Ottoman Empire was often inclusive in nature. For example, the *al-Ma'aref* newspaper published a series of articles debating the concept of a 'nation'. In so doing it was reflecting the political spirit of the times: the Young Turks' ascension to power in Constantinople in 1908 had paved the way for the spread of political secret societies throughout the region and the rise of a pan-Arab nationalist movement.[1] The discussion about nation and identity in the 'Amili publication was neither exclusive nor sectarian; rather, it encompassed a general Islamic identity. The sectarian nationalism of the Shi'i community started to take more coherent shape following the French colonial authorities' recognition of their sect and, as mentioned earlier, the establishment of religious courts in January 1926 (Weiss 2010, p. 157).[2] It was through these newly established institutions and the daily interactions between members of the Shiʿa faith that the earliest form of Shiʿi nationalism found root during the 1920s and 1930s. The corpus of court documents, correspondence, and letters during this period demonstrates a growing consciousness among the Shiʿa of their distinct identity. Hizbullah used a similar form of institutionalisation, but one that was more intense and comprehensive, to reconstruct Shiʿi history and national identity.

The following section therefore focuses on the contentious issue of the written historical record in Lebanon, including Jabal ʿAmil's early history, and provides a more nuanced view of the debates and controversies behind what was subsequently presented as a coherent history vindicating Hizbullah's agenda. This is followed by an analysis of the historical situation of the Shiʿa within the wider socio-economic framework of the Levant under Ottoman and colonial rule, highlighting the significance of the feudal or *iqtaʿ* system in what was predominantly an agrarian society.

3.1 Writing Lebanese History

Lebanon's written historical record remains a contentious issue in its deeply divided society[3]; it has been highly politicised, and historical studies have generally been, with a few exceptions, split along partisan lines between a Christian nationalist narrative of Lebanon's non-Arabic roots and a largely Muslim Arabist current (Salibi 1979, p. 11). However, the focus in most instances is on the Mount Lebanon area (the Western Mountains), whose population over the past five centuries has been predominantly Christian and Druze. While the remaining regions, annexed to Lebanon under the French Mandate in 1920, shared some of Mount Lebanon's history, they remained, for the most part, connected to Greater Syria (which included Palestine).[4] Added to this division, the widely accepted Sunni narrative of Arab and Islamic history is also at odds with the dominant Shiʿi version. While Sunnis generally revere the caliphs in the Islamic Umayyad, Abbasid, and later Ottoman periods, Shiʿi histories and *Hadith* collections portray them as illegitimate rulers and, quite often, as 'butchers'.[5] Indeed, the belief in the sole political authority of the Twelve Imams underpins the Shiʿa's overarching condemnation of the Umayyad and Abbasid caliphs. By the same token, the historical narrative of predominantly Shiʿi South Lebanon, or Jabal ʿAmil, has found itself at odds at various times with the national (mostly Christian and Druze) historical story.[6]

While the two major sources of Mount Lebanon's history are the Druze and Maronite's church records, Jabal 'Amil's history is largely dependent on the works of the Shi'i religious scholars, on poetry and on oral history. Oral history of battles, truces, and internal feuds inspired local poetry. However, the main problem with oral history is that it is second hand, not based on witnesses or first-hand accounts, rendering it more vulnerable to politically motivated perceptions. Such oral accounts are near impossible to corroborate, as current events tend to influence the narrators' perceptions and cloud their objectivity. Jaber, as well as Hizbullah's historians, acknowledged the difficulty of finding valid sources for their accounts due to hardships and political repression in these times. Under the subtitle 'The obscurity of Jabal 'Amil's history', Jaber writes: "I do not hide that research into Jabal 'Amil's history, specifically, is very difficult, and hard work, shrouded by ambiguity and vagueness due to the [lack of] evidence and loss of documents" (Jaber 1981, p. 15). Jaber wonders in his preface why the 'genius[es]' of the *ulama* of Jabal 'Amil, despite their huge output on religion, Arabic literature, philosophy, and the natural sciences, never produced a history of the region (Jaber 1981, pp. 15–17). The answer to this, in his opinion, lies in the lack of evidence, which he attributes to the persecution of the *ulama*, referring specifically to two *ulama*, known in the Shi'i narratives as the Shahid Awwal and Shahid Thani (the First and Second Martyrs), who were killed by Sunni rulers (Jaber 1981, p. 17). Despite his awareness of the danger of relying on unattributable evidence, however, Jaber refers in his account of Jabal 'Amil's history to "some documents I found among the dispersed papers of Jabal 'Amil's historians", without naming these sources (Jaber 1981, p. 37). Some of his accounts of entire historical periods in Jabal 'Amil, such as the Sodon era, are based on evidence that cannot be corroborated.

As a result, Kamal Salibi, a renowned Lebanese historian, maintains that Lebanese written history is confined to documenting the Druze and Christians from the twelfth century onwards, despite the existence of other confessional groups, including the Shi'a (Salibi 1979, p. 77). But although Salibi's judgement of the Shi'a's scant historical record presides over a number of other significant studies of Lebanese national history, there was a movement of Shi'i historians known as the 'Amili Trio (comprising Jaber, a layman, and two clerics, Sheikh Suleiman al-Dahir and Ahmad Reda) that attempted to construct the history of Jabal 'Amil (Chalabi 2006, p. 33). These historians, who were active in opposing Ottoman rule during the late nineteenth and early twentieth centuries, had a pronounced political agenda: they wanted to see the establishment of Jabal ʿAmil as an autonomous region within a unified Arab Syria, and this project required a degree of historical legitimacy. Their agenda emanated from their activism in secret Arab societies, which served as opposition groups to Ottoman rule, and later organised demonstrations in support of Prince Faysal's Arab government.[7] For this reason, the ʿAmili Trio's historical accounts dwelt on the distinct character of Jabal ʿAmil, but in so doing they also offered a glimpse of the divisive feudal rule and fractured loyalties in the area during the different Islamic eras. For instance, in his attempt to accentuate the Shiʿi demands for autonomy under Ottoman rule, Jaber never actually uses the word 'autonomy' or refers to its context, but turns to examples of the feudal landowners (and tax collectors) who, at times, defied the Ottoman caliphate, with often bloody consequences. The Ottoman Empire's administrative policy required the assistance of local leaders to ensure the flow of tax revenues back to Constantinople, but some of these leaders occasionally resisted Ottoman control in sporadic, short-lived rebellions. Jaber, among other historians, glorified these periods of 'independent rule'. Such clashes were not specific to Shiʿi communities; however, tensions between the Ottoman centre and local feudal lords were common throughout the Levant, and the dominant historical narratives of the Christians and Druze were similarly built on the story of resistance to Turkish rule.

The emergence of the Maronite Christian and Druze sub-nationalisms is generally recognised by historians of Lebanon as primarily due to the Ottoman reforms of the eighteenth and nineteenth centuries. As Makdisi notes, "sectarianism was a practice that developed out of, and must be understood in the context of, nineteenth century Ottoman reform" (Makdisi 2000, p. 6). However, while the Christian and Druze communities competed for power, often violently, the Sunni elites were part of the Ottoman cadres, and it was they who later established Arab nationalist societies, following the coup by the Young Turks in Constantinople. These societies or associations included Ottoman officers, such as Nouri el-Saʿid, ʿAziz al-Masri, and Jameel Madfaʿi, many of whom went on to participate in the governments of the Arab states during the colonial era (Sharara 1996, p. 51). In 1910, two Arab Sunni officials, Muhammad Rafiq and Muhammad Bahjat, completed an Ottoman-commissioned survey of Lebanon known as the *Wilayat Bayrut*, in which the Shiʿa are referred to as *mitwalis*, and which notes the absolute nature of the feudal leadership in Shiʻi society and the tension between the local leaders and the clerics.

> This class of people [the clerics] is well known; standing between confined knowledge and great power. They like to have publications that describe in detail God, the sanctity of the twelve imams, welcome the arrival of the Mahdi and praise their leaders ... [I]n fact, they have nothing else to do. If they don't do this, they lose their power vis a vis the leaders, *al-bakawat*, and their elevated position in society. (Rafiq and Bahjit cited in Chalabi 2006, p. 55)

The two authors, aware of the security interests of their Ottoman bosses, were careful to note the limitations of the clergy's intellectual activities: "What they write does not go beyond this parameter, there is no one else who can value writing" (Chalabi 2006, pp. 14–15). In response to some of the discriminatory language used to describe the Shiʻa in the survey, al-Dahir, a leading cleric and one of the "ʻAmili trio", asked, "Is it the aim of such a book to insult specific peoples/communities?" (Chalabi 2006, p. 16). However, the influence of the Shiʻi feudal lords—armed with Ottoman support and the ownership of large swathes of land, and aided by widespread illiteracy among the general population—dwarfed that of al-Dahir and the other activist religious scholars. These powerful landowners managed to sustain their influence right up to the advent of urbanisation and the decline of agrarian society in the 1960s.

Shiʻi narratives of Jabal ʻAmil's history, therefore, remained limited to chronicling the tensions between the feudal landholding families and the Ottoman *walis* (local governors). The construction of a specifically Shiʻi history in the early twentieth century suffered from the lack of any popular movements or symbols, and was thus confined to a small number of individuals. This gap in the source material was in fact widely acknowledged and much debated among clerical scholars and historians at the time. Jaber blamed the lack of historical sources on the Umayyad and Abbasid repression of the Yemenis and Shiʻa (both are elements in Lebanese Shiʻi identity) (Jaber 1981, p. 33).

The sectarian violence between the Druze and the Christians in the nineteenth century, meanwhile, played a major role in forming their subsequent sectarian identities—but this alone does not explain the exception of the Shiʻa. The answer to the difference lies in the factor that fuelled this tension: the class struggle between the Druze, who were landowners and warriors, and the Christians, who constituted the large peasant base. This accentuated the sub-national consciousness of each group (Traboulsi 2007, pp. 10–15). By contrast, both the feudal lords of South Lebanon and the peasants they dominated were Shiʿa, and this, coupled with the region's mountainous terrain, delayed the formation of a Shiʿi sectarian identity.[8] The under-development of Jabal ʿAmil, in comparison with the lands of the Druze and Christians, also contributed—the lack of infrastructure rendered transportation, and consequently connections between communities, extremely difficult over the region's 1,200 square miles. According to an edition of the *Jabal ʿAmil* newspaper, published on 14 March 1912, it took between nine and ten hours to travel between the central towns of the three *cazas* (districts), as the roads were not maintained and were unpassable by either truck or car.[9] The different areas were basically disconnected, further weakening sectarian claims of coherence.[10]

3.2   Geography, Economy, and Classes

While the accounts of certain Shiʿi clerics, such as Ali Al-Zein, expanded Jabal ʿAmil's geography to include vast areas reaching as far as modern Jordan, the region is generally defined as the area bounded by the ʿAwwali River to the north, Galilee to the south, and the northern part of the Biqaʿ Valley, particularly around the towns of Hermel and Baalbek (Shanahan 2005, p. 15). The southern part was chiefly dominated by feudal landowners, known locally as the *zuʿama*, while in the northeastern Biqaʿ Valley the Shiʿa population was largely formed of nomadic tribes, under the leadership of the Harfoush and Hamade feudal clans.[11] Although the al-Assʿad family, descendants of the Ali al-Sagheers, was the dominant clan amongst the *zuʿama*, it also included the al-Khalil clan in Tyr, the al-Fadl in Nabatieh, and the al-ʿAbdallah in al-Khiyam, one of Jabal ʿAmil's largest towns.[12] At the local level, the *ulama* class was subservient to the landowners, who were also the Ottoman Empire's representatives or *multazim*.

The population of this region remained scant until the mid-twentieth century. In 1912, *Jabal ʿAmil* estimated that it numbered around 150,000, including a large Christian minority; the *Wilayat Bayrut* set the number at 126,759; and a census in 1964 estimated the Shiʿi population to be 404,000 (Chalabi 2006, p. 17). The demographics of any multi-faith state will always be a highly politicised and sensitive issue, and this is particularly the case in Lebanon, with its 18 official religious sects—which explains why the last official census was held in 1932. This census, however, confirmed that Maronite Christians constituted the largest confessional group, followed by Sunnis, and then the Shiʿa, and this defined their respective political roles under the French Mandate and later in post-independence

Lebanon, with Maronite Christians controlling the senior positions in state institutions. This "hegemony of Lebanese Christians and conservative Sunni financial and mercantile elites" only began to break by the early 1970s (Chalcraft 2009, p. 104).

Jabal ʿAmil remained a predominantly rural society. Grain, mostly wheat, was the most important crop. Peasants had what was termed *muʿashara* agreements with the landowners, whereby they received one-tenth share of the harvest, with some exceptions. This arrangement guaranteed that the *zuʿama* class, the well-known landowning families such as the al-Khalil and al-Sagheer, maintained their control over the peasant population in a fashion similar to that found in Wadi Hauran (the Huran Valley) in southern Syria, although on a smaller scale. The highly labour-intensive cultivation of tobacco began in South Lebanon in the eighteenth century, and increased in importance in the mid-nineteenth century after the Ottoman Empire provided access to the Egyptian market. Its later regulation by the French colonialists intensified the pressure on the peasants, leading to violent clashes, casualties, and arrests—events that were documented in Jaber's history, but disregarded in Hizbullah's.

The nineteenth-century French traveller and physician, Louis Lortet, noted in 1870 that the remains of olive presses, ancient mills, and wells suggested that agriculture dated back centuries in Jabal ʿAmil.[13] Early twentieth-century (mostly Arabist) intellectuals used such observations by European travellers to emphasise the ancient origins and practices of the people of Jabal ʿAmil—an important theme in modernist nationalism. The dominance of agriculture in Jabal ʿAmil's economy, however, meant that the *ulama* class had little effective power, a fact that remained unchanged until mass urbanisation drove the Shiʿi peasant population into the cities in the 1960s. Lescot, a French officer, writing in 1936, described the clerics' meagre influence in comparison to that of the powerful landowners:

> There is a strange thing in [this] Shiʿi country, the religious authorities did not enjoy the authority that one expected. The influence of the 'Sayyids' or the 'Cheikhs' remains for the most part local. If they have some credit among the peasants, then the more evolved classes were increasingly outside their control and merely represented external symbols of respect. (Lescot cited in Chalabi 2006, p. 17)[14]

This relationship between the *ulama* and their constituency contradicts Jaber's claim that they played a leading role in Shiʿi society, an assertion that was fundamental to Hizbullah's later narrative. Lescot's observations could have applied equally well to similar contexts in Iraq and Iran, where the landowners' religious tax, the *khoms*, comprised the *ulama*'s sole source of income, rendering them dependent on, and subservient to, the feudal authorities.[15]

3.3 The Myth of Shiʿi Origins

Jaber strongly endorsed the myth of the origins of Lebanon's Shiʿi population; he focussed in his work on the Arab roots and historical continuity of the "Amili people'. According to him, Jabal ʿAmil dates back to the first Arab settlers in the Levant, while the name "Amil' comes from the ʿAmila, an Arab-Yemeni tribe that moved to the region in 300 BC (Jaber 1981, p. 29).[16] However, as Salibi explains, the Islamic conquest of the Levant was not completed until 641 AD, and the region of Jabal ʿAmil was then annexed as a Jordanian province in the new administrative arrangement introduced by the second Muslim caliph (Salibi 1979, p. 33). Shiʿa Islam began to spread in the Levant under the Abbasid caliphate of Al-Mutawakel. During this time, the Turkish Tollon family ruled the Levant as a reward for successfully heading off a rebellion in Egypt against Umayyad and Abbasid rule (Jaber 1981, pp. 61–65).

The figure of Abu Dhar al-Ghifari, one of the Prophet's confidants and a loyal supporter of Imam Ali, was integral to both Shiʿi modern oral history and Hizbullah's historical narratives and propaganda.[17] What could be called, in essence, the 'Abu Dhar al-Ghifari origin myth' in South Lebanon also appeared in some early, pre-Hizbullah historical accounts, but it was (and remains) both uncorroborated and incoherent, and was almost always based on oral evidence. According to the Shiʿi religious scholars' (mainly oral) narratives, the tribe of ʿAmela Ben Sabaʿ emigrated from Yemen to Jabal ʿAmil following the collapse of Sadd Maʿreb and the kingdom of Saba' (an ancient Semitic civilisation) in 300 BC. What is seen as the ancient phase of the region's history ended with the Ottoman's assumption of control over the region in 1517 AD (Jaber 1981, p. 29). When the renowned Persian traveller Nasser Khosro visited the region in the eleventh century, he noted that "most of Tyr's [a city in southern Lebanon] people are Shiʿi in faith, and so is Tripoli [in the north]. The Shiʿa have built fine mosques all over the country" (Khosro, pp. 49–50).[18] Shiʿi scholar Ali Al-Zein argued in 1954 that the Shiʿa in the region date back to the Umayyad era, referring to mosques carrying the name of Abu Dharr and ʿAli Ben Abi Taleb, the first Shiʿi imam (Al-Zein 1954, p. 36).[19]

Some Shi'i scholars have contested the Abu Dharr origin claims, citing the centuries-wide gap between Abu Dharr's life (he died in 652AD) and the first accounts of Shi'i existence in Jabal 'Amil. Jaafar Al-Muhajer, a leading figure among these scholars, notes that "the Shi'a existed in regions close to Jabal 'Amil towards the late tenth century ... Tyr was for a long time a Shi'i stronghold; the city was home [to] the renowned Shi'i cleric al Caracji Abul Fateh Ben 'Ali Ben Uthman who died in 449 Hijra (1058AD), and [the] poet Abdul Hassan al Suri" (Al-Muhajer 1992, p. 203). According to various historical accounts, the northern city of Tripoli was Shi'i until the Crusaders' conquest in 1109 AD, as were the Kesrwain Mountains (in now-Christian Mount Lebanon) and the Northern Metn district until the fourteenth and fifteenth centuries (Al-Muhajer 1992, p. 11). Accordingly, the northern Biqa' Valley was Shi'i, except for Baalbek, which remained a major Sunni Hanbali centre up to the fifteenth century.[20] As such, Abu Dharr's presence in the history of the Shi'a is purely symbolic, as one of Mohamed's four loyal companions who remained true to his cousin and 'legitimate heir', Imam 'Ali Ben Abi Taleb.[21] Al-Muhajer traces the beginning of the Shi'i presence in the Levant to immigration from Kufa, the Shi'i centre in Iraq, Imam 'Ali's capital of choice during his caliphate years. The tribe of Hamadan, loyal to 'Ali Ben Abi Taleb, embarked on the first Shi'i migration to historical Syria.

While the origins of the Shi'a in the Levant remain a subject of controversy, the popular myth of Abu Dharr preaching the Shi'i faith in South Lebanon (also known as the Western Levant) remains dubious, in spite of Hizbullah's continued efforts at reviving it as an established fact.[22] Roger Shanahan argues that Abu Dharr clearly served the Shi'i clerics' need to establish their authenticity, especially because his narrative provides them with a direct link to the Prophet. "The motivation for such claims that link the establishment of Shi'a with someone as noteworthy as one of the companions [of Mohamed] is not difficult to decipher; they are designed to substantiate the Lebanese Shi'i community's authenticity" (Shanahan 2005, p. 15). In any account, it appears that by the eleventh century, Shi'a Islam existed across the area now known as Lebanon.

3.3.1 Fighters with the Imam

Among the main themes of Hizbullah's reconstructed history is the myth that Jabal 'Amil's Shi'a fought with Imam Husayn (who, as the Prophet's grandson and the third Shi'i imam, is among the most revered figures in

Shiʿa Islam) in the epic battle of Karbala, in southern Iraq.[23] By consulting the historical evidence and analysing Shiʿi tribal demographics at the time, however, Al-Muhajer confirms the predominantly Sunni narratives that mention the Levantine Shiʿi tribes who fought against Imam Husayn; he contends that one of these tribes, the al-Humeir, converted to the Shiʿa faith only following their participation alongside Muʿaweya Ben Sufyan, the founder of the Umayyad dynasty, in the battle against Imam ʿAli (Al-Muhajer 1992, p. 95). This evidence is based on a tale from the ninth-century book, *Tareekh Abi Zaraa al-Demashki*, but Al-Muhajer, when tracing the Shiʿi community's origins, relies more on the fact of the notable population decreases in the Kufa tribes; he notes the disappearance of the great Shiʿi Hamadan tribe, which has ceased to exist in today's Kufa, while previously less numerous tribes like the Bani Assad "are now everywhere" (Al-Muhajer 1992, p. 79). The Hamadan appears to have left Kufa for the Levant following Umayyad repression.

3.3.2 Banu ʿAmmar and the Mamluks

When the Abbasid dynasty began to collapse, historical Syria (the Levant) was separated from the empire and governed by a series of short-lived dynasties from 970 AD. According to Jaber, the Beni Tolon, Beni Ekhshid, Beni Hamdan, Fatimid, Nureyeh, Ayyubi, Mamluk, and Barjeya Sharkaseya dynasties governed the Levant until the advent of the Ottomans, and under these dynasties, the feudal families consolidated their dominant position in Jabal ʿAmil (Jaber 1981, p. 33). Before the Mamluk era in the thirteenth century, Shiʿi rulers enjoyed wide power: they held sway over the northern part of Levant during the assumption of power by the Banu ʿAmmar dynasty and had the support of the Beni Hamdan dynasty. The Crusaders, however, ended all Shiʿi privileges and launched a campaign of repression, driving the Shiʿi populations from most of historical Syria into South Lebanon and the Biqaʿ Valley. Added to this twist of fate, the decline of the Fatimid dynasty, the rise of the Sunni sultans, and the advent of the Mamluk dynasty led to further decreases in the Shiʿi population. The Mamluks, according to Salibi, launched a drive to either expel the Shiʿa from the north and Mount Lebanon or forcibly convert them to Sunni Islam (Salibi 1976, p. xvi).

Jaber documented one of the tragedies recited among the Shiʿa during the Mamluk period (1478–1639), which tells of the 'foreign' families that were brought in to govern the region. One of the incidents related by this oral history involved the Sodon family, which presided over Jabal ʿAmil (Jaber 1981, pp. 38–39). According to Jaber's narrative, the Sodon era ended after members of the family fed a Shiʿi infant to their hungry dogs after an unsuccessful hunting trip. The child's family succeeded in notifying the sultan's deputy in Damascus, sparing none of the incident's graphic details. "The child's father was a wise man, as he avoided challenging the family publicly, but instead recorded in detail the child's kidnapping, his slaughter and subsequent slicing [up] to feed the hungry hunting dogs in front of his grieving mother" (Jaber 1981, p. 42). The account of the victim's complaint to the caliph, and his subsequent response, carried an underlying message about the efficacy of central governance. Jaber, by narrating this story, which was derived from both oral and written sources, draws an analogy between what he terms 'autonomous rule' by the Shiʿi feudal landowners and 'foreign' governance. The end of one dynasty and the beginning of another was usually signalled by a purge of the Shiʿa and their forced displacement, and this meant that few traces of symbols of communal solidarity can be found in Jabal ʿAmil, where the newly uprooted populations merged with the dispersed peasant population within its feudal social structure.

What Jaber calls Jabal ʿAmil's first period of autonomous rule began before the Ottomans gained control of Syria. The Waʾel family, later known as Ali Sagheer, dominated the leadership in South Lebanon (Jaber 1981, p. 36).[24] Nevertheless, stronger tribes such as the Shokr clan rose to power, challenging the Waʿel's authority, at times nearly exterminating the family (Jaber 1981, p. 42). The Shokr wiped out the direct family of Waʿel leader Sheikh Hussein Ben Ahmad Nassar, for example, and Nassar's pregnant wife was forced to seek shelter in her tribal region in the Syrian desert. Her son, known as Ali Sagheer (Ali the Young), was later encouraged to return to Jabal ʿAmil, where he launched a campaign against the Shokr. He succeeded in ambushing and killing dozens of members of the family during a wedding, and subsequently took over the reins of power, founding the Ali Sagheer dynasty (Jaber 1981, p. 43). This story lacks sufficient sources to confirm the detail, but it highlights the significance of the clans and feudal landowners from early on in Shiʿi history; the clerics were marginalised. Hudson, for example, notes the following about the social power of the Shiʿi family structure: "The extended family is the basic political as well as social unit in Lebanon. This structure—patrilineal, patriarchal, and endogamous—comprises the power base of nearly all the important politicians in modern Lebanon" (Hudson 1968, p. 19).

During this pre-Ottoman era, Jabal ʿAmil was mostly administered from Damascus or northern Palestine (Acre or Safad) according to the *ajnad* system (Shanahan 2005, p. 16). The relationship between the rulers and the local feudal landowners was tax-based, and the Ottomans retained this system.

3.4 Ottoman Rule: 'Direct' and 'Indirect' Phases

During Ottoman rule, Jabal ʿAmil was always a small and mostly forgotten part of the *wilayet* of Damascus or Beirut. The Ottoman centre only recalled the region when in need of recruits and funds, as one nineteenth-century Belgian Orientalist noted:

> The Metoualis are Moslem Shiʿa or partisans of Ali, the son-in-law and cousin of the Prophet. For this reason, they cordially detest the Sunnis or orthodox Moslems, who well return it to them. The Turkish government remembers them when it feels the need to fill the vacuums of its coffers or military cadres. (Lammens cited in Weiss 2010, p. 42)

While there was no pact or written agreement defining this relationship with the Ottoman centre, the Amili group of historians, including Jaber, divided the region's Ottoman history into two phases: direct (central) and indirect (autonomous) rule.

When speaking of indirect rule (1517–1865) in Jabal ʿAmil, Jaber is referring to the Ali Al-Sagheer dynasty's semi-autonomous status. Nineteenth- and twentieth-century Shiʿi clerics and historians considered this long period a 'golden age', largely due to the region's relative autonomy (Jaber 1981, p. 55). The formerly Shiʿi region of Mount Lebanon developed a local leadership culture based on the authority of the 'wise prince' Al-Ameer Al Hakeem. As these feudal lords and hereditary leaders grew in strength, they sought to establish greater independence from the Ottoman court (Shanahan 2005, p. 19). Their authority, however, was at times contested by other Shiʿi feudal leaders, specifically the Harfoush dynasty in the Biqaʿ Valley, leading to bloody rivalry and recurrent internecine warfare (Jaber 1981, pp. 19–20). Jaber's claims of an entrenched Shiʿi identity among these feudal families, however, are not well supported; historical evidence suggests that they were willing to change their sectarian allegiances and even convert if it appeared in their interests to do so. For example, even Jaber acknowledges that the Harfoush family's links to its Shi'i roots declined and its members later converted to Christianity (Jaber 1981, p. 21). However, the feudal families' ownership of vast swathes of land in Jabal 'Amil was rarely mentioned in Jaber's *History of Jabal 'Amil*, nor the fact that it was common for the Ottoman authorities to rely on these feudal lords to levy taxes and govern its districts. Yet it was for this reason that it was only these *walis* who represented any real threat to Ottoman power in the region.

The Ali Sagheer family retained its influence in Jabal 'Amil for centuries. Its status is evident in its written communications with the Ottoman centre. Official Ottoman letters to Ali Bey Al-Ass'ad (grandchild of Ali Sagheer and a much-celebrated feudal leader in South Lebanon) addressed him as the "President of [the] Tribes and the Supreme Sheikh" (Jaber 1981, p. 55). This relationship was based on the fact that the Ottoman state was predominantly interested in collecting taxes from the regional governors and feudal landowners, and it was greatly aided in this by gaining the loyalty of a single influential feudal leader (Jaber 1981, pp. 88–89). The Ottoman provincial governor would visit Jabal 'Amil two or three times a year to collect taxes and levies, often raising the bar in order to win the favour of his ministerial superiors (Jaber 1981, p. 90).

The tribal and feudal rulers of South Lebanon were also divided over their regional alliances. Hamad El-Beik (who died in 1852), another descendant of the Ali Sagheer dynasty, allied himself with the Ottoman Empire and partook in the Ottomans' battle against Egyptian advances (Jaber 1981, pp. 53–55). However, Tamer El-Hussein, another member of the family, despite being well renumerated by the Ottomans, had close ties with Egypt, and disputed the leadership of Jabal 'Amil with his cousin Ali. The Ottomans, showing an utter disregard of the family's political and local values, incarcerated both cousins. They died of tuberculosis while in prison in 1865 (Jaber 1981, pp. 60–61). Kamel Bey Al-Ass'ad (1870–1924), on the other hand, was one of the feudal leaders who showed extreme loyalty to the Ottoman Empire. The Arabist bloc in Jabal 'Amil, namely, the 'Amili Trio, accused him of appeasing his Ottoman overlords and rejecting pan-Arabism, and even of acting as informer against Shi'i anti-Ottoman intellectuals. Later, because of his Ottoman connections, the French colonial administration sought to have him arrested, and sent soldiers to ransack his home in Taybeh in South Lebanon (Jaber 1981, pp. 62–63).[25]

Jaber further divided the feudal rule of South Lebanon into three phases: 1780–1804, 1804–1832, and 1841–1865. The first phase, which he dubbed 'direct rule', commenced in 1780 with the battle of Yaroun (a village in Jabal ʿAmil). Between the second and third phases, the Egyptian Ibrahim Pacha's army occupied Jabal ʿAmil for nine years. The end of feudal governments in 1865 did not mark the end of feudalism, however, but rather the death of Jabal ʿAmil's perceived 'autonomy'.

The 'foreign' families who ruled Jabal ʿAmil during the Ottoman period were the Ma'ns and the Shehabs. The latter family did not last long, according to Jaber, as their role was solely restricted to enforcing Ottoman power in the case of mutiny or refusal to pay taxes. However, Jaber noted that the Shiʿa saw in Prince Fakhreddine the Second, a member of the Maʿn dynasty, a man of strategic vision, who sought independence from the Ottoman Turks; despite this, Jabar criticised the Maʿn rulers' collaboration with the Ottomans against the Shiʿa of Jabal ʿAmil, referring to the eruption of bouts of warfare between them (Jaber 1981, pp. 108–113). "When under heavy pressure, unable to avert their foes, and facing many soldiers, Shiʿa in Jabal ʿAmil resorted to guerrilla warfare, military tricks and surprising the enemy at night" (Jaber 1981, p. 113). The Ottomans gave Fakhreddine jurisdiction over the Safad District, which included Jabal ʿAmil, but a relative of Fakhreddine, Younes Harfoush, the Shiʿi ruler of the Baʿlbek region (in Biqaʿ), disputed the Ottoman's decision.[26] The feud continued until Fakhreddine killed Younes. When Jaber describes the death of Younes, he says that Fakhreddine "killed him treacherously" (Jaber 1981, pp. 112–113), but in official Lebanese history, which is part of the national school curriculum, Fakhreddine is portrayed as a national hero who sought independence from the Ottoman Empire. The Shiʿi feudal families' authority suffered under his government as he tried to consolidate his local power and increase tax revenues.

In passing, it is important to note that Jaber had no scruples about differentiating between the 'Lebanese', by which he means the Christians and Druze, and the Shiʿa ʿAmilis in the south, calling the latter the "ʿAmili people'. In one case, he speaks of attacks mounted by "the Lebanese from the North, and the Palestinian Bedouins from the South" on Ottoman orders, referring to "ethnic and sectarian differences" (Jaber 1981, p. 80). He fails to explain, however, how the "ʿAmilis' differed ethnically from the northern 'Lebanese' or southern Palestinian Bedouins.

3.4.1 Thaher Al-ʿOmar

One of the chief figures in the early twentieth-century accounts of Jabal ʿAmil's history is Sheikh Thaher al-ʿOmar (1686–1776), a tribal Sunni leader from Palestine who "descends from Imam Husayn's bloodline" (Jaber 1981, pp. 113–115).[27] According to Jaber, al-ʿOmar's tribe moved from Medina to Palestine, and al-ʿOmar established a local fiefdom in Acre in northern Palestine, securing his power base through his monopoly of the cotton trade. In Acre, he set about building fortresses and establishing alliances with neighbouring tribes. After a battle between al-ʿOmar and Nassif al-Nassar, a Shiʿi tribal leader in South Lebanon, the opposing forces drew up a treaty whereby they formed a united front against their Ottoman overlords. Together, these local chiefs opposed the Ottoman Empire in order to preserve their independent status. There followed three battles between the Ottoman army, led by Youssef al-Shehabi, and the allied armies led by al-Omar (Jaber 1981, pp. 122–134). The allies won all these battles—the most celebrated victory was their defeat of the Ottoman *wali*'s army in 1771. However, the Ottoman Ahmed Pasha, known in Shiʿi legend as 'the butcher', finally succeeded in defeating the allied armies in Acre, where al-ʿOmar met his death (Jaber 1981, p. 137).[28]

Jaber's focus on al-ʿOmar may have concealed another agenda besides valorising the part the Shiʿi forces played in these military victories. The Arab nationalists among the Shiʿa, Jaber included, were looking at the time to the leadership of another Sunni, Reda Bey al-Solh, from Sidon in South Lebanon. Recreating al-ʿOmar's alliance with Jabal ʿAmil's Shiʿi leaders reinforced the legitimacy of the ʿAmili Trio's contemporary political allegiances. They portrayed the potential power of their pan-Arab nationalist activism as bearing a strong resemblance to that actualised in al-ʿOmar's alliances and subsequent victories, thus helping enhance their legitimacy in the face of their traditional foe, Kamel al-Assʿad, the leading Shiʿi feudal lord in South Lebanon.

3.4.2 Tribal and Feudal Infighting

During the period of direct Ottoman rule, Jabal ʿAmil witnessed an unprecedented period of feudal and tribal infighting (Jaber 1981, p. 169). Jaber, arguing from a nationalist pro-unity perspective, notes that there is "no doubt that these internal differences were among the major reasons behind the 'backwardness' of the Shiʿi Sect, breaking its unity, weakening both sides, and strengthening the government's authority" (Jaber 1981, p. 170). According to Jaber, certain Ottoman rulers were more favourable than others in Jabal ʿAmil; he specifically names Medhat Pasha, a reformer, who governed the Levant region in 1876. Under his rule, a Shiʿi, Khalil Bey Al-Assʿad, was appointed governor of the predominantly Sunni province of Al-Balkaa, whose capital was Nablus (Jaber 1981, p. 172), while Nagiub Al-Assʿad, the son of another Shiʿi leader, became the mayor of Sahion (Zion), a region in the province of Latakia.

With Medhat Pasha's death, increasing Ottoman interference led to the spread of Arab nationalism in the region; this local 'awakening' intersected with an international interest in breaking up and further weakening the Ottoman Empire—a policy formed in response to what was known in colonial circles as the 'Arab question' (Jaber 1981, pp. 174–175). This also coincided with the increasing influence of Turkish nationalists in Constantinople. In this Arabist era, the Sunni Solh family rose to prominence in South Lebanon. But Jaber states that with the onset of the First World War, Arab nationalists united behind the Ottoman Empire, as the logic ran that "Turkish rule remains lighter than colonialism". This position changed, however, with the appointment of the Ottoman military leader, Gamal Pasha, known as the 'butcher' for his exceptional brutality, to run Lebanon. Gamal was granted special emergency powers, and his mission was focused on two goals: eliminating Lebanon's special status (*almutasarefeya*) and eradicating the Arab nationalist movement (Jaber 1981, p. 198).

3.5 Arab Nationalism in Jabal ʿAmil[29]

Most nationalist movements in Lebanon were elitist, partly because political forms of mass protest were little known in the region—there were few means to transmit such ideas to a wider public given the lack of a mass media—until the early twentieth century, when small demonstrations began to occur and nationalist publications started to circulate in Jabal ʿAmil. The authorship of nationalist historical narratives (examined in this chapter), however, was mostly restricted to the ʿAmili Trio.

Jaber's narrative, in accord with those of his co-historians in the Trio, al-Dahir and Reda, traces Arab nationalism in Jabal ʿAmil to the era of the Ottoman sultan Selim the First (1512–1520), whose forces killed many thousands of Shiʿa in Iran, Anatolia, and the Arab regions. The massacres occurred in the context of the war between Selim and the Persian Safavid ruler, Ismail. The Ottoman emperor avenged his defeat by ordering mass killings of Shiʿa in the Levant—the victims were perceived to be loyal to the Safavid Empire because they shared the same faith. These massacres defined the turbulent relationship between the inhabitants of the region and the Ottoman Empire, leading to a long phase of indirect rule. "This region [Jabal ʿAmil] in spite of its small area and sparse population, fiercely resisted the Turks ... it did not fall under direct Turkish rule [apart from] a short period, half a century between 1865 and 1918" (Jaber 1981, pp. 206–207). Jaber, who was descended from a Safavid family, displayed strong anti-Turkish sentiments in his writings, expressing sympathy towards the Shiʿa in Iran. Arabist sentiments in South Lebanon were thus a reaction to Turkish repression, rather than a 'nationalist awakening', a phenomenon that was manifested in the growth of political secret societies and nationalist literary societies in the early twentieth century.

At the political level, Shiʿi representatives of Jabal ʿAmil participated in a secret conference in Damascus in 1877 to discuss Syrian independence during the last phase of the Turko–Russian war.[30] The Russian advances stirred the hopes of the Arab nationalists—hopes that were soon dispelled by the Ottoman success in averting a decisive defeat. The Shiʿa had agreed at the conference to accept Abdul Alqader al Jazaʿery as prince of Syria in the event of a Russian victory (Jaber 1981, p. 208), but as the much-anticipated Ottoman defeat did not occur, the conference was rendered obsolete. Nevertheless, other Shiʿi intellectuals in the early twentieth century took a somewhat different line to Jaber's. A weekly newspaper, *Al ʿErfan,* was established following the Young Turks' coup, in the hope of gaining more freedom within the Ottoman Empire. Ahmad ʿAref Al-Zein, the publication's founder, argued in his editorials that the new Ottoman state would find strength in decentralisation (Sharara 1996, p. 9). The coup, according to Al-Zein, had lifted the barrier between the Ottoman state and the civilian populations of the empire, and he compared the situation to that of Japan, which, by developing economically and socially, was able to defeat the Russia of the Czars (Sharara 1996, p. 10). The journal, in fact, struggled to define its identity: in an editorial, it described its mission as "a forum between Iraq and Jabal ʿAmil's poets and scholars, on one hand, [and] the scholars and poets of the remaining regions, on the other hand; the magazine is especially concerned with the ancient and modern affairs of [the] Shiʿa" (Sharara 1996, p. 12). *Al ʿErfan*'s call for decentralisation in the empire, however, was the norm among the various segments of the Arab population. For example, following the accession to power of the Young Turks in Constantinople and the promulgation of the 1908 constitution, George Antonius, a leading Arab nationalist, noted that it would "integrate the different ethnicities in a single populous Ottoman rule, in which Turkish would be the special language" (Antonius 1939, p. 177).

Sharara remarks that *Al ʿErfan*'s writers might have been cautious about defining the Arab 'nation' and incorporated the Ottoman Empire in its calls for change either to avoid the closure of the publication or because they wished to be realistic in their aspirations (Sharara 1996, pp. 29–30). The key to strengthening the Ottoman Empire lay in the establishment of a strong education system throughout its territories, *Al ʿErfan* argued; decentralisation, freedom, and education would guarantee the empire enough strength to defend itself against Western aggression (Sharara 1996, p. 20). This realism would soon fade in Ahmad Reda's work (one of the members of the ʿAmili Trio, who contributed to the journal), as it did in nationalist writings in the Arab world more generally. Reda instead focused on the myth of Shiʿi existence in Jabal ʿAmil since ancient times, referring to the Abu Dharr legend (Sharara 1996, p. 32). In another article, he argued that the Shiʿa of South Lebanon embraced Shiʿism even earlier than the Iranians, claiming their conversion followed that of the first Shiʿa of Medina in the Arab Peninsula (Sharara 1996, p. 33).

Meanwhile, a number of secret Arab nationalist societies were established in the wake of the Young Turks' coup; their members were mostly from the Sunni urban elites and included a large Christian minority (Sharara 1996, p. 51). A few Shiʿi names emerged in these societies, among them Abdul Kareem Khalil, a Beirut resident who claimed descent from Jabal ʿAmil, and Hussein Haidar, a physician from the Biqa' Valley, a relative of two major local landowners and Ottoman tax collectors, Said Pasha Haidar and Majid Bey Haidar (Sharara 1996, p. 52). In Jabal ʿAmil, Jaber, Reda, and Sheikh Sleiman Thaher founded a society, which called on the region's residents to oppose Ottoman rule and demand autonomy for the region as part of a decentralised state (Jaber 1981, p. 210). The Shiʿi members of these secret societies were either descended from clerical families or were residents of Beirut, with feudal roots in Jabal ʿAmil or the Biqaʿ Valley. Such movements were therefore elitist in composition, and lacked the mass support of the Shiʿi population, with its large peasant base.

The peasantry, meanwhile, was firmly under the control of the feudal leader Kamel al-Assʿad, who opposed the rise of any rival who might influence the population. Al-Assʿad, in pursuit of his own interests, sided with the Ottoman ruler, and was heavily criticised for exposing Abdul Karim al-Khalil's Arab nationalist anti-Ottoman activities, leading to his execution. Al-Assʿad was further criticised for receiving the Ottoman sultan in his palace in his hometown of Altaybeh (Sharara 1996, p. 54). Al-Assʿad, however, had seen an opportunity to rid himself of yet more enemies, and his informants helped Gamal Pasha arrest activists from these nationalist societies, the most prominent being the Sunni leader al-Solh[31] (Jaber 1981, p. 213). Jaber notes that because Al-Assʿad was an aristocrat, a descendant of traditional Shiʿi leaders, he was "dissatisfied with the rising status of Reda Bey al-Solh in Jabal ʿAmil; he considered his interference in the region's matters an attack on [his] traditional authority", which was why his policy was to oppose al-Solh in every way. The latter, Jaber noted, "always emerged [the] winner" (Jabal 1981, p. 214). On 28 July 1915, the Ottoman authorities released most of the activists of Jabal ʿAmil, except for Al-Khalil, who was hanged in August of that year, and al-Solh and Shaykh (cleric) Bahaʾuddine Al-Zein, who were exiled to Izmir (Jabal 1981, p. 218). In the aftermath of the Young Turk regime's crackdown on secret societies, the Jabal ʿAmil elite lapsed into political inactivity (Sharara 1996, p. 55).

The reinterpretation of the historical phase that followed is particularly important, as Jaber attempted to magnify the role the Shiʿa played in the Arab revolt. After the Allies defeated the Ottoman Empire in the First World War, Jaber emphasises that the Shiʿa joined in the call for an independent Syria under the rule of the Hashemite Prince Faysal. In January 1920, the Allies were ambushed in several regions (Jaber 1981, p. 228), but the resistance faded, according to Jaber, after the French forces incited the Christians in the region to support French colonial occupation (Jaber 1981, p. 218). There is little evidence to lend credence to Jaber's claim of the Shiʿa's remarkable participation in the struggle for Syrian independence, however, while there is much to suggest that this support was purely symbolic.

It was when the French Mandate authorities granted the Shi'i community recognition in January 1926, leading to the establishment of its own religious courts, that an institutional process was set in train in which ordinary Shi'a began to interact and identify with one another. These Shi'i courts therefore were integral to forging a Shi'i sense of sectarian identity, which was only sharpened by the fact that the Sunni and Christian communities began to play an increasingly significant political role in the new Lebanese state (established by the French Mandate in 1920), both before and after independence.

3.5.1 The 'Tobacco Revolt'

A small but significant incident indicated this shift in the sense of collective identity amongst South Lebanon's Shi'a. The Ottoman's 1858 land code had perpetuated the landowners' dominance in Jabal 'Amil at the same time as Mount Lebanon and Beirut were experiencing economic expansion and transformation. The French Mandate authorities further regulated tobacco production through the Regie, a parastatal company, and this concurrently increased the landowners' control and the pressure on the Shi'i peasants. The establishment of the *banderole* system (placing an official stamp on the wrapping) in June 1930 resulted in even tighter monopolistic control over the tobacco industry (Weiss 2010, p. 190). These colonial policies, added to a further decrease in the price of tobacco, paved the way for the 'effervescence' or upsurge of protest in Bint Jubayl, a large Shi'i town. The clashes were followed by the introduction of a new French law in 1935, aimed at increasing the efficiency of tax collection in South Lebanon. The French High Commissioner dispatched reinforcements to Shi'i towns, especially Bint Jubayl, and launched an investigation. The investigating officers' report, published in the local *L'Orient* newspaper, claimed that while tobacco was the chief 'alibi', Arab nationalists—called 'secessionists' by the French—were behind the clashes (Weiss 2010, p. 193). While there were only a few dozen participants, the revolt did illustrate that Arab nationalist and socialist ideas had started to gain ground amongst a small but growing Shi'i urban class.[32] As Weiss argues:

> The French colonial state contributed to rendering the Shi'i community in Jabal 'Amil and Beirut more visible, more empowered, but also more sectarian, in ways that it had never quite been before … To be sure, the Shi'i

community was relatively quiescent politically speaking and culturally marginal during the French Mandate period, with occasional exceptions ... the transformation of Shiʿi sectarian identity in the Lebanese context was gradual, so subtle, in fact, as to appear unremarkable for most historians. (Weiss 2010, p. 4)

3.6 Conclusion

During the colonial administration of the region, Shiʿi intellectuals and clerics in Jabal ʿAmil who espoused Arab nationalist ideas constructed a history of the region, in order to validate the demand for self-rule. Although lacking historical sources, the work of this intellectual group, which was centred around the ʿAmili Trio, claimed the existence of a distinct ʿAmili Shiʿi identity and history within the larger Arab nation. Hizbullah's later historical narrative was based on these earlier histories, especially that of Jaber, a leading member of the group. While Jaber only completed his history in the second half of the twentieth century, sections of his work and references to it appeared in Jabal ʿAmil publications such as *al-Maʿaref* and *Jabal ʿAmil*.[33] Jaber's book, examined at length in this chapter, stressed the importance of Shiʿi ʿAmili unity, highlighted what it called the Shiʿi 'golden age' (in the context of calls for autonomy from the Ottoman Empire), re-established the myth of the ancient origins of the Lebanese Shiʿa, and sought to create Shiʿi symbols of resistance out of historical figures such as Thaher al-ʿOmar and Nassif al-Nassar. The ʿAmili Trio's approach bore many similarities to the agenda common to all nationalists—the construction of a historical pedigree for an emerging 'nation', or as Smith puts it, "the re-appropriation of the ethnie" (Smith 2009, p. 37).

Although Jaber's narrative stressed Jabal ʿAmil's Arab identity and the sacrifices made by Lebanon's Shiʿa for the Arab cause, his main focus was the production of a history of the ʿAmili Shiʿa that would show the historical continuity of their nation. His creation of Shiʿi symbols of resistance and his glorification of the role played by the *ulama* in this history formed a significant launch pad for Hizbullah's subsequent narratives. However, Jaber's recognition of the extent of feudal domination in Jabal ʿAmil and his emphasis on a common Arab identity were jettisoned by Hizbullah's historians. Yet the common denominator in both chronicles is the lack of verifiable sources to corroborate their claims. Jaber lamented the lack of sources for his work as a way of justifying his reliance on oral history, and he criticised the pervasive omission of the story of the Shiʿa of Jabal ʿAmil in Lebanese written history. In similar fashion, Hizbullah's subsequent reconstructed history relied heavily on Jaber's (uncorroborated) historical account, and it blamed its further dependence on oral sources on the pervasive omission of the history of the Lebanese Shi'a in official Ottoman and Arab documentation. In this way, the 'Amili historical narrative reveals Hizbullah's double-layered construction of Shi'i history and national symbols.

Notes

1. The accusation of anti-Arab bias against the Young Turk government, though common in Arab and some Western histories, is widely contested. Khalidi, for instance, refers to the appointment of Arab ministers and officials during the Young Turk era (Khalidi 1991, pp. 18–19).
2. Makdisi uses the term 'sectarian nationalism'; however, 'sub-nationalism' is also appropriate. In Hizbullah's eyes, the Shi'i 'Amili identity is superior to all other forms, including Arab and Lebanese.
3. On 10 March 2012, 14 protesters were injured at a Christian demonstration against the proposed inclusion in the Lebanese school curriculum of a work of history that focuses on the Palestinian resistance to Israeli occupation and disregards the Christian narrative of resistance against Palestinian and Syrian hegemony over Lebanon. The potential introduction of the book into the school system remains one of the most controversial subjects in Lebanese politics today.
4. The borders of modern-day Lebanon were drawn up by the French, in consultation with the British, following the defeat of the Ottoman Empire.
5. Shi'i literature refers to Yazid, Mu'awiya's son and caliph, as 'the butcher' after the battle of Karbala. The books of *hadith* (in the Shi'i Twelver tradition) contain collections of the Prophet's sayings, and those of the Twelve Imams.
6. The much-celebrated "national heroes" in official Lebanese history, Princes Bashir and Fakhreddine, both fought for direct control over the Shi'a in South Lebanon. Due to this, they were portrayed in a very different light in Shi'i historical narratives such as Jaber's.
7. Prince Faisal established the Arab government in Damascus in 1918.
8. This partially explains the large Shi'i enrollment in the Lebanese Communist Party, Fatah (the Palestinian organisation), and other secular movements.
9. *Jabal 'Amel* was issued for two years after an Ottoman ban on *Al 'Erfan*. The latter's editor, 'Aref Al-Zein, was *Jabal 'Amel*'s publisher (Chalabi 2006, p. 176).

10. These claims are further disproved by the wide array of feudal families in South Lebanon, such as the Al-Zein, different branches of the al-Sagheer, and the al-Khalil (in the coastal areas).
11. To this day, the tribes of the northern Biqaʿ Valley dominate most walks of life, unlike in the more urban south.
12. Al-Khiyam became better known during the years of Israeli occupation as the location of the most notorious prison, known for its regime of torture and its inhumane conditions.
13. His remarks on agriculture were mentioned in the ʿAmili Trio's historical accounts.
14. Roger, Lescot (1936) *Les Chiites du Liban Sud*. Report to the Centre des Hautes Etues de l'Aise Moderne. Paris: CHEAM.
15. This relationship will be further examined in Chap. 4.
16. Jaber wrote his history of Jabal ʿAmil during the French Mandate, long before it was eventually published in 1981.
17. Imam Ali was the first Shiʿi imam, and any association with him carries considerable religious weight.
18. Khosro's book is downloadable online in Arabic.
19. Al-Zein, Ali (1954) *Maa alTareekh Al ʿAmili*. Sidon: Al ʿErfan Publishing.
20. Al-Hanbali is the most conservative and puritanical of the four major Sunni schools of jurisprudence. Adherents of this sect led purges against non-Sunni Muslim minorities.
21. Imam ʿAli was Mohamad's brother-in-law and cousin, and the first infallible imam. The four 'Companions of Mohamad', revered by the Shiʿa for their loyalty to ʿAli, are Abu Dhar al-Ghaffari, Salman Al Farsi, Al-Mokdad Ben al-Aswad, and ʿAmmar Ben Yasser. Sunnis categorically deny the Shiʿi claims in this regard.
22. Hizbollah-affiliated historians have treated the Abu Dharr myth as a known fact, even teaching it in schools and disseminating it in their media outlets.
23. The battle of Karbala, in which Imam Hussein died with his followers and family, is revered in Shiʿi Islam and commemorated annually.
24. This dynasty continued throughout the following centuries up to the mid-1980s, when the Syrian regime and its allies sidelined the last descendent, the former speaker of parliament, Kamel al-Assʿad.
25. These narratives from the Ottoman era are present in detail in both Jaber's and Sheik Ali Reda's work; the latter's house was ransacked by, he believed, al-Assʿad's men.
26. Prince Ahmed Harfoush, Younes' son, was married to Princess Fakhera, the daughter of Prince Fakhreddine.
27. The descendants of Imam Hussein, the third imam, are revered in Shiʿi Islam, and along with other descendants of his grandfather, the Prophet Mohamed, receive exclusive financial assistance.

28. The Sunni leadership of Thaher Al-Omar, like the voluntary conversion of the Harfoush clan to Christianity, does not feature in Hizbullah's historical narratives.
29. The history of Arab nationalism in Jabal ʿAmil is downplayed by Hizbullah's historians, as it is in Kourani's narrative; they emphasise instead the themes of resistance and anti-colonialism.
30. Until the French Mandate, the whole of Lebanon was considered to be part of Syria, in literature and in political discourse.
31. According to Jaber, Gamal Pasha wrote in his diary that Kamal Bey Al-Assʿad notified him of Arab nationalist activism in South Lebanon.
32. The ʿAmili Trio were the pioneers of Arab nationalism in Jabal ʿAmil, but when more ideological and well-established movements started to spread elsewhere in Lebanon and Syria during the French Mandate, the influence of these ideas grew, gaining momentum among the urban Shiʿa.
33. While working on this book, I collected a number of these rare publications from old bookstores in South Lebanon and Beirut. They remain in my possession.

REFERENCES

BOOKS

Al-Muhajer, J. (1992). *Al-Taʾsis Litareekh al-Shiʿa* (The Foundation of Shiʿa History). Beirut: Dar Al Malak.

Al-Zein, A. (1954). *Maʿ al-Tareekh Al-ʿAmili*. Sidon: Al Erfan Publishing.

Antonius, G. (1939). *The Arab Awakening*. Philadelphia: J.B. Lippincott.

Chalabi, T. (2006). *The Shiʿis of Jabal ʿAmil and the New Lebanon*. New York: Palgrave.

Chalcraft, J. (2009). *The Invisible Cage: Syrian Migrant Workers in Lebanon*. Stanford, CA: Stanford University Press.

Hudson, M. (1968). *The Precarious Republic: Political Mobilization in Lebanon*. New York: Random House.

Jaber Al Safa, M. (1981). *Jabal ʿAmel Fi alTareekh*. Beirut: Dar Al-Nahar.

Makdisi, U. (2000). *The Culture of Sectarianism: Community, History, and Violence in Nineteenth-Century Ottoman Lebanon*. Berkeley: University of California Press.

Salibi, K. (1976). *Cross Roads to Civil War: Lebanon, 1958–1976*. Delmar, NY: Caravan Books.

Salibi, K. (1979). *Muntalaq Tarikh Lubnan* (The Basis of Lebanon's History). Beirut: Muʾassasat Nawfal.

Shanahan, R. (2005). *The Shiʾa of Lebanon: Clans, Parties and Clerics*. London, UK and New York: I.B. Tauris.

Sharara, W. (1996). *Al-Umma al-Qaliqa, Al-'Amiliyun wal-'Asabiyya Al Amiliya 'Ala 'Atabat Al Dawla Al-Lubnaniya* (The Concerned Nation, The 'Amilis and the 'Amili Solidarity in the Doorstep of the Lebanese State). Beirut: Dar Annahar.

Traboulsi, F. (2007). *A History of Modern Lebanon*. London: Pluto Press.

Weiss, M. (2010). *In the Shadow of Sectarianism*. Cambridge, MA and London, UK: Harvard University Press.

CHAPTER 4

Hizbullah's Reconstruction of History

Since its 'open letter' in 1985 that outlined its ideology and goals, Hizbullah has presented a constructed narrative of Shiʻi history in line with its identity of resistance and *Wilayat al-Faqih* (doctrine). This chapter examines Hizbullah's historical narratives by evaluating either official party discourse or studies by affiliated historians. The chapter demonstrates that the main themes of Hizbullah's history of Lebanon's Shiʻa are consistent with common features of nationalist histories: claims of origins, resistance to threats, decline and disappearance, national character, and 'golden ages' (Breuilly 2007, pp. 10–17). Unlike Islamic organisations' transnational narratives, there is a distinct territorial and ethnic element in Hizbullah's historiographies, pertaining to either the southern Lebanese region of Jabal ʻAmil or to Lebanese Shiʻa in general.[1] The process, if not the particularities, is similar to Iran's Cultural Revolution in the early 1980s, when the national curricula were overhauled to fit the new ruling elite's Islamic ideology. Tensions between the transnational *Wilayat al-Faqih* and the territorial/ethnic elements in Hizbullah's historical narratives are reconciled by highlighting historical links of solidarity and exchanges.[2] These are closely tied to Iran's 'superior' Persian narrative, which is also associated with Islamic transnational doctrine through its claim to Islamic leadership. Similarly, presenting Hizbullah's 'Islamic resistance' as the leading force in a weak nation justifies the ethnic/territorial elements in the organisation's historical narratives and discourse.

This chapter illustrates how Hizbullah deploys earlier histories, discussed in detail in Chap. 3, to reconstruct Shiʿi history. The nuances of the earlier historical narratives are replaced with a more targeted version, creating a dual layer in its narration of history, a reconstruction of the constructed. This chapter examines Hizbullah's historical narrative at length, highlighting how the organisation's official discourse connects to the present. It illustrates the wide range of invented narratives, mostly based on 'oral histories'—these were represented in two popular television series aired on Hizbullah's Al-Manar channel.

4.1 Source Materials

The primary sources used here come from two main categories: Hizbullah's direct stance and that of allied third parties, propagated by the organisation's affiliated publishing houses. The first category entails official statements, party publications, or television productions and books written by party cadres or members; the second includes non-party intellectual publications from Hizbullah's publishing houses. In the first category, Mohamad Kourani's *Al-Jozoor al-Tarikheya Lel Moqawama al-Islamiya* (*The Historical Roots of the Islamic Resistance*), published in 1993, is a leading source, primarily due to its popularity and its consistency with Hizbullah's official rhetoric, suggesting a wide influence. Kourani, widely associated with Hizbullah, remains the organisation's primary historian, regularly featured on Al-Manar.[3] Since Kourani's book was published, many books by other authors have covered the modern phase of Hizbullah's resistance against Israeli occupation, especially the 2000 Israeli withdrawal and the 2006 war against Israeli aggression. In other sources, mostly covering the post-1993 history, the use of the aforementioned historiography to reconstruct the meanings of recent political and military events is examined. In certain instances, Hizbullah officials endorse Kourani's book through an introduction in Shaʿlan's book on the July War,[4] such as that by Shaykh Hassan ʿIzzeddine, the organisation's political chief in the south. While the number of books on the July War is large, the most popular among them concern supernatural events. Kourani's book is more significant in its influence on discourse and subsequent intellectual output than the remaining historiographies.

4.2 Potential Limitations

The major limitation in evaluating any reconstruction of history is the possibility of overstating specific books or various forms of literature in the process of creating or narrating 'the nation's history'. In discussing the study of nationalists' reconstruction of history, Smith cautioned against such a limitation (as did Herder) (Smith 1993, p. 362). To contain these limitations in this case study, a wider variety of official discourses and affiliated publications are examined to highlight the organisation's points of emphasis. Kourani's book constitutes the premises of the first two parts of this chapter: the reverberation of his main themes throughout official party discourse and media production are examined to validate their use in the organisation's politics and rhetoric. However, Kourani's influence is evident from the organisation's discourse: his articles are featured on party websites and he regularly appears on Al-Manar (Moqawama 2010). A second limitation relates to drawing political assumptions based on these narratives. The examination of historical narratives is not a substitute for causal explanations; however, their study contributes to the debate on the extent of nationalism's modernity—in this case, 'sectarian nationalism'—and the extent to which these 'intellectual brokers' draw on pre-existing ethnic ties and traditions (Smith 1993, p. 362).

The construction or reconstruction of history is not confined to a particular timeframe, as the process and contestations continue. In the post-Soviet era, Eastern European countries engaged in the construction of national histories, creating tension between the yearning to westernise and emphasising a distinct identity (Breuilly 2007, p. 8). In Lebanon, however, Hizbullah's historiography could be considered the most organised and systematic contestation of the official Maronite history of the country. As discussed in Chaps. 2 and 3, Hizbullah's historians and clergy have rewritten Shiʿi and Lebanese history, emphasising its Islamic and resistance elements. Those rewriting the history, however, admitted their lack of sources, which they blamed on the Lebanese Maronite hegemony over Lebanon since 1920.[5]

4.3 Hizbullah's Historians: Inventing Continuity

The historians examined are mostly 'intellectual brokers' frequently claiming independence and neutrality, although some are Hizbullah members. In some instances, the historians are independent or non-Shiʿi writers, but the common denominator is the Hizbullah-affiliated publishing houses. Since the 1980s, these Shi'i publishers have transformed the once weak sector in Lebanon, doubling its size and acquiring nearly 45 per cent of the national market (Rosiny 2000, p. 8). The organisation's influence over these publishing houses is usually indirect, as Rosiny notes:

> Hizbullah seems to control and harness the book market more indirectly. For example, the party's subsidiary organization like al-Wahda al-I'lamiyya al Markaziyya (Central Media Unit) or Mu'assasat al-Shahid (Martyr's Foundation) and the already mentioned Markaz al-Istishari li l-Dirasat wa-l-tauthiq commission their printed works from private companies like Dar al-Nada, Manshurat al-Wala or Dar al-Wasila. In this way they may subsidize these ideologically friendly companies. (Rosiny 2000, p. 26)

This subtle subsidy is clear in the book prices, as there is a wide discrepancy between Hizbullah-affiliated books and other Arabic publications, although they are rarely for sale in the same outlet.[6]

Hizbullah's publishing revolution bears similarities to other nationalist historiographies: nationalist political elites engage in reconstructing history to foster a sense of continuity "to re-socialize uprooted populations and inculcate new values of order and hierarchy" (Smith 1993, p. 356). Like archaeologists, nationalist historians, as Smith illustrates, magnify certain aspects and events, many times selectively, to weave a national history and mythology worthy of the nation. This reconstructed history is central to the group's capacity for mobilisation and claims to legitimacy.

Hobsbawm, a historian himself, noted in a striking analogy the relation between historians and nationalism:

> For historians are to nationalism what poppy-growers in Pakistan are to heroin-addicts: we supply the essential raw material for the market. Nations without a past are contradictions in terms. What makes a nation is the past, what justifies one nation against others is the past, and historians are the people who produce it. So my profession, which has always been mixed up in politics, becomes an essential component of nationalism. (Hobsbawm 1992, p. 3)

The major role of nationalist historians, whether in secular or religious contexts, is transforming local symbols, myths, memories, customs, and traditions into a worthy national history. This process involves exaggerations, inaccuracies, a selective approach, and, in certain instances, forgery

(Smith 2009, pp. 71–72). Rather scattered and incoherent local elements need to be 'pruned', or assembled, in such a way to allow nationalist organisations or groups to appeal to the wider populace and garner support for their agenda, which, in the case of Hizbullah, is resistance and loyalty to the leadership.[7]

While acknowledging the occurrence of forgery and arbitrary selection in nationalist movements' reconstruction of history, Smith maintains that the "cultural nationalists were intent on recreating a vernacular culture and history that would meet the two basic criteria of historical plausibility and popular resonance" (Smith 2009, p. 71). The historical continuity of Hizbullah's basic elements of identity is important for reasons of legitimacy, as the party's name (the 'Party of God') and concept stem from a Qurʾanic verse referring to its holy representation. In this regard, there is a subtle contention that the group, representing a holy organisation of the faithful people, has existed in different forms throughout history, as Allah's thesis fighting its antithesis.

4.3.1 Jabal ʿAmil: The 'Holy Origins'

Saints, prophets, and sages, writes Smith (2009, p. 97), offer sanctity to homelands, whether in Ireland, the land of St. Patrick, St. Gregory's Armenia, or the Virgin Mary's holy presence in Mexico and Poland. Hizbullah's version of history, which selectively reproduced the myth of Shiʿi origins in Lebanon, is based on the immigration of Abu Dharr, one of the Prophet Muhammad's companions and a loyalist of his cousin ʿAli Ben Abi Taleb, the first Shiʿi Imam and the fourth Muslim caliph. This myth has been largely disputed due to the lack of sufficient resources and inconsistencies in the Abu Dharr story.[8] Jabal ʿAmil gained its historical significance from 'ancient' times when this "great mountain was a breeding ground for the call of prophets due to its proximity to Palestine" (Kourani 1993, p. 23).[9] In a 2014 speech from the southern town of Aynata, Hizbullah's Secretary General Nasrallah referred to Jabal ʿAmil as "this blessed and holy land" (Al-Manar 2014). The 'holiness' of Jabal ʿAmil is a recurrent theme in the organisation's local festivals and conventions; in one instance, the region is named the birthplace of saints and the 'chapel of the prophets' (Al-Manar 2014). Kourani's book is even less apologetic on this theme, naming Jabal ʿAmil a 'holy and blessed' land, home to 'geniuses' and notable scholars (Kourani 1993, p. 23).

According to Hizbullah's narrative, Jabal ʿAmil was distinguished from neighbouring lands and regions by four major factors. The first lies in the sanctity of its land, as a number of Qurʾanic verses and their Shiʿi interpretations demonstrate (Kourani 1993, pp. 23–24). The Qurʾanic verse "O my people, enter the Holy Land which Allah has assigned to you and do not turn back [from fighting in Allah's cause] and [thus] become losers", is interpreted in Kourani's historical narrative as 'a holy land in the Levant' (Kourani 1993, p. 24). The Levant is vast, but the author selectively interprets the verse to refer to Jabal ʿAmil. The second verse is that of the *Al Israa*, a significant event in Islam, in which God miraculously lifted the Prophet Muhammad from his mosque in Mecca to Jerusalem. The verse states: "Exalted is He who took His Servant by night from al-Masjid al-Haram to al-Masjid al-Aqsa, whose surroundings We have blessed, to show him of Our signs. Indeed, He is the Hearing, the Seeing" (*Al Israa*, Verse 1). In popular and written Hizbullah narratives, the 'blessed surroundings' include Jabal ʿAmil in the south of Lebanon, also known as the *aljaleel alaʾaʿla* (Upper Galilee) (Kourani 1993, p. 24). The presence of many shrines of prophets and saints, though controversial, accentuates the claim to sanctity.[10]

The second reason for Jabal ʿAmil's sanctity is its early conversion to Shiʿi Islam: "After the Prophet Muhammad passed away, only four of Imam Ali's Shiʿa existed: Salman (the Persian), Al Muqdad, Abu Dharr and Ammar. Then in the time of Usman, Abu Dharr went to the Levant where he stayed several days, and many converted to Shiʿi Islam" (Kourani 1993, p. 24). Abu Dharr's name became synonymous with that of Jabal ʿAmil, further enforcing Hizbullah's claims of its historical continuity in Islamic resistance (Al-Manar 2014). Abu Dharr, portrayed as a rebel against the Umayyad ruler, resembles both defiance and holy origins, being one of the Prophet Muhammad's and Imam ʿAli's senior companions.

Serving the 'myth of election', as it is called by Smith, the reconstructed history of Lebanese Shiʿa also claims that following the death of the Prophet, two Shiʿi communities existed in Jabal ʿAmil and Medina, Islam's first city (Kourani 1993, pp. 24–25). The earlier, better documented and methodologically valid historical narratives, like Jaʿfar Al Muhajer's book on Shiʿi origins, note that Shiʿi Islam arrived in the Levant with later immigration from Iraq, centuries after the myth claims. The third reason is the presence of senior and 'knowledgeable' clergymen in Jabal ʿAmil; their presence is connected to governance in the time of the last Shiʿi imam's great absence, the age of Imam Mehdi (Kourani 1993, p. 25). The fourth is Jabal ʿAmil's claimed mention in the imams' *Hadeeth*, the sayings of the Prophet Muhammad's cousin and his 11 descendants. Kourani mentions one statement by the sixth imam, Jaʿfar al Sadeq (d. 765), referring to a 'holy' land in the Levant, even naming a town known as Shqeef, and its surrounding valleys and mountains (Kourani 1993, p. 26). In the narrative, the imam says of the people of this 'holy' region: "They are our true Shiʿa, our followers and brothers … [they have] soft hearts for us, tough for our enemies" (Kourani 1993, p. 26).

4.3.2 *Resistance Against the Crusades*

Although widely contested and uncorroborated, the Shiʿi resistance against the Crusades features in the organisation's narratives and discourse. The narrative has been constructed from 'oral', undocumented stories and has been effectively used to justify policy in terms of historical continuity.[11] The ongoing conflict in Syria is justified by this claimed historical continuity: for example, Mohamad Fneish, a Hizbullah cadre and government minister, presented the historical basis for the Syrian conflict through the Crusades in a 2014 speech:

> The effect and influence of Jabal ʿAmil's geographical location was both active and reactive, as it has not departed from its position of resistance to invaders throughout its historical periods … [T]his Jabal's Sectarian peculiarity retains its uniqueness in understanding, belonging and commitment to the Ummah's unity and causes, and remains a force and a guarantee in preserving identity, defending rights, rejecting prejudice and facing falsehood (*albatel*) and authoritarianism. The role of this Jabal in resisting the Crusaders' invasion, the Ottoman injustice, confronting French colonialism and the Zionist project and its occupation of land, the support of liberation movements and standing against *takfiri* crimes and deviations (in Syria). This continued history's connection to the present is not a continuation of those frozen in past glories … it is the continuity of those knowledgeable of the reality's equations, committed to their apostolic goals, and exerting every effort, useful for the homeland and the entire nation, even if this requires sacrificing souls. (Al-Manar 2014)

A school textbook published by Hizbullah's *Almaʿaref* claims that Shiʿi resistance against the Crusaders commenced with Tripoli, which 'strived' under the Bani ʿAmmar rule, until surrendering in 1109 (*Almaʿaref* 2014,

p. 53). According to Kourani (1993, pp. 32–35), the Fatimid-era resistance against the Crusader campaigns in the twelfth century culminated in the siege of Tyr, a coastal city, for 25 years. The account of the siege of Tyr makes underlying assumptions more relevant and suitable to contemporary politics: first, the inhabitants of Jabal ʿAmil are portrayed as a unified entity or a bloc, acting and planning as such, and second, this entity's acts imply the existence of a unified nation, worthy of the ultimate sacrifice. The *Almaʿaref* states:

> This phase was characterised by the focus on defending Jabal ʿAmil's largest metropolis to prevent it from falling to the Franks (*alferanj*).[12] This occurred under a complete parallelised let-down state of the Islamic world's military and political power after the Crusaders' campaign succeeded in penetrating it and reaching its heart, occupying the city of al-Quds, where it committed one of the ugliest massacres in history, exposing the extent of the Islamic world's weakness and powerlessness. (*Almaʿaref* 2014, p. 54)

In this context, Tyr's resistance, just like Hizbullah's nine centuries later, reinstalled hope and morale 'in Muslim hearts', although its fall after 'this glorious steadfastness' also greatly affected them (*Almaʿaref* 2014).

Kourani contrasts Tyr's resistance against the Crusaders with Sunni-dominated Sidon's rapid surrender and concludes that the Islamic Resistance was and continues to be the only capable anti-colonial force:

> The Islamic Resistance has proven throughout history, and to this day, that it remains the only force capable of perseverance and persistence, as its foundations are the ideological and Sharia principles, and what the live human conscience requires, even if it led to the sacrifice of the Mujahideens' heads. (Kourani 1993, p. 39)

Furthermore, with the fall of Tyr, "all of Jabal ʿAmil fell under Crusader occupation" (*Almaʿaref* 2014). Jabal ʿAmil is presented as a political entity: under the title *Jabal ʿAmil the Base of Jihad*, the book argues for the centrality of the 'ʿAmili land' in the definitive battle against the Crusaders, although there is no mention of specific examples of the local contribution to the battle (*Almaʿaref* 2014, p. 55). There is, however, criticism of Salahuddin's truce with the Crusaders (*Almaʿaref* 2014, p. 55). Such criticisms of the much-celebrated Islamic figure fall within the general Shiʿi tradition recounting Salahuddin's role in ending the Fatimid dynasty. Another side to this resistance is the city of Jizzine, which "remained purified, un-desecrated by the Crusaders ... [I]n brief, ʿAmilis conquered the ordeal of occupation, and succeeded in establishing their schools, completely preserve their existence ... and remained faithful to their authentic intellectual message" (*Almaʿaref* 2014, p. 55). The ʿAmilis, *Almaʿaref* continues, "have guarded the Arabic language, preserved its studies in this domineering foreign sea, they guarded the studies of Shariʿa, preserved it and bequeathed it to coming generations as an eternal trust" (*Almaʿaref* 2014, p. 57).

4.3.3 Inventing Symbols of Resistance

ʿAmili heroic figures are a common theme in Hizbullah's historical accounts, as they highlight the extent of invention in the organisation's constructed Shiʿi identity. In the case of the Crusades, the story of two previously unknown heroes emerges: *Almaʿaref*'s narrative refers to the "unknown ʿAmili hero Husameddine Beshara", attributing to him and his soldiers participation in the battle of Hattin (1187) between the Crusader kingdom of Jerusalem and Salahuddin's forces.[13] Beshara, the "ʿAmili hero', died in 1201, "after a life full of *Jihad*" (*Almaʿaref* 2014, p. 56).

Without sources or citations, Kourani narrates in detail the story of an unnamed old man from Tyr, who burned down three wooden towers of military significance. In Kourani's account of this ʿAmili 'hero', myth and reality are mixed. Each of these mobile wooden towers, Kourani writes, had 1,000 men inside; the old man used a liquid to set them on fire, thus sending 3,000 men to their death on his own (Kourani 1993, p. 33). The 'people of Tyr' fought the Crusaders, and their resistance outlived Baldwin I, and continued into the reign of his cousin Baldwin II, the king of Jerusalem, who subsequently succeeded in controlling the 'defiant' city (Kourani 1993, p. 36).[14] While its source remains unclear, the story upgrades the Shiʿi ʿAmili presence in resisting the Crusaders to the level of the remaining history. As such, the Shiʿi response to the crusaders' campaigns, the Ottoman occupation, and colonial and Israeli aggression is unified under the banner of resistance and a commitment to the Shiʿi Islamic ideals.

4.3.4 The Jihad of the ʿUlamaʾ

In a similar approach to that in the Crusader campaigns, the Shiʿi clergy's dominant role in Hizbullah's leadership, nearly filling its entire top tier, reflects itself in the organisation's historical narratives, revealing

4 HIZBULLAH'S RECONSTRUCTION OF HISTORY

another aspect of the reconstructed history. Hizbullah's various narratives and histories, both official and affiliated, claim a continuity in the *ulama*'s leadership from ancient times to today. This approach is manifest in the words of a Hizbullah member of the Lebanese parliament, who speaks of "their leading role in the creation of Jabal ʿAmil's renaissance" (Al-Manar 2014). The "understanding between the *ulama* and the princes", specifically between the feudal leader Nassif Nassar and Sayyid ʿAbd al-Hassan Musa al-Husseini, resulted in the semi-independence of Jabal ʿAmil, paving the way for "economic and cultural prosperity" (Al-Manar 2014). The magnification of the *ulama*'s role is seen most clearly in a Hizbullah-funded television series, *Qiyamat al-Banadeq* (*The Rise of Rifles*), which aired on Al-Manar in 2013. The series narrates the story of a group of young men in a Jabal ʿAmil village who form a resistance movement under the auspices of the Shiʿi *ulama*. Continuity in the series, a relatively large production effort, combines the various elements of Hizbullah's identity, especially resistance and the *ulama*'s leadership.

The significance of the *ulama* lies primarily in their efforts to preserve or 'save' the faith. The capture and crucifixion of Shiʿi cleric Shamsuddine Mohammad Ben Makki Al Jizini, Kourani writes, left its mark on Jabal ʿAmil's politics from the fourteenth to sixteenth centuries; the Shaykh had risen to prominence in 1383 "to save Shiʿism" (Kourani 1993, p. 60). During the time when the Shiʿa suffered under Mamluk repression, the faith went underground, paving the way for what were considered exaggerations in faith, including a claim to prophethood by Shaykh Mohamad Al-Yalushi. Al-Jizini, widely known as *Al-Shaheed Al-Awal* (the 'First Martyr'), rebelled against this 'distortion' of religion, through preaching the 'true call' of Shiʿi Islam, and then by taking up arms against Al-Yalushi in the battle of Nabatieh al-Fawqa in Jabal ʿAmil. His foes reported him to the Sunni rulers, leading to his captivity and crucifixion in 1384 (Kourani 1993, p. 60). The primary explanation for the failure of the First Martyr's movement was the "departure [conversion] of coastal Shiʿa to the Sunni Islam's sects" (Kourani 1993, p. 61).[15] The consequence of this failure was the appearance of the feudal lords and the 'evaporation' of the efforts to "organize the Shiʿi community and resurrect them as an independent sect" (Kourani 1993, p. 61). The Shiʿi are thus portrayed as an oppressed population who, guided by their Islamic beliefs, chose the path of resistance.

4.3.5 Islamic Governments

Quite unreservedly, Kourani connects Hizbullah's Islamic governmental ideology to Jabal ʿAmil's history, claiming that three 'Islamic governments' existed in different time frames in the region: Mashghara (the eastern Biqaʿ Valley), Jezzine (South Lebanon), and Bani Bechara in the southern part of Jabal ʿAmil.[16] They are portrayed as part of a continuous Shiʿi historical line, which leads to today's *Wilayat al-Faqih* structure. The evidence provided for the first so-called Islamic Shiʿi state of Mashghara is scant: while there have been no historical accounts of a Shiʿi government in Mashghara, the author presents the tensions and differences between Shiʿi feudal lords and the dominant Shihabi family as evidence of its existence (Kourani 1993, p. 63). Jezzine's 'Islamic government' refers to the First Martyr's leadership and his war against perceived distortions in Islam. The local and often feudal leadership, such as that of the Sobh family in the Biqaʿ Valley or Shaykh Zeinulabiddine Ben Bechara in the town of Zebqin (South Jabal ʿAmil and the Litani River), are all listed as examples of Islamic government (Kourani 1993, pp. 63–65). Uncorroborated and lacking references, the extraordinary claims in Kourani's section on 'Islamic governments' stand out in comparison with Jaber's historical account.

4.3.6 Resisting Ottoman Rule

The ancient Islamic governments' narrative carries an underlying assumption of a prosperous people; this phase, however, ended with the Ottoman occupation. The Shiʿa bore the brunt of repression, destitution, and injustice under Ottoman rule, Kourani asserts: their scholars were tortured, libraries burnt, and calls to kill them were pronounced (Kourani 1993, p. 69). While the Ottoman repression of the Shiʿa occurred especially during its war with the Safavid Empire, Kourani's historical account and Hizbullah's rhetoric in this regard are selective, exaggerated, and more dramatic.[17] Although most of Kourani's chapter on Ottoman era is based on Jaber's history of Jabal ʿAmil, the Hizbullah historian glosses over the early phase of Jaber's indirect rule; this approach highlights the political differences between the historians. Jaber's praise was politically motivated, as he wanted to make the case for indirect rule: Jabal ʿAmil's early twentieth-century historians and intellectuals sought federalism or autonomy within the Ottoman Empire; this agenda is not compatible with Hizbullah's ideology or political programme.

Resistance against Ottoman rule is sketched down to the smallest detail, drawing comparisons with the contemporary resistance in Jabal ʿAmil. This theme of the continuity of resistance resonated in a Hizbullah-sponsored conference: "From the al-Tayaha which resisted the Army of Ahmad Pasha Jazzar at the end of the eighteenth century, to the resistance that defeated the Israelis in the early twenty-first century, Jabal ʿAmil remains reconciled with its history of rejection of injustice and occupation" (Al-Akhbar and Al-Manar 2013).

4.3.7 Al-Muqawim (the 'Resistor') Melhem Qassim

In a similar approach to the section on the Crusades, Hizbullah's historical narratives weave heroic tales of resistance against Ottoman rule. In this case, in the late nineteenth century, Melhem Qassim, a shepherd's son who was born in a cave, is a larger-than-life character in al-Hajj Hassan's history of Lebanon's '100 years of resistance'. In an act of selflessness for the sake of resistance, Qassim, whose story is based on oral sources, sold 40 of his father's sheep to buy four pistols and four hunting rifles (Al-Hajj Hassan 2008, p. 26). Qassim's character featured in Al-Manar's television series, *Qiyamat al Banade*, on the roots of resistance in Lebanon (Al-Manar 2013). While the 31-episode series tells the story of the anti-Ottoman resistance, the leading and enlightening role of *ulama* is a recurrent theme. In the second episode, a *sayyid* is shown preaching a message of resistance, condemning Ottoman rule and warning against falling for Western promises of freedom and happiness (*Qiyamat al-Banadeq* 2013). He predicts the failure of diplomatic conferences and the colonial betrayal of the Arabs following their revolution against the Ottomans. The *sayyid*'s speech encapsulates the organisation's desired image of the Shiʿi cleric as an enlightened, insightful leader, capable of foreseeing danger and exposing colonial conspiracies. The *sayyid*'s diverse audience, both economically and demographically, reflects a continuity with the influence of the *ulama* in the current age.

The series highlights other symbolic figures of resistance, such as Mahmoud Bazzi, and showcases the territorial elements in Hizbullah's identity. In the third episode, Bazzi and his men trap a fugitive from the Ottomans and ask him whether he is an *Ittihadi* (Young Turks supporter) or *Hamidi* (an Ottoman sultan supporter); the man replies: "None, I am an Arab from Jabal ʿAmil" (*Qiyamat al-Banadeq* 2013). As such, this anti-Ottoman resistance is seen to resemble contemporary Islamic resistance in its sectarian, ethnic, and territorial identity, in addition to the significance of the *ulama* leadership. The television series was presented as a historical account of this phase, although its director acknowledged in an interview with the *Assafir* newspaper that the production's narratives are partially based on oral histories by "elderly people in Jabal ʿAmil" (*Qiyamat al-Banadeq* 2013, p. 9). However, the series is based on the period 1912–1926, making it highly unlikely that the producers would have found any elderly people who had witnessed this phase.

Also based on oral history, al-Hajj Hassan builds up Qassim's story. Born in 1858 in the Biqaʿ Valley, Qassim killed five Ottoman soldiers in the summer of 1911, subsequently becoming a fugitive (Al-Hajj Hassan 2008, p. 27). In al-Hajj Hassan's narrative, he rejected the Ottoman government's offer of reconciliation, *alsolh*:

> After he rejected the reconciliation, they threatened to burn his town Bretal and Hor Taʿla, and they called on him to surrender in Taʿla's police station, they pledged him peace, and returned him to his family unscathed. Melhem, well-intentioned, obeyed. He fell into their trap, they arrested him, tied his hands. They assembled a firing squad, but Melhem escaped from in-between the soldiers. (Al-Hajj Hassan 2008, p. 30)

Al-Hajj Hassan narrates in detail Qassim's heroic escape, dodging Ottoman bullets, biting the ear of a soldier, and "returning to his men to continue on the path of resistance" (Al-Hajj Hassan 2008, p. 30). The author equates Qassim's growing resistance with the fall of the Ottoman Empire, as if the former was a factor in the decay of the latter: "The days passed between the two sides, a day of attack and a day of retreat, till the historical moment arrived, and the Ottoman Empire disintegrated in November 1918" (Al-Hajj Hassan 2008, p. 30).

4.3.8 *Debunking Lebanon's Maronite-Druze History*

Hizbullah's view of internal politics as a dichotomy between resistance and local collaboration with the aggressors applies to the historical narrative of Lebanon's two most respected figures in official history: Fakhreddine II and Bashir al-Shihabi. "The official Lebanese history portrayed Prince Fakhreddine II as a man of independence, and described him as grand and the wise politician", writes Kourani (1993, p. 76). In the Maronite-dominated national history, Prince Fakhreddine II is a national hero who liberated Lebanon from the Ottomans after forcing his authority on feudal chieftains (Jamil 1948, pp. 19–20). In a statement resonating with Hizbullah's general contemporary discourse, Kourani claims that the much-celebrated Lebanese prince had "suspicious relations" with Paul V.[18] Communications between the two men constitute "good evidence of the connection between this ruler with the spiteful West, which was trying to return to the Islamic Levant" (Kourani 1993, p. 75). Although publicly a Muslim Druze, Fakhreddine was a Christian at heart; his strong sympathy with Christian interests evoked Shiʻi fears of a pogrom following their expulsion from Mount Lebanon, and the 'Islamic resistance' against Fakhreddine took the form of guerrilla warfare and scattered attacks against his representatives (Kourani 1993, p. 76).

Bashir Al Shihabi, known in Lebanese national history as *al-kabeer* ('The Grand'), took after Fakhreddine in terms of power and his antagonistic policy against the Shiʻa of Jabal ʻAmil (Kourani 1993, p. 99). Al-Shihabi's 'animosity' towards Muslims became apparent in the assistance he gave to the Napoleonic invasions in the late eighteenth and early nineteenth centuries; the 'anti-Muslim' ruler provided the French armies with food supplies during their siege of Jafa, where Muslim prisoners were executed (Kourani 1993, p. 100). Similar to Fakhreddine, Al-Shihabi, who later converted from Sunni Islam to Christianity, enjoyed a strong relationship with Pope Pius VII, and exchanged letters with Napoleon, who in turn gave him a gift of a sword—his acceptance of the gift is portrayed as a sign of his subservience to the French ruler. Bashir helped the 'new Crusaders', who like their ancestors wanted to pillage, destroy, and control Muslims, especially the armed Shiʻa of Jabal ʻAmil (Kourani 1993, p. 101).

According to this narrative of betrayal, the common or recurrent thread in Bashir's alliances was the protection of Christians and their superiority over the Shiʻa. Mohamad Ali Pacha, leader of the Ottoman campaign to liberate Egypt, took power and built a strong army with Western help, and his son Ibrahim Pacha led a campaign in 1831 to 'liberate' the Levant. Bashir, who recognising that Pacha "solidified the status of Christians and Jews on every land he controlled", decided to support the new military campaign (Kourani 1993, p. 103). The Egyptian rule of Jabal ʻAmil was 'unjust', as it included higher taxes, servitude, compulsory military service, and the disarmament of the population (Kourani 1993, p. 105). As in the various other polarised narratives, Bashir and Fakhreddine II were both conspirators against Jabal ʿAmil's resistance and the 'Islamic government'.

4.3.9 Resistance and Revolution Against 'Egyptian Injustices'

In the vein of the recurrent theme of injustice and resistance, the discriminatory treatment of Jabal ʿAmil's people resulted in skirmishes with the local population, which developed into a three-year revolution in 1836 (Kourani 1993, pp. 104–105). Without referencing any sources, Kourani places the *ulama* in the forefront of this revolt: aided by his brother Mohamad ʿAli, Shaykh Shbib Ben Shaykh ʿAli Alfares Alsaʿbi led the 'revolution'; they attacked government posts, expelled its workers, and tortured its soldiers. Ibrahim Pacha learnt of the rebellion and dispatched soldiers to help Bashir Al-Shihabi, who ordered his inexperienced son Majid to launch a campaign. Majid's soldiers failed to repress the hit-and-run fighters, and the army then sought to take collective punishment on the population. The Wujahaʾ of Jabal ʿAmil asked the rebels to surrender, but they chose to leave to southern Syria. Another tale of heroism occurred in their new hideout, according to Kourani, which represents the *ulama* ideal of selflessness for the cause: Shaykh Shbib became very ill and asked his brother Mohamad Ali to flee Pacha's army, but a follower named Musa Qleit decided to take over, telling the soldiers he was Mohamad Ali. Shbib and Qleit were executed, while Mohamad ʿAli lived another 40 years (Kourani 1993, pp. 105–106).

Bashir continued to repress the Shiʿa, incarcerating and torturing the grandchild of one of Jabal ʿAmil's leaders, Shaykh Haidar Al-Fares, for one month (Kourani 1993, p. 106). While Ibrahim Pacha was occupied in trying to take over the Ottoman Empire, Bashir Al Shihabi and Sherif Pacha, a relative of the Egyptian rulers, governed the Levant. Christians of Jabal ʿAmil were mobilised and armed, ready to fight the Shiʿi rebels. The Al-Shihabis, therefore, not the Egyptians, were responsible: "The Al-Shihabis portrayed Jabal ʿAmil to Egyptians as a revolutionary land and rebellious people who had to be ruled by … oppression, so they poured their wrath on them, tortured their leaders and elites, incarcerated most of them" (Kourani 1993, p. 107). According to this account of events, Jabal ʿAmil's binary identity of resistance and Islam invited clashes with the era's powerful empires and their agents. The narrative of the battles between

Jabal ʿAmil, portrayed as a political entity, and Fakhreddine II and Al-Shihabis, has similarities to Hizbullah's contemporary view of Lebanese politics: the party's conflict with the Western- and Saudi-funded blocs is presented as a continuation of Lebanon's history of betrayals and alliances with external forces against Jabal ʿAmil.

Hizbullah's historians, specifically Kourani, adopt no criteria in differentiating between a revolt and more commonplace clashes between feudal lords and the Ottoman Empire's enforcers, whether these were the army or local representatives and tax collectors. The Egyptian invasion of South Lebanon again is represented as a period of clergy-led revolutions against injustices. For instance, Kourani says that following the illness of Mohamad Ali Pacha, the local Shiʿi leader Shaykh Hamad Mahmoud Nassar launched a rebellion against the Egyptian rule of Jabal ʿAmil. Shaykh Hamad, who studied at *alkawthariya* religious school under the supervision of Shaykh Hassan Kobeissi, a notable clergyman, scored a victory against the army of Prince Majid, Bashir al Shihabi's son. He then advanced towards northern Palestine, taking control of Safad, Al Nassera (Nazareth), and Tabaraya (Kourani 1993, p. 107). The 'Jabal ʿAmil rebels', as Kourani calls them, freed prisoners in *ʿAkka* (Acre). The continued use of the terms "ʿAmili rebels' or "ʿAmili resistance' implies the historical continuity of this movement, as manifest in Hizbullah today.

4.3.10 The Neo-Crusades: Colonial Hegemony

In speaking of the era of the weakening Ottoman Empire, Kourani reaffirms Jabal ʿAmil's leading role in the resistance and the preservation of Shiʿi Islam under the *ulama*'s leadership, blaming betrayals for their failures. The first of these betrayals or disappointments was the Christians' abuse of hospitality. Following the retreat of Ibrahim Pacha's armies from Lebanon in 1840, his ally Bashir Al-Shihabi surrendered to the English and was exiled to Malta, only to be replaced by the 'weak' Bashir III. The new prince's weakness and misjudgements paved the way for a 20-year-long phase of chaos in Lebanon, inviting more French, British, and Austrian incursions. The Ottoman Empire was dubbed 'the sick man of Europe', while the French and British were competing for control and influence in the Levant (Kourani 1993, p. 109).

Foreign powers were the sole instigators of the 1860 civil war between the Druze and Christians, partly in order to restore the old Crusader influence:

> Britain and France found the right circumstances for their ambitions in Lebanon, where they incited people, and ignited an abhorrent Sectarian war between Christians and Moslems, which carried dire consequences for citizens, destroying their towns and properties. In spite of this, the Moslem wise men in Syria and Lebanon took a stance characterized by awareness and appreciation of the situation to extinguish this *fitna* (discord), ignited by spiteful Crusader hands. (Kourani 1993, p. 110)

The majority of Jabal ʿAmil's tribes decided to receive Christian refugees as 'welcome guests', and they were protected and sheltered by ʿAmil's Muslims (the Shiʿa). This act of benevolence was not reciprocated, but instead was met by Christian acts of violence: "They [the Christians], unfortunately, were not duty-bound in 1920 [during the French Occupation], and in 1975 in Nabaʾ and Dahia [Beirut's eastern and southern suburbs], in Jabal ʿAmil and other Shiʿi regions" (Kourani 1993, p. 110).

Direct Ottoman rule of Jabal ʿAmil returned and with it the progress referred to as the 'time wheel' was reversed; the region began to regress after an 'independent' phase "full of noble deeds" (Kourani 1993, p. 110). While the Ottoman Empire was disintegrating, "European countries were in continuous development and prosperity". The 'canines' of *'Altakalob alʾistiʿmary'* (colonial insatiability) began to appear.[19] When France occupied Algeria in 1830, the *mujahed* ʿAbd al-Qader Aljazaʾri led a revolution against them (Kourani 1993, p. 111). After the European colonial powers agreed at the Berlin conference in 1878 to divide the territories of the Ottoman Empire among themselves, France occupied Tunisia in 1881, Britain occupied Egypt in 1882 and Sudan in 1899, Italy occupied Libya in 1911, while the Spanish and French took control of Morocco in 1912 (Kourani 1993, p. 112).[20]

Kourani reasserts the selflessness of the *ulama* during the following difficult periods of conflict and famine. The First World War took its toll on Jabal ʿAmil, as famine and Ottoman conscription left many dead and the survivors in desperate straits[21]; the bodies of the dead were left abandoned at the roadside and in the bushes, while "land and honour" were sold for "a pinch of flour or a meal" (Kourani 1993, p. 120). ʿAbd al-Hussein Sharafeddine, the *marjaʾ* (senior cleric), successfully pressurised the rich of Jabal ʿAmil to help its starving poor, lessening some of their pain and saving many lives (Kourani 1993, pp. 121–122). The common, recurrent theme of the various Hizbullah-affiliated histories of the era is that the Shiʿa of Jabal ʿAmil found strength in their unity and the *ulama*'s 'sacred word'. Kourani's narrative, among others, professes to see a continuity with the present day, not only in relation to the authority of the *ulama*, but also in the voluntary public obedience to their *fatwas*—the Shiʿi clerics of the time constituted a supreme authority and their *fatwas* a final judgement that the Shiʿi leader or ruler had to obey (Kourani 1993, p. 80). However, the *ulama* also shared in the sufferings of the Shiʿi laity: denied official Ottoman recognition as imams, they were conscripted into the Ottoman army during the First World War (Kourani 1993, pp. 120–121).

4.3.11 Sharafeddine: The Marjaʿ Leader

Ayatollah ʿAbd al-Hussein Sharafeddine (1872–1957), a leading Shiʿi cleric from Tyr, features strongly in Hizbullah's historical discourse on Jabal ʿAmil and Lebanon during the twentieth century. The roles attributed to Sharafeddine fit with the theme of the *ulama*'s leadership and Islamic resistance; this narrative thrusts Jabal ʿAmil's resistance and the *ulama* into the centre of events in the colonial Arab world. Contrary to other historical accounts of the era, Kourani portrays the Shiʿi-Christian violence in 1920 as an 'Islamic revolution' and refers to the ensuing attacks against the French occupation as 'Islamic resistance'.[22] The story of the revolt is one of betrayal and resistance under the auspices of the *ulama*. Sharif Hussein Ben ʿAli, the Prince of Mecca, declared his independence from the Ottoman Empire on 27 June 1916 and launched an Arab revolt against Turkish rule. Following the empire's defeat and subsequent withdrawal from the Levant, Prince Faisal, Sharif Hussein's son, entered Damascus where he declared an Arab government, and asked the leaders of Jabal ʿAmil and Beirut to raise the Arab flag, thus inaugurating a new era (Kourani 1993, p. 125). Kourani here equates Beirut with Jabal ʿAmil and accordingly recreates the showdown between Damascus and the French colonialists, but replaces the former with Jabal ʿAmil. Although flags were raised in Bʿabda, Beirut, Sidon, Nabatieh, Tyr, and Marjaʿyoun, Sharif Hussein fell victim to French and British plots, entrusting T. E. Lawrence, known as Lawrence of Arabia and a 'British spy', with the Arab revolution (Kourani 1993, pp. 126–127). Although the betrayal itself is historically factual and well corroborated, it is used to contrast the Prince of Mecca's failed leadership with Sharafeddine's perseverance. In this historically recurrent image, the *ulama*, unlike the lay leaders, possess an insight into, and awareness of, foreign conspiracies, as well as a willingness to share their people's plight.

Sharafeddine had established a local government in Tyr to preserve security following Sharif Hussein's call; however, the British annulled it, stating: "But we, and those faithful to religion, nationalism and patriotism, will not to surrender to force" (Kourani 1993, p. 127). Kourani's account of this phase contradicts that of Traboulsi, who states that "Kamel al-Asʿad, Shiite Zaʿim of the south, was declared governor-general of Jabal ʿAmil" (Traboulsi 2007, p. 77). After the French entered Jabal ʿAmil, they banned public gatherings and political demonstrations in a written statement hung in Nabatieh's main square (Kourani 1993, p. 126). "The French showed clear favoritism to the Maronites and started preparing to establish an expanded Maronite state by including the four Cazas [regional districts in Jabal ʿAmil]", Kourani asserts, "but ʿAmilis strongly rejected this, because the new colonial power adopted the ways of Ibrahim Pacha the Egyptian. Wars and battles erupted between the occupation army and the Muslim ʿAmilis" (Kourani 1993, p. 128). Clashes did erupt, although historians such as Traboulsi confines them to two attacks, stating that the 'armed bandits' of Adham Khanjar and Sadeq Hamza "attacked French troops stationed in the Christian villages of Judayda (Marjaʿyun) and ʿAyn Ibil" (Traboulsi 2007, p. 77).[23]

Embodying the continuity of the *ulama*'s leadership, Sharafeddine is highly regarded in Hizbullah's reconstructed history, whether in television productions or intellectual/cultural forums and ideological/historical indoctrination. The Jabal ʿAmil imam is portrayed as "firm in his certainty, persevering in his movement, chasing occupiers or defending against them, wherever they went" (Kourani 1993, p. 132). On the other hand, nationalists, like the feudal lords before them, fell into the traps set by the colonial forces. When the British and French entered Jabal ʿAmil, the nationalists thought the allies would grant them complete independence in the same way as they had previously encouraged the establishment of local governments in Syria and Iraq (Kourani 1993, p. 131). While the local governments ignited disputes between the feudal lords, Jabal ʿAmil's politicians opposed France and called for independence. When the Allies' intentions were exposed and France started conspiring against the Syrians and Lebanese, including the ʿAmilis, battles erupted, and the French troops were defeated in certain areas, leading to their concentration in cities (Kourani 1993, p. 131). According to Kourani, ʿAbd al-Hussein Sharafeddine played a vital role in resisting the French through a *fatwa* declaring *jihad* (holy war) against the occupation; his call earned him a death sentence (Kourani 1993, p. 132).

Kourani quotes Hassan Nasrallah on the issue of Sharafeddine and the way in which the role of '*ulama mujahedeen*' was downplayed or ignored:

> Lebanon's crisis on the internal level is connected to the past that goes through the Umayyad and Abbassid rule to the Ayubis, Hamadanis, Mamluks, Ottomans, until one reaches the French Mandate era that we consider the nearest historical and political period resisted by Moslems. The symbol of the resistance against the French was Imam Sayyid Abdul Hussein Sharafeddine. But as it is usual in political action, France showcased those it wanted to stand out as heroes of resistance. (Kourani 1993, pp. 132–133)

The French used pro-mandate Christians to fight dissent in Jabal ʿAmil—for example, George Hallaj, a Christian officer, stormed Sharafeddine's house with his soldiers, pointed his pistol at the cleric's head, and asked for a letter authorising Prince Faisal to speak on behalf of Jabal ʿAmil at the League of Nations. Sharafeddine fought back and managed to expel the soldiers from his house, following which, "[t]housands marched from the coast and Jabal ʿAmil in wonderful historical demonstrations" (Kourani 1993, p. 134). The reasons for the revolt against the French occupation thus lay in the use of Christians against Jabal ʿAmil's Muslims and the attack on Sharafeddine (Kourani 1993, p. 135).

4.3.12 *The Wadi al-Hujair Conference: The Mujahideen and the ʿUlama*

The Wadi al-Hujair Conference in 1920 features in Hizbullah's discourse and its historical narratives as a major event, bringing together the resistance, *almoqawama*, and the clergy. According to the organisation's narrative, the conference demonstrated both the religious leadership's dominance over the military figures of the resistance and the latter's obedience to the *ulama*; the power of the feudal landowners faded in light of this loyalty to the senior *marjeʿ* ʿAbdul Hussein Sharafeddine. This leadership resonates with both the doctrine of *Wilayat al-Faqih* and its manifestation in Hizbullah's clerical leadership. This was clear in *Assafir*'s coverage of the ninth anniversary of Hizbullah's 'holy victory' in the July 2006 war; the event was held in Wadi al-Hujair. In a poetic tone, *Assafir* wrote:

> Everyone who entered Wadi al-Hujair yesterday comprehended the meaning and connotation of the Hizbullah-chosen slogan for the ninth annual celebration of the historical victory in the July 2006 war: 'Your Victory is Permanent', because the soil's odour in Wadi al-Hujair is still intact in spite of the years and consecutive pages of heroism from the gate of Jabal ʿAmila. (*Assafir* 2015)

The article in *Assafir* establishes a continuity between the two events in the 'blessed valley', where everything predicts 'permanent victory': "the victory is for Lebanon and the Arabs since this stubborn valley hosted the ʿabayas of ʿAmila's men and its spiritual and historical leaders on the 24 April 1920" (*Assafir* 2015).

Accordingly, Kourani's narration of the event also suggests there is a continuity. On the above date, the clerics, leaders, and fighters of Jabal ʿAmil convened in Wadi al-Hujair, known as the 'fortress of resistance' (Kourani 1993, p. 136). Sharafeddine led the conference, while the feudal lord Kamil al-Assʿad was 'extremely distressed' at the rise of new leaders, the two *mujahideen* of Jabal ʿAmil: Sadeq Hamza and Adham Khanjar (Kourani 1993, p. 137). Khanjar attended the conference with 200 armed men, and Sadeq attended with 50. The meeting between the two men and Kamil Al-Assʿad was 'cold' due to rising tensions over the latter's leadership (Kourani 1993, p. 137).[24]

On the other hand, the *ulama* held the ultimate authority at the conference, Kourani claims. "Nothing surpasses the *ulama*'s authority in Jabal ʿAmil; their words are dictums", Kourani notes in absolute terms, referring to an ʿAmili tradition of "revering them, which still stands to this day" (Kourani 1993, p. 138). In the aforementioned *Assafir* article, the consensus achieved at the conference was made manifest in Sharafeddine, "with whose ink the conveners signed the declaration of resistance against the French occupier" (*Assafir* 2015). This assertion of the clerical and Islamic character of the rebellious movement is highlighted in Kourani's detailed descriptions: for example, Sadeq Hamza's oath on the Qurʾan to commit to a clause demanding security for both Muslims and Christians, making an exception for collaborators of the French occupation (Kourani 1993, p. 141). The strictly Islamic character of the conference is downplayed in Traboulsi's account, which places the *ulama* as one group among many attendees, listing them after the powerful notables: "On 24 April 1920, some 600 Shiite notables, *ulamas* and leaders of the armed partisans of the Arab revolt met at the Hujayr Valley Congress to declare Jabal ʿAmil an independent district linked to the Syrian federation" (Traboulsi 2007, pp. 77–78).

4.3.13 The 'Islamic Revolution'

Without supplying references, Kourani invents the Islamic character of the 'revolution', known in other more neutral texts as simply attacks or rebellions (Traboulsi 2007, p. 76). Kourani acknowledges the role of lay revolutionaries, who were connected or claimed connections to the Syrian leadership (Prince Faisal); however, ignoring his own findings and remarks, and based on earlier works recounting the history of Jabal ʿAmil, Kourani's portrayal of events focuses on the relentless 'Islamic resistance' and the clergy:

> The honorable clerical stance was a dazzling proof of the presence of ʿAmili Jihad in its deeply rooted Islamic roots. Sayyid ʿAbd al-Hussein Sharafeddine played a prominent role in the confrontation, alongside a number of *ulama*, *Muʿmineen* (the faithful), and youth. They confronted the colonial tide, represented by France and its aides … against the Hussayni tide deeply rooted in history. This fighting *Muʿmina* vanguard responded in Jabal ʿAmil, took up arms … to defend the basins of this proud Mountain, to protect religion, preserve dignities, honour [*alʾaʿrad*] and sanctities. They were inspired by the honorable history of the grandfathers in Albahra, Kfarruman, the Alghazieh plain, Yarun, Tyr, Ansar, Ainata and other arenas of honour and glory. They took their [grandfathers'] steps because they never ensconced a day in front of an invader (*fateh*), nor surrendered to a usurper or aggressor, their lives were cheap if compared to their honour and freedom, careless about calamities when they occurred, or [in] battle if their enemy surpassed them in numbers and armour/equipment. From each village, the best, strongest, bravest and most faithful youth departed, they were stationed in valleys, road junctions, exhausting their enemies with their strikes, rejecting his tyranny, authoritarianism and the so-called colonialism. (Kourani 1993, pp. 147–148)

Perhaps the most extraordinary claim of his book is that of the existence of the 'Islamic resistance'. Kourani identifies three major Islamic resistance groups, whose leaders were Adham Khanjar, Sadeq Hamza, and Mahmoud Bazzi. This claim is widely contested, especially among the region's Christians. For instance, Shukrallah Shoufani writes in his history of the Christian town of Rumaish that some of the 'bandits' were engaged in resisting the French occupation, while others such as Mahmoud Bazzi never clashed with the French, but were solely engaged in criminal activity (Shoufani 1996, pp. 101–102). The Shiʿi elites were unsettled by the 'random violence', especially the attacks on Christian towns, which culminated in the massacre of ʿAyn Ibil (Abi Saab 2014, pp. 15–16). However, the bandits' attacks on the French did garner admiration of some Shiʿa, such as Hasan Mohsen al-Amine, who wrote of Khanjar's heroism in his short story, 'The Lute of Fire' (Abi Saab 2014, p. 15).[25]

Sadeq Hamza al-Faʿur represents a leading figure in Hizbullah's narrative of Islamic resistance, from Kourani's book to the Al-Manar television production of *Qiyamat al-Banadeq*. In spite of al-Faʿur's declared allegiance to Prince Faysal, Kourani creates an Islamist character, more suitable perhaps to modern Hizbullah ideals: apparently, Al-Faʿur, a local Shaykh's son from the village of Debʿal in Tyr Province, taught children how to memorise the Qurʾan and was also swift, fit, and skilled in the use of weapons (Kourani 1993, p. 148). Sadeq decided to continue fighting against the French army in spite of other local leaders' efforts to reconcile with the Christian community and French authorities (Kourani 1993, pp. 195–196). The 'Islamic ʿAmili resistance', as Kourani calls it, took over the strategic Khardeli Bridge, although no French casualties were recorded. Shiʿi clerics called on Sadeq's men and their allies to stop their attacks, as the Shiʿa "have worn the robe of shame in the eyes of civilized world" (Kourani 1993, p. 197). Sadeq in this narrative complies with the *ulama*, but declares he cannot guarantee that the other men involved in the battle against the French will do so, considering the scale of French injustice and their discrimination in favour of the Christians in Jabal ʿAmil.[26]

Adham Khanjar al Sa'bi is another legendary figure in Hizbullah's reconstructed history. Born in 1895 in Marwanieh, in today's Nabatieh district, he lost his father at a young age—Kourani instils an Islamic element into Khanjar's story, portraying him as an Islamic fighter. According to this account, Khanjar studied the Qurʾan, then moved to Sidon (Saida) to continue his education (Kourani 1993, p. 199), and, subsequently, after continuously complaining to his friends about the French occupation, he killed a French soldier in a feud. Pursued by the French,

Khanjar took refuge at the home of his relative Mahmoud Bey Al Saʿbi, who in turn took him to Sadeq Hamza (Kourani 1993, p. 200). Khanjar's most significant battle was in Kherbet Ain, where he and his men killed 30 French soldiers, loosening the Mandate's control in parts of Jabal ʿAmil (Kourani 1993, p. 201). He attacked Christian towns loyal to the French and punished Youssef Bey al-Zein for refusing to pay Sadeq Hamza by burning his crops (Kourani 1993, p. 202). In these narratives, Khanjar is portrayed as a heroic figure, with stories of his attacks against the French and his exploits saving civilians from armed robbers (Kourani 1993, p. 203).

In an attempt to link this early twentieth-century movement to today's 'Islamic resistance', Kourani mentions Shaykh Abdallah Harb, grandfather of Ragheb Harb, one of Hizbullah's symbolic leaders, as "one of Adham's men" (Kourani 1993, p. 203). Such a connection is common in Hizbullah's contemporary discourse: for example, in an event commemorating the martyrdom of three Hizbullah leaders, Sayyid Abbas Al-Musawi, Shaykh Ragheb Harb, and Imad Mughniyeh, a Hizbullah member of parliament drew an analogy between the contemporary debate on resistance and the negative press coverage of Khanjar's resistance. Nawaf al-Musawi said in front of a memorial stone for the three men:

> We have the right to be proud of sacrificing these martyrs defending the nation, without expecting a return from anyone. We work to preserve their history, to avoid repeating the experience of Sadeq Hamza and Adham Khanjar, transformed by the colonial-era Lebanese press into bandits, criminals and gangs. (NNA 2015)

Learning a historical lesson requires the sanctity of resistance, thus affirming its stature in society and state. For this reason, al-Musawi asserts: "We will not allow in this age, when the banner is in our hands, that our leaders encounter what the resistors Adham Khanjar and Sadeq Hamza encountered". Al-Musawi's connection is not made in general terms, but is related to justifying a specific event, that of the dialogue with the Saudi-backed Lebanese Future movement, which Hizbullah had resorted to in order to spare the resistance leaders the fate of their predecessors through guaranteeing their position in the state.

While such an analogy seems far-fetched, it is a recurrent theme in the organisation's discourse. "Did not the French authorities execute Khanjar after charging him with burglary, when he was arrested while preparing for the assassination of General [Henri] Gouraud?" al-Musawi asked at the memorial, comparing French colonial charges to the Future movement's accusations against Hizbullah (NNA 2015).[27] Khanjar accepted an invitation to visit the home of Sultan Pacha al-Atrash, the Syrian Druze leader, in Al-Karya, a town in al-Suweida Druze province, where French soldiers seized him after an informant's tip-off, possibly due to the offer of a large bounty (Kourani 1993, p. 206). The Sultan, a much-respected Syrian figure, was on a hunting trip, and upon his return, he learned of his guest's fate. According to Kourani, as an expression of his anger "[h]e [al-Atrash] set his own house on fire", while Khanjar's arrest and subsequent execution "played a significant role in igniting the Syrian revolution" (Kourani 1993, pp. 206–207). The French authorities executed the 28-year-old Khanjar in Raouche in West Beirut on 29 May 1923; the 'Islamic martyr' refused to be blindfolded during the execution (Kourani 1993, pp. 207–208). The dominant theme in this historical narrative is that the French colonial raid on al-Atrash's house amounted to an insult to a man of his stature, thus triggering the Syrian revolt.[28]

As in Khanjar's story, the defeat of Jabal Khanjar 'Amil carried implications beyond its borders to the entire Islamic and Arab *ummah* (nation). The French colonial authorities sealed their repression of Jabal 'Amil by extracting a heavy fine from the Shi'a of the region: originally 100,000 lira, the fine increased fivefold to half a million golden lira. Subsequently, the Shi'a lost their cattle and money, while men and even children "were hunted down in the streets" (Kourani 1993, p. 216). Their revolution may have been in support of the Arab cause, but none of the Arabs supplied them with weapons when they were needed (Kourani 1993, p. 216). Due to the dire economic situation and the French punishments, Jabal 'Amil sunk further into poverty, leading its youth and most talented members to migrate in search of a better life (Kourani 1993, pp. 215–216). Kourani takes the defeat's implications beyond the country's borders:

> The defeat of revolutionaries in Jabal 'Amil was the experience that encouraged the colonialists, so Maysaloun [a French-Arab battle to conquer Syria] occurred. It [the Jabal 'Amil defeat] paved the way for the Jewish immigration to Palestine, with English encouragement, and so the colonialists extended their claws to rip apart al Umma [the nation], and swallow its pieces. (Kourani 1993, p. 216)

In this view, the 'Amili defeat, culminating in Khanjar's execution, paved the way for the growth of the Zionist project in Palestine.[29]

4.3.14 The Zionist Project in Lebanon

In Hizbullah's discourse, the leaders of the resistance against the French occupation, Khanjar and Sadeq, were pioneers in resisting Israeli occupation. The aforementioned Christian alliance with the French occupation against the Shiʿi ʿAmili resistance continued in its attitude towards resistance in every phase of Lebanese history until today. Hizbullah's Secretary General Nasrallah maintains that the resistance, embodied in the organisation's military arm, has never enjoyed a consensus in Lebanon:

> There was never a national consensus over the resistance in Lebanon, in any day, and anything said to the contrary to this is incorrect. Even at the peak of the 2000 victory, while the resistance was dedicating it to all the Lebanese, there was no consensus ... [S]ome people do not know that there is a resistance in Lebanon since 1948, because they do not know what resistance means. (Al-Manar 2014)

The lack of consensus that Nasrallah speaks of refers to the opposition to the organisation's involvement in Syria's conflict.[30] The early Jabal ʿAmil resistance against Israel mentioned by Nasrallah remains largely undocumented and difficult to corroborate due to both over-dependence on local sources and the politicisation of the issue. For Nasrallah, the resistance in Jabal ʿAmil started "in the first moment of occupation ... One form of Jabal ʿAmil population's resistance was to stay in this land, guard their fields, and die under their roofs" (Al-Manar 2014). The resistance, he continues, comprises "every house in these villages and border towns, and every mosque, olive tree and tobacco crop" (Al-Manar 2014).

As with Hizbullah's general discourse, Nasrallah's speech is in line with Kourani's historical narrative. For Kourani, the French Mandate's policy intersected with the Zionist project in Lebanon, as both sought to establish a Christian-dominated state (Kourani 1993, pp. 235–239). However, the Zionist project included the occupation of Jabal ʿAmil up to the Litani River (Kourani 1993, p. 239). Here, Kourani counters the national historical narrative, portraying the celebrated "heroes of Lebanese independence" as collaborators with the Zionists: the Maronite leaders in Lebanon, Bechara Khouri and Emile Edde, both of whom played leading political roles during the French Mandate and the era of independence, communicated with Zionist leaders, according to Kourani; these communications defined the relations between Maronites and Jabal ʿAmil (Kourani 1993, pp. 241–250).[31] Eliyahu Sasson, leader of the Jewish Agency, held meetings with Bechara Khouri, Lebanon's first post-independence president, in 1941. During one of these meetings, Khouri proposed the ethnic cleansing of Jabal ʿAmil of its Shiʿi residents, "because they constitute a threat to both our countries, and they have collaborated with the gangs of the Mufti during the unrest in Palestine" (Kourani 1993, p. 249). Khouri proposed resettling Maronite immigrants currently in America following the war, and he asked Eliyahu to provide the patriarch with enough money to buy land in Jabal ʿAmil. Maronites would then be the neighbours of the future State of Israel, thus facilitating 'cooperation' without any further disturbances (Kourani 1993, p. 249). However, the Zionist project in the Levant faced local resistance, with Jabal ʿAmil in the lead, according to Kourani's account. Jewish settlers accused Khanjar of killing two men and a woman in a northern Palestinian settlement during clashes between his group and the French military (Kourani 1993, p. 204). A total of "50 armed Jewish men" attacked Khanjar's house, but he managed to escape through the window and surprise the group's leader from behind. He pointed his pistol at the back of the leader's head and forced him to retreat (Kourani 1993, p. 204).

4.3.15 *The 'Real Face' of Lebanese Independence*

In his narrative, Kourani contests the "official Lebanese history of independence taught at school" (Kourani 1993, pp. 278–279). The official story of independence from the French Mandate—following a demonstration and the imprisonment of nationalist figures belonging to all religious sects—Kourani believes is 'selective', as the main concern of the French was securing Maronite domination over Lebanon through control of state institutions: a 32-member majority in a 54-seat parliament (Kourani 1993, p. 273). The military, by contrast, was established along sectarian lines, granting Christian Maronites the post of chief of staff and other highly sensitive positions: "Maronites considered the army a guarantee ... of power" (Kourani 1993, p. 279). The post-colonial National Pact between Muslim and Christian leaders, the basis of the Lebanese government since independence, "is in fact a suicide pact, in which Muslims [agreed] that Maronites are the undisputed rulers. In return, they received trivial gains" (Kourani 1993, p. 278). For instance, out of five Lebanese provincial officials, none were Shiʿi, an under-representation noted by the *Al ʿIrfan Shiʿi* newspaper (Kourani 1993, p. 283).

While neither Nasrallah nor Kourani specify exactly what they mean when referring to anti-Zionist armed resistance in Jabal ʿAmil, the latter repeats statements or calls (*daʿwat*) made by Shiʿi clerics (Kourani 1993, pp. 319–322). These calls are presented as major historical events, although both their effect and their constituency remain unknown. For instance, when a delegation from the US embassy visited a Shiʿi cleric in 1953 to invite him onboard the *Roosevelt*, an American aircraft carrier, the cleric, Mohamad Jawad Moghnieh, rejected both the 'luxurious' car that was offered and the visit to the warship "because our sons and brothers in Palestine are being killed by the criminal weapons that America pours into Israel" (Kourani 1993, pp. 319–320). Moghnieh apparently informed the American visitors that "America is the Arab nation's and Islam's bitterest enemy; it established Israel, [and] killed and displaced our people in Palestine" (Kourani 1993, p. 320).[32]

4.3.16 The 1958 Popular Revolution: Islamic or Feudal?

In 1957, the pro-Western Lebanese President Camille Chamʿoun allied his government with the Eisenhower administration, gaining a US commitment to his regime's survival in the face of "any communist threat". In this narrative, Kourani (1993, p. 324) asserts the break with the current Lebanese system or status quo through emphasising the US and Israeli connection. Following the establishment of the United Arab Republic, comprising Syria and Egypt, Muslim–Christian clashes erupted in 1958. The 'revolution' in which "a number of Jabal ʿAmil's youth from border towns participated and were martyred" occurred when the US forces landed on Beirut's shores to support its ally (Kourani 1993, p. 325).[33] Kourani, however, does not mention that Shiʿi regions witnessed less fighting in comparison with the Arab Sunni regions, or that Chamʿoun, in spite of his Christian bias, enjoyed some popularity among the Shiʿi population. On the contrary, Kourani claims that "[t]he revolution started first in Jabal ʿAmil, Tyr, accompanied by a popular explosion in Lebanon's Islamic regions" (Kourani 1993, p. 325). Kourani fails to mention the role of Ahmad al-Assʿad, Jabal ʿAmil's feudal and political leader, who hails from the al-Saghir family, historical landowners in the region. Al-Assʿad's supporters played a major role in the uprising against Chamoun; his apparent loss in the elections against a traditional foe factored in his pan-Arab stance (Nir 2004, pp. 117–118).

According to Kourani, the US ambassador's interference played an integral role in containing and diminishing the revolution's goals. The US army remained in Beirut for three months and only left "after a deal with sectarian emirs who connived against the revolutionaries, martyrs and the whole nation" (Kourani 1993, p. 330). In his condemnation of the deal, which ended the 1958 'mini' civil war, Kourani blames the local sectarian leaders for wasting the opportunity and reinstating the status quo "as if the war did not harvest anyone. families were not deprived of their youths, the country's economy was not destroyed" (Kourani 1993, p. 331). Denying the feudal leaders' role in the uprising magnifies their condemnation as conspiratorial.[34]

When looking at the 1967 defeat of the Syrian, Egyptian, and Jordanian armies against Israel, Kourani notes "Jabal ʿAmil managed, alone and due to the faith of its sacrificial youths, to defeat Israel and destroy the myth of the undefeatable army" (Kourani 1993, p. 334). The myth of Jabal ʿAmil is thus magnified in comparison with the defeated Arab world: "ʿAmilis have proved that they possess enough psychological, social, cultural, civilized, historical and traditional immunity to foil the Zionist enemy's plots, however diversified and branched his tools and methods are" (Kourani 1993, p. 343). Following Black September (the civil war) in Jordan, Jabal ʿAmil's towns received Palestinian resistance fighters with roses and flowers, according to Kourani: "Jabal ʿAmil embraced them with love and compassion" (Kourani 1993, p. 346). While the Palestinian movement was overwhelmingly secular, Kourani notes that thousands joined the *jihad* as an Islamic *farida* (obligation) (Kourani 1993, p. 346). Kourani therefore glorifies Jabal ʿAmil's Islamic resistance and sacrifices, while condemning both the Lebanese government's stance and the Palestinian non-Islamic and divisive politics (Kourani 1993, pp. 347–348). The Palestinians also failed, according to the same narrative, "to preserve their good relations with Lebanese Muslims. and they failed to commit to the security and stability of the land that received them" (Kourani 1993, p. 348).

4.3.17 *Musa Sadr's Call for Resistance*

In line with their earlier insightful politics during the Ottoman, French, and post-independence eras, the *ulama* played a similar role in saving the resistance from the failures of the Palestinian Liberation Organisation (PLO). Following the transfer of PLO fighters from Jordan to Lebanon, Musa Sadr, an Iranian-born cleric and head of the Lebanese Islamic Shiʿi

Higher Council, called on the Palestinian leadership to train Shi'i Muslims (Kourani 1993, p. 347).[35] Following Sadr, Iranian Ayatollah Ruhollah Khomeini issued a statement in 1977 denouncing the commission of atrocities against the Shi'a, among them the massacre in Nabaa (6 July 1976), a poor Shi'i neighbourhood surrounded by Christian areas (Kourani 1993, pp. 357–358). Khomeini's statement, prior to Iran's Islamic Revolution, focussed on caring for the war's orphans and siding with Lebanon's Shi'a against the Christian militias, whom he refers to as 'barbarian medieval gangs' (Kourani 1993, p. 357). Khomeini urged Iranian Muslims to help their brethren in Lebanon (Kourani 1993, p. 358).

4.3.18 *The 1978 Israeli Invasion*

Assisted by local Christian militias and Lebanese army units that defected, both led by Saad Haddad, the Israeli army invaded large parts of South Lebanon in 1978 following a Palestinian operation against Haifa. Kourani emphasises the Christians' collaboration in this operation:

> From the onset of the Israeli invasion to occupy Jabal 'Amil, it was clear that Christian forces in Mount Lebanon and in the battlefields were coordinating, militarily and politically, with the Zionists, and the Israeli Radio stated clearly during the offensive: "As for the Christian fighters, they are playing their role/part, and the land is theirs and their towns and houses". (Kourani 1993, p. 360)

Following the invasion, another Khomeini 'call' is noted in Kourani's book, condemning the Israeli invasion and the Islamic countries' inaction in the face of, or even collusion with, the Zionists in their 'crimes' (Kourani 1993, p. 364). The same theme reverberated throughout Sadr's calls, also quoted in Kourani's book: "Oh Arabs, what did you do with South Lebanon? ... [T]he conspiracy commenced in 1948 with the ethnic cleansing of Palestinians from their own land and terror in South Lebanon" (Kourani 1993, pp. 367–368). Kourani also mentions Sadr's statements on the importance of South Lebanon, "one of the richest [regions] in the world ... Israel has yearned for it since its inception" (Kourani 1993, p. 366). Sadr further magnifies South Lebanon's importance: "The land of civilizations, the spring of cultures, teacher of alphabets, discoverer of lawyers and international relations ... it is the land of the human being and faith" (Kourani 1993, p. 369). As such, losing South Lebanon means "the fall of the whole of Lebanon and its breakdown ... the spread of the spark of tension in the whole Arab world, the whole world, even inside the United States itself" (Kourani 1993, p. 369).

Following Sadr's disappearance in Libya, the 1979 Islamic Revolution in Iran is romanticised as the moment the weak, the poor, and the oppressed rose against the whole world, the East (the Soviet Union) and the West (the USA). The Islamic Revolution reverberated in Lebanon, paving the way for the 'golden age' of resistance in Jabal 'Amil: "The first voice of the Islamic Revolution in Iran spread around, echoed instantly in Lebanon ... Revolutionary Islam in Lebanon became a model for revolutionary freedom movements in the entire Islamic world" (Kourani 1993, p. 381). With no elaboration on the 1979 revolution's spontaneous effect, Kourani skips more than three years to the 1982 Israeli invasion, when Tehran dispatched revolutionary guards to establish the local Islamic resistance (Kourani 1993, p. 381). The Islamic resistance became a model on its own account, offering a 'successful adaptation' of a 'wonderful experience' in Iran (Kourani 1993, p. 380). Although trained and supported by the Islamic Republic, Hizbullah became a 'titanic' force. In the words of Imam Khomeini: "The Jihad of Hizbullah in Lebanon is an allegory for the Muslims of the whole world" (Kourani 1993, p. 382).

4.4 Making History: The 'Divine' Continuity

While the reconstruction of history mainly concerns the pre–twenty-first century period, more recent publications have covered the years of Islamic resistance up until the Israeli withdrawal in 2000 and the 2006 conflict, in a similar vein to both Kourani's historical narrative and Hizbullah's official discourse. These narratives place the events in a historical perspective as the culmination of a long struggle or as a 'golden age' at the end of centuries of repression, suffering, and resistance. Despite the difficulty of constructing late twentieth- and twenty-first-century histories, Hizbullah's historical account of this phase remains controversial, even among its allies. For instance, following the broadcasting of the television series *Alghalibun (The Victorious)*, many Amal movement supporters took to Twitter, demanding that Al-Manar interrupt the popular broadcast "to extinguish the *fitna* [sedition] that it *alghalibun* [awakened]" (*Al-Akhbar* 2011). Amal maintains that its militants fought the battle of Khalde against the Israeli occupation in 1982, and not Hizbullah's, since the latter was not officially established until 1985.

4.4.1 The 1982 Israeli Invasion

The Israeli invasion of Lebanon in 1982 is the crucial point in the establishment of Hizbullah, and therefore occupies pride of place in its historical narrative. *Alghalibun*, which proved very popular, claims that the 'Islamic resistance' led the Khalde battle against the advancing Israeli army (*Al-Akhbar* 2011).[36] Amal, however, claims that its own fighters led the fight against the Israeli forces, portraying it as a major event in its history. As with the later *Alghalibun* series, Kourani also tells of a solely Islamic resistance, ignoring the role of the Lebanese National Resistance Front (which included nationalist and communist parties), despite the fact that it dominated the resistance following the Palestinian Liberation Front's withdrawal in 1982. According to Kourani, 100,000 Israeli soldiers were distributed among eight corps and entered Jabal ʿAmil, where they embarked on a campaign of destruction "with an intensity [never before] witnessed in this world" (Kourani 1993, p. 383).

In this narrative, the Iranian Supreme Leader Ayatollah Khomeini has a central part; in a letter to Muslims after the Israeli invasion of Lebanon, Khomeini noted the Arab betrayal and the significance of resistance (Kourani 1993, pp. 388–390). Israel's Christian allies played a vital role in the invasion, and the Palestinians withdrew, emptying the battlefield of "protection from Zionist rifles" (Kourani 1993, p. 386). The condemnation of the Palestinian withdrawal goes hand in hand with the glorification of the Islamic resistance, namely, at Beirut's southern gate of Khalde, where 'faithful Islamist fighters', who had learned from the Iranian Islamic Revolution "to rely on the people in revolution until victory", led the battle against the Israeli advance (Kourani 1993, pp. 386–387). Hizbullah's resistance surprised the Israeli army who thought "its dream [had] become reality following its swallowing of more than half Lebanon ... thinking that Jabal ʿAmil [had] become a part of the Jewish State" (Kourani 1993, pp. 396–397). These 'dreams' evaporated due to the "Islamic revolutionaries' consecutive successful *jihadist* operations against Zionist forces and patrols, instilling fear in their hearts" (Kourani 1993, p. 397). Ahmad Qassir's 'magnificent' suicide bombing against Israeli forces on 11 November 1982 marked a new era, as it led to the destruction of the Israeli forces' Tyr headquarters, killing 75 and injuring 150 (Kourani 1993, p. 398).

This new era, according to Kourani, suffered no setbacks like the Palestinian withdrawal in 1982, but was consistent in its resistance against the Israeli occupation, leading to "revenge against the superpowers who thought they were residing in their own home" (Kourani 1993, p. 398). This revenge manifested itself in the bombing of the multinational forces' headquarters in a suicide operation that killed 239 US marines in 1983, paving the way for their rapid departure from Beirut (Kourani 1993, p. 398). This bombing, alongside the Ahmad Qassir and Abu Zainab operations, constitutes one of Hizbullah's founding legends. The previous phase of weak and fragile resistance, under Palestinian revolutionary leadership, temporarily granted the Israelis "no way other than escape, they scurried to withdraw to the so-called security belt, and most of Jabal ʿAmil was liberated" (Kourani 1993, p. 402). Kourani's prophetic ending to his book connects the ancient with the modern: "And so the Islamic resistance continues to make one victory after another, determined to liberate the land … until Allah allows the awaited Mahdi … to appear, raising the sword of right" (Kourani 1993, p. 402).

4.4.2 2000: The Year of Victory

Since the Israeli invasion in 1982, the Israeli military has suffered fatal blows from various resistance movements, including Amal and Hizbullah; consequently, by 1983, the Israeli army had withdrawn from Beirut, and then further southwards to the 'security belt'. On 24 May 2000, the Israeli occupation army withdrew completely from South Lebanon, while Hizbullah declared victory after nearly two decades of resistance. Prior to the Israeli War in 2006, the organisation's discourse on the withdrawal was based on the 'divine' element. According to Nasrallah, "Allah granted you victory" on that day and will grant more (*Assafir* 2001). The 25 May became a national holiday in Lebanon, a day celebrated annually with speeches by Hizbullah's secretary general: on 25 May 2012, for example, Nasrallah stressed the continuity in the organisation's stance on resistance with the days of Sharafeddine, who repeatedly demanded that the government resist Israeli aggression after 1948 (Al-Manar 2012). Israel's expansionist plan of building a state from the Nile to the Euphrates, Nasrallah asserted, died on 25 May 2000 (Al-Manar 2012). On the same date the following year, Hizbullah's leader called it "one of Allah's days, during which his mercy, blessings, victory, generosity and support manifested themselves to our patient and resisting people" (Al-Manar 2013).

4.4.3 *The July 2006 'Divine Victory'*

In Hizbullah's reconstructed history, the July 2006 conflict with the Israeli army, known in Lebanon as *Harb Tammuz*, resulted in a great 'divine victory' (*nasr ilahi kabir*). The organisation commemorates the event annually on 15 August, a day after the 34-day conflict ended. There are two trends in presenting the war: the first pertains to documenting in detail every single event, portraying each as a miraculous victory. Such an approach is quite similar to that of the Egyptian and Syrian efforts to immortalise the 1973 war with Israel. The second focuses on the manifestations and results of the July 'divine victory', portraying it as a 'game changer' with global implications as well as a victory against the USA, unprecedented since the Cold War (*Al-Akhbar* 2014).

4.5 Conclusion

Since the 1980s, Hizbullah's intellectuals have been engaged in the reconstruction of Lebanese Shi'i history. Their historical narrative bears similarities to nationalism's reconstructed histories: claims of origins, threat and resistance, decline and disappearance, national character, and 'golden ages'. These themes appear in political discourse, television dramas, written and oral histories, and various party publications. The organisation's television station, Al-Manar, produced two drama series on the history of Jabal ʿAmil and Islamic resistance. However, there is a strong reliance on print and the organisation's educational network in disseminating this history.

Through examining the various sources of Hizbullah's historical discourse, this chapter has highlighted two trends: first, Hizbullah's historical reconstruction is holistic, and encompasses the intellectual, media, educational, and political spheres; second, the recurrent historical themes consistently emphasise 'Islamic resistance', as well as the crucial importance of the group's clerical leadership. In certain instances, especially when narrating the stories of resistance figures, Hizbullah's historical accounts are hardly referenced, and are at times even inventive. Although Jaber noted his lack of sources, presenting dispersed stories as a coherent history of the "Amili people', Kourani still quotes him unreservedly, while justifying an uncorroborated narrative of Islamic resistance and the situation in Jabal ʿAmil based on oral histories. As such, Kourani's narrative is built on two sources, both of which are invented in their presentation: Jaber's history and oral accounts.

In reconstructing Shiʿi history, Hizbullah operated as a functional equivalent of modern nationalism, seeking a new unified identity for the Lebanese Shiʿa. In this holistic effort, the organisation contested the predominant historical narratives in Lebanon, most specifically that of the Maronites. To what extent does Hizbullah's historiography serve its desire for state power? While it is empirically impossible to verify or quantify this effort, the organisation's politics reveal a drive to maintain its quasi-state apparatuses, which it often uses as a leverage to acquire more state power. Within the context of the sect-based politics of Lebanon, Hizbullah's historical narratives emphasise the so-called ancient Shiʿi geographic claims to the whole state's modern borders. The organisation's historiography presents the Lebanese Shiʿa as a leading resistance movement and political force throughout its history, subtly pushing forward claims to the state based on their high levels of sacrifice.

Notes

1. In one of his recorded speeches from the 1980s, Hassan Nasrallah, Hizbullah's current secretary general, warned Christian militias against separatism, noting that the Shiʿa are the original inhabitants of Mount Lebanon.
2. The main ideological nuance between Hizbullah's and other Islamic groups, whether in Iraq (Islamic al-Daʾwa) or Egypt's Muslim Brotherhood, is territorial. Hizbullah emphasises the territorial ideological continuity, extending legitimacy over the Lebanese Shiʿi community's history. Considering the state's weakness, geopolitics, and sectarian history, Hizbullah remains a unique case among other Shiʿi groups, many of which were either underground (until 2003 in Iraq, 2001 in Afghanistan) or remain so in the Gulf. While the Amal movement's historical narratives converge at times with Hizbullah's, the latter's approach retains a distinct Islamic character, pertaining to the doctrine of *Welayat al-Faqih*.
3. Kourani hails from a Hizbullah-affiliated family, with many relatives assuming leading roles. Shaykh Ali Kourani is a founding member. For instance, on 5 May 2015, Al-Manar television broadcast an interview with Kourani, along with a florid musical introduction, usually reserved for major officials/guests. While Kourani is publicly presented as an independent figure, a Hizbullah official told me there is an unofficial affiliation.
4. ʿIzzeddine showers praise on the author of this 'blessed' book, noting his 'objectivity' and patriotism (Shaʿlan 2007, p. 6).
5. The Lebanese Maronite politicians focused on the Phoenician origins of Lebanon as a measure against Arab nationalists. The latter group sought to

unite Lebanon, either with Syria or Egypt or the whole region, thus destroying the proportionally strong Christian presence.
6. During fieldwork for this book, the bookstores and publishing houses I visited were more prone to offer discounts on Hizbullah-affiliated books than were the usual bookshops in West Beirut.
7. The Islamic leadership is governed by a learned clergy, which is viewed as a representative of the hidden twelfth infallible imam (the Shiʿi messiah or saviour).
8. In Chap. 2, in the discussion of Al Muhajer's discursive research, the Abu Dharr story is treated as a myth.
9. Kourani, author of this book and a Hizbullah figure, descends from a traditional clerical family.
10. The repeated reference to Jabal ʿAmil as 'holy' in Hizbullah discourse is mostly rooted in this interpretation of the Qurʾanic verse.
11. Whenever Kourani and other historians fail to provide sources, they refer to 'oral' histories, which are undocumented discussions with witnesses or their descendants.
12. *Al-Feranj* is either translated as Franks, Westerners, or Europeans in general.
13. The battle of Hattin marked a decisive Muslim victory against the Crusades, and it carries significance into the modern age, especially pertaining to the struggle against Israeli occupation. The battle freed Jerusalem from the Crusaders.
14. In a story about archaeological excavations in the region, a Fatimid era tower is claimed to have been found under a Crusader-era castle in Jabal ʿAmil, known as Beaufort Castle or *Qalaʾat Al-Shaqif* in Arabic (Al-Manar 2014). According to this Hizbullah narrative, Shaykh Nassif Nassar, a local feudal leader, renovated the castle in order to confront al-Jazzar, the Ottoman ruler (Al-Manar 2012).
15. Kourani's narrative of massacres of the Shiʿa in Mount Lebanon and the north of the country has its roots in history and was featured in a 1980 speech by Nasrallah during the height of Lebanon's civil war. The massacres of Shiʿa in Kesrouen, Mount Lebanon, following a *fatwa* (edict) by Sunni scholar Ibn Taymiya, occurred during the Mamluk period in the fourteenth century. The stories of 'horrible' massacres are narrated in detail in Kourani's book (1993, p. 57). For instance, during the massacres, hundreds of Shiʿa took refuge in a cave, resisting the army's attempts to take over the area, but the Mamluks built a concrete wall, starving their enemies to death (Kourani 1993, p. 57). Narrations of the massacres and heroic resistance of the victims against the Mamluk army are consistent both with the ancient Islamic and later histories of the Shiʿa. The massacres and the oppressed existence of the Shiʿa in different parts of modern

Lebanon meant there was no mention of them throughout the fourteenth century (Kourani 1993, p 58).
16. Hizbullah's initial programme included a plan to establish an Islamic government in Lebanon. While it remained part of the organisation's ideology, Hizbullah removed the clause from its programme.
17. This assessment is made in comparison with Jaber's claims in this regard.
18. The Arabic word *mashboha* (suspicious) is recurrent in Hizbullah's discourse, and it relates to their general approach of accusing their foes of conspiratorial links to external forces.
19. The phrase 'the canines began to appear', a direct translation of the Arabic, is a metaphor suggesting an animal-like appetite. Here it is deployed to demonstrate the colonial desire to control and divide the region.
20. The colonial conquest of the region is connected to today's Israeli occupation in Palestine and Lebanon, and, as such, the focus on the Islamic nature of resistance carries underlying assumptions for the present time.
21. The famine of the First World War is a major event in Lebanon's official history, which greatly influenced the country's early literature.
22. The Islamic revolution term resonates with the 1979 Iranian Revolution, which bought Khomeini to power.
23. Traboulsi (2007, p. 77) employs the term 'armed bandits' as a cautionary measure because banditry existed in different areas of the Ottoman Empire, and tales of resistance often converged with other forms of armed banditry.
24. Many criticisms of the narratives outlined earlier had emerged on different occasions; Kourani devotes a section to debunk each of them. Among these criticisms were the numerous allegations of ʿAbd al-Hussein Sharafeddine's relations with the French, namely, his Beirut meeting with General Henri Gouraud, commander of the French forces in the Levant. Sharafeddine's relations with the French came into question after he hosted a 'generous dinner' for French officers. Kourani dismisses allegations of sectarianism and nepotism against the "heroes of Jabal ʿAmil's Islamic resistance". For instance, a family member had written that Mahmoud Bazzi's attack on the Christian town of Ain Ibil was organised not for political reasons related to French collaboration, but as a retaliation against his uncle Mohamad Saʿid Bazzi. The latter rejected his nephew's engagement to his daughter, leading to a family feud; Mahmoud sought to embarrass his uncle through an attack on a Christian town (Kourani 1993, p. 226). In his refutation of these allegations, Kourani unconvincingly blames the traditional feudal leaders, hinting at their collaboration with the French Mandate in order to preserve their status (Kourani 1993, p. 228).

25. Al-Amine, a historian himself, was later dismayed by the sectarian acts of violence against Christians in South Lebanon.
26. Kourani tells a heroic tale during dinner at his friend's house of how Sadeq downed a French plane. No doubt is cast over the story, even though it is entirely based on oral history.
27. The Sunni Future Movement accuses Hizbullah of involvement in assassinations and of using its arsenal to impose its politics in spite of the elections' results, which gave the 14 March Coalition a clear majority.
28. Khanjar's execution in its own right did not trigger the Syrian revolution, but the raid on al-Atrash's house did.
29. While colonial repression factored in weakening the local capacity to resist the Zionist Project, it is difficult to assess the impact of French policies in Jabal ʿAmil on the subsequent resistance and the general morale of the Arab world. Kourani's underlying assumption is that Jabal ʿAmil's resistance was at the centre of events in the region.
30. Hizbullah's involvement in the Syrian conflict started with political support for the Assad regime in 2011 and developed in later years into a controversial military intervention.
31. The official Maronite-dominated history celebrated these figures as the "brave" founders of modern Lebanon.
32. During the Suez War in 1956, Sharafeddine issued a call through the Egyptian Asharq Al-Awsat Radio to all clerics in the world, without specifying a certain religion. Sharafeddine urged "clerics everywhere to say their word ... and declare war on colonialism that made the Universal Declaration of Human Rights a law of pirates" (Kourani 1993, p. 322).
33. Al-Assʿad was an ally of the Sharafeddine family from which the cleric ʿAbd al-Hussein hails.
34. Kourani also condemns Fouad Chehab, the much-celebrated reformist Lebanese president, as 'sectarian' (Kourani 1993, p. 331). The reason cited is an uncorroborated Algerian request to arm border villages in Lebanon; Chehab rejected the offer, citing one reason: "They are Muslims" (Kourani 1993, p. 332).
35. Sadr's slogan, "Jerusalem only wants to be liberated by the faithful" is usually interpreted as the inevitability of the Shiʿi role in the liberation process.
36. Hizbullah's Al-Manar television station produced the series *Alghalibun* (*The Victorious*), which narrates the story of the Israeli invasion and the subsequent resistance against the occupation.

REFERENCES

BOOKS

Abisaab, R., & Abisaab, M. (2014). *The Shiʿites of Lebanon: Modernism, Communism, and Hizbullah's Islamists*. Syracuse: Syracuse University Press.

Al-Hajj Hassan, A. (2008). *Tareekh Lubnan Al Muqawama: Fee Miʾat ʿAm* (The History of Resistor Lebanon: A Hundred Years). Dar Al-Wala: Beirut.

Breuilly, J. (2007). Nationalism and Historians: Some Reflections. The Formations on Nationalist Historiographical Discourse. In C. Norton (Ed.), *Nationalism, Historiography and the (Re)Construction of the Past* (pp. 1–28). Washington, DC: New Academia Publishing.

Jamil, R. (1948). *Beirut and the Republic of Lebanon*. Beirut: Librairie Universelle.

Kourani, M. (1993). *Al Jozoor Al Tarikheya Lel Moqawama Al Islamiya* (The Historical Roots of the Islamic Resistance). Beirut: Dar Al Waseela.

Noun Centre for Writing and Translating (2014). *Manar Al-Huda*. Beirut: Jamʿiat Al-Maʿaref Al-Islamiya Al-Thakafia.

Rosiny, S. (2000). *Shiʾa Publishing in Lebanon: With Special Reference to Islamic and Islamist Publications*. Berlin: Verlag Das Arabische Buch.

Shaʿlan, R. (2007). *Al-Waʿd al-Sadeq: Iʿsar Wa Intisar* (Al-Waʿd al-Sadeq—July War: A Hurricane and a Victory). Lebanon: Dar al-Janub.

Shoufani, S. (1996). *Tareekh Rumeish* (The History of Rumeish). Beirut: Deir Sayyidat Al-Bishara.

Smith, A. (2009). *Ethno-symbolism and Nationalism: A Cultural Approach*. London: Routledge.

Smith, A. D. (1993). The Nation: Invented, Imagined, Reconstructed? In M. Ringrose & A. J. Lerner (Eds.), *Reimagining the Nation* (pp. 159–175). Philadelphia: Open University Press.

Traboulsi, F. (2007). *A History of Modern Lebanon*. London: Pluto Press.

JOURNAL ARTICLES

Hobsbawm, E.J. (1992, February). Ethnicity and nationalism in Europe Today. *Anthropology Today 8*(1), 3–8.

Nir, O. (2004, November). The Shiʾites During the 1958 Lebanese Crisis. *Middle Eastern Studies, 40*(6), 109–129.

NEWS ARTICLES

Al-Hakim, B. (2011, August 9). Hamla ʿala alghalibun: Kafa Tazwiran lil Tarikh (A Campaign Against Alghalibun: Enough with this Forgery of History). *Al-Akhbar*, p. 14.

Assafir. (2001, December 15). *Ihtifalat Wa Massirat Wa Oroodat Fi al-Dahiya Wa Bʿalbak Wa Sour*. *Assafir*, p. 2.

Mohsen, A. (2014, August 15). *'Harb Tamuz ... Noqtat Tahawol'* (July War ... Transformation Point). *Al-Akhbar*, p. 8.

Obeid, H. (2015, August 15). *'Nasrallah: Noreed al-Dawla al-ʿadila ... al-Mabniya ʿala al-Sharaka al-Haqiqiya'* (Nasralla: We Want the Just State Based on True Partnership). *Assafir*, p. 3.

Links

Al-Musawi, N. (2015, February 15). *Limowasalat al-Hiwar Wal Wosol Ila Tafahomat L'injaz al-Istihqaqat Wabelʾakhas al-Reʾasa* (To Continue Dialogue and Reach Understandings to Accomplish the Requirements, Especially the Presidential Elections). Retrieved June 23, 2015, from http://goo.gl/kDh0WY

Jabal ʿAmil yahtafel bel faizin wal mubdein fee mosabaqat Midad al Jabal al Sheriya (Jabal ʿAmil Celebrates the Winners and Innovators in the Midad al Jabal al Sheriya Contest), June 30, 2014. Retrieved October 30, 2014, from http://www.Al-Manar.com.lb/wapadetails.php?eid=885377

Kourani, M. (2010, May 19). *'Intilaq al-Moqawama al-Islamiya ʿabr al-Tareekh Mina al-Mabdaʾ al-ʿaqaʾidi Wal Tashreeʿ Daleel Aʿla Nasaʿatiha Wa Istimrariyatiha'* (The Launch of the Islamic Resistance Throughout History from the Islamic Ideology and Laws Is a Proof of Its Purity and Continuity). Retrieved November 21, 2013, from http://www.moqawama.org/essaydetails.php?eid=16901%26cid=199

Omsiya Sheʿriya fee Tebnin Bereʿayat Layon (A Layon-Sponsored Poetic Evening in Tebnin), July 14, 2012. Retrieved November 23, 2013, from http://www.Al-Manar.com.lb/wapadetails.php?eid=268069

Videos

Al-Manar. (2013). *Qaherat al-Ghozat: Tareekh al-Madina al-Moqawem* [Online]. Retrieved May 8, 2014, from http://www.almanar.com.lb/programs/pdetails.php?pid=5531%26eid=77174%26wid=2660

MEDLEBANON2. (2013). *Qeyamat AL-Banadeq Episode 02* [Online]. Retrieved May 10, 2014, from https://www.youtube.com/watch?v=9Q5NE9yox0E%26index=2%26list=PLxu8Ui2VLloMVBjbiBqybUj6FAseCpAq6

Noon, M. (2004). *Manar Al-Huda: Durus Tamhidiya Fi Al-Maʿaref al-Islamiya*. Beirut: Jamʿiat al-Maʿaref al-Islamiya.

CHAPTER 5

The Supernatural in Hizbullah's Identity

This chapter looks at Hizbullah's dissemination of supernatural narratives in Lebanon's Shiʻi community, sanctifying its mission and actions. Through examining the dissemination of supernatural literature on contemporary events—miracles or divine connections pertaining to Hizbullah's resistance and *Wilayat al-Faqih*—the chapter demonstrates that the religious and spiritual aspects of the organisation's identity are novel. In a way similar to the organisation's historical narratives, discussed in the previous chapter, the contemporary supernatural narratives are constructed upon the foundations laid by the theological works of Ayatollah Mohamad Baqer Majlesi, a senior cleric in the early period of Safavid rule. The party's supernatural propaganda is based on a revival of Majlesi's theological tradition, which remains controversial and contested in mainstream Shiʻi theological schools—for instance, Ali Shariʻati, a leading ideologue of the Islamic Revolution, wrote extensively against Majlesi and the dissemination of supernatural narratives, denouncing its creation of credulous and malleable individuals.

In line with the Islamic Republic's official (Iran–Iraq) war and post-war propaganda, the Lebanon-based organisation's institutions and affiliated publishing houses diffuse a vast array of supernatural stories on Hizbullah's connection to the 'Hidden Imam' and to its fighters' victorious battles. The first part of the chapter will review theories on the political usefulness of such supernatural narratives, providing comparative examples where possible. The second part will review the tensions between Islamic reformists

© The Author(s) 2018
M. Hage Ali, *Nationalism, Transnationalism, and Political Islam*,
DOI 10.1007/978-3-319-60426-8_5

and supernatural sects and trends; it will argue that reviving supernatural narratives goes against mainstream Islamic reforms, both Sunni and Shiʻi.[1] The third part will examine different trends in Hizbullah's supernatural literature. Through historical and comparative means, the chapter will argue that the dissemination of supernatural narratives could contribute to understanding the organisation's success in mass mobilisation and the modern transformation of ancient religious beliefs.

5.1 Supernatural Narratives as a Political Tool

Taking into consideration the unavoidable limitations involved in measuring supernatural narratives' effects on the Lebanese Shiʻi community, this section reviews the studies and theories related to their political usefulness and application and demonstrates that the political deployment of supernatural narratives, whether religious or 'superstitious', is an ancient activity; however, Hizbullah's modern use of these stories is more sophisticated than organised religion and has an influence on the Shiʻi sense of identity.

The boundary between supernatural narratives and religion cannot be generally defined in terms of mainstream trends, but only in historical and case-specific contexts.[2] Religion after all is fundamentally a belief in the supernatural; however, the post-reformist clerical establishment condemns any unconventional supernatural beliefs and happenings as 'superstition' (Hodgson 1974, p. 252). The term 'superstition' had political connotations, since the early modern Protestants employed it to condemn pre-Reformation Catholicism. Francis Bacon expressed these undefined and elastic boundaries by noting that "there is a superstition in avoiding superstition" (Parish and Naphy 2002, p. 4, 20). This chapter uses the term 'supernatural' or 'supernatural narratives' rather than 'superstition', since it is more concerned with Hizbullah's accentuation and production of supernatural narratives in religion for political purposes. In Islamic scholarship, traditionally, there has been a general scepticism towards ongoing miracles or supernatural events, and its critique of Christianity commences from the latter's belief in the Godly nature of Jesus. According to the prevalent Sunni and Shiʻi narratives, the Qurʾan was the Prophet Muhammad's most significant miracle; his human nature and subservience to God are central to the Islamic faith, as his status as the Prophet is usually paired with that of the 'worshipper'.[3] Islam's often strict stance on the issue of supernatural narratives, condemned as 'superstition', helps draw a line under what is deemed acceptable in the mainstream, and can thus illustrate how varied or even overstated the superstitions under examination are (Moazzam 1984, p. 7).[4]

Another limitation in looking at the political usefulness of supernatural narratives lies in the parallels to the general utility of religion. Throughout history, rulers have sought divine legitimacy through their links to the clerical establishment. The task of separating the political use of supernatural narratives from that of their religious use could be difficult; however, the variations in the application of the supernatural narratives, and how they are emphasised, are better defined in the historical Shiʿi context. The clerical establishment's praise for certain rulers, bestowing them with religious legitimacy, is common in Islamic history. However, this chapter argues that the scale of the supernatural in Hizbullah's rhetoric has reached unprecedented levels in intensity and scale, applying older traditions in a contemporary context. For instance, the Shiʿi Safavid Empire, although it employed the clerical establishment for legitimating purposes, arguably did not produce supernatural propaganda on Hizbullah's scale. The Safavid shahs employed 'Twelver Shiʿism' for political purposes, claiming to be the representatives of the 'Hidden Imam' (Savory 2007, p. 27). Clerics, such as Majlesi, linked the Shiʿi imams to the Iranian monarchy, through emphasising Imam Husayn's marriage to the daughter of Yazdegerd III, the Sassanid king (Savory 2007, p. 27). Hizbullah, on the other hand, indirectly produced supernatural literature on its battles and actions, while accentuating its claims of links with the 'Hidden Imam'. The organisation has produced on a large scale literature linking the *Wilayat al-Faqih* leadership and hierarchy to Imam Mahdi, the hidden legitimate authority in Shiʿi doctrines. In a similar approach to the examples narrated in the second chapter, the organisation's various institutions remodel this claimed link between the divine and Hizbullah's hierarchy to suit its various audiences in the Lebanese Shiʿi community. This millennialism is not restricted to Shiʿi doctrines, as Holt points out in his work on the Mahdist movement in Sudan. In "Sunni Mahdism", al-Mahdi is the "guided one" who possesses "a particular measure of divine guidance and is the repository of esoteric secrets" (Holt 1970, p. 22). In Shiʿi Islam, Mahdi is alive and hidden, while in Sunni Islam he is not yet born. Upon his birth, the Mahdi will initiate the end of the world after restoring right governance and filling earth "with equity and justice" (Holt 1970, p. 22).

The supernatural, being more primordial, is more effective as a tool for legitimacy and mobilisation. The primordial elements in supernatural narratives elevate their bearer above any rational questioning: for instance, while Hizbullah considered the 2006 Israeli War on Lebanon a 'divine victory', its participation in the Syrian civil war was automatically considered *alwajeb al-Jihadi* (the *jihadi* duty) (Al-ʿAhd 2013). Since the conflict against Israeli aggression had been established as 'holy', Hizbullah extended this sanctity to its involvement in Syria, connecting the 'martyrs' of both wars (Al-ʿAhd 2013). This chapter attempts to define the political use of the supernatural and the nuances between this practice in Hizbullah's case, and the general deployment of religious discourse in politics. As discussed in part three, the scale of the supernatural propaganda sponsored by Hizbullah is great. While most religious beliefs are rooted in Shiʿi theology, many of the associations between the divine and politics, whether in scale or type, are modern.

The political utility of superstition, particularly through numbing or controlling the masses, was thoroughly discussed in pre-enlightenment philosophy and by nineteenth- and twentieth-century Marxists. In the former era, Baruch Spinoza, himself an outcast from his religious community, linked superstition to the individual relinquishing of reason, referring subtly to its utility to the elite. Through accepting superstition, in an act of subservience, the masses or 'common folk' surrender control over their own affairs in order to increase their life chances. Hence, superstition, Spinoza argued, is the last resort of dependent and less-knowledgeable individuals: "If men could manage all their affairs by a certain plan (*consilium cer tum*), or if fortune were always favorable (*fortuna semper prospera*) to them, they would never be in the grip of superstition" (Frankel 1999, p. 902).

"Ordinary people", Spinoza noted, "have found no stronger proof of God's providence and rule than that based on the ignorance of causes"; this misconception "has been the sole cause of superstition, and perhaps of much knavery" (Frankel 1999, p. 903). Spinoza remarked that superstitions, being "delusions of the imagination", result in ignorance and confusion, and so "turn men from rational beings into beasts since they completely prevent everyone from using his free judgment... and distinguishing between true and false". Superstition thus prevents men from governing their affairs wisely, condemning them to misery (Frankel 1999, p. 905), and arises "when hope and fear are struggling for mastery" (Rahnema 2011, p. 9). In such circumstances, whether during Lebanon's devastating 2006 war and its aftermath, or due to the sanctions and various challenges Iran has faced, superstition thrives under the auspices of the clerics. Rahnema, an Iranian scholar who worked on the subject of superstition and ideology, notes that in times of crisis, the population grants the clergy a powerful agency, often establishing an alleged association with the divine:

> Once society accepts a leader as divinely selected and supported, an unfettered sociopolitical control mechanism, the ultimate objective of such politically inspired superstitious claims, is put in place. The self-proclaimed vicegerent of God arrogates absolutist rule and demands unquestioned obedience and allegiance from his believing and complying subjects. (Rahnema 2011, p. 14)[5]

Unlike Spinoza's general concern with the human being's freedom for rational reasoning, Karl Marx focussed on the elite's conscious use of religion to conceal and divert class tensions. Religion acts as a pacifier to human suffering: as it is "the illusory happiness of the people", the abolition of religion is "the demand for their real happiness" (Marx in Raines 1998, p. 167). Marx takes issue with the powerful elite's use of religion to gain legitimacy and construct 'meaning' in the face of personal tragedy (Marx in Raines 1998, p. 168).[6] Marx and Engels made several references to the 'usefulness' of religion and superstition in politics, calling it "numbing the masses". Engels noted in a letter on American society:

> Though the Americans… have not taken over Europe medieval institutions, they did take over lots of medieval tradition, religion, English Common (feudal) law, superstition, spiritualism, in short, all nonsense that was not directly harmful to business, and now is very useful to dull the masses.[7] (Engels in de Tollenaere 1996, p. 139)

Marxism, self-identified as scientific and comprehensive in nature, was generally deemed incompatible with religion, in spite of various attempts at reconciliation with Christianity in the late nineteenth century (McLellan 1987, pp. 1–2).[8] This incompatibility was also attributed to the Marxist materialist metaphysics and, most importantly, the function of religion as "an instrument of class rule, an ideological bulwark of the dominant class" (McLellan 1987, p. 2). The general Marxist view of religion is more nuanced, especially if one notes Gramsci's attempt to differentiate between the simple forms of faith in comparison to the Jesuitical form. Engels' analysis of American superstition highlights the nuances in comparison to religion.

The political usefulness of religion, in its simple or traditional form, is accentuated in its more popular superstitious form.[9] Unlike in the Christian world where peasant uprisings had worn a religious mask, the rise of supernatural 'saviours' in Muslim Arab societies occurred at periods of collision between merchants and Bedouins, according to Engels:

> A peculiar antithesis to this [thesis of the Christian world's uprisings] was the religious risings in the Mohammedan world, particularly in Africa. Islam is a religion adapted to Orientals, especially Arabs, i.e., on the one hand to townsmen engaged in trade and industry, on the other to nomadic Bedouins. Therein lies, however, the embryo of a periodically recurring collision. The townspeople grow rich, luxurious and lax in the observation of the 'law'. The Bedouins, poor and hence of strict morals, contemplate with envy and covetousness these riches and pleasures. Then they unite under a prophet, a Mahdi, to chastise the apostates and restore the observation of the ritual and the true faith and to appropriate in recompense the treasures of the renegades. In a hundred years they are naturally in the same position as the renegades were: a new purge of the faith is required, a new Mahdi arises and the game starts again from the beginning. That is what happened from the conquest campaigns of the African Almoravids and Almohads in Spain to the last Mahdi of Khartoum who so successfully thwarted the English. It happened in the same way or similarly with the risings in Persia and other Mohammedan countries. (Engels 1894)

Engels observes that the economic causes behind these recurrent uprisings endure, while religion serves as a disguise for a form of class war, though it fails to provide an alternative system:

> All these movements are clothed in religion but they have their source in economic causes; and yet, even when they are victorious, they allow the old economic conditions to persist untouched. So the old situation remains unchanged and the collision recurs periodically. In the popular risings of the Christian West, on the contrary, the religious disguise is only a flag and a mask for attacks on an economic order which is becoming antiquated. This is finally overthrown, a new one arises and the world progresses. (Engels 1894)

While Spinoza writes on the effects of superstition on the popular level, Marx and Engels look into the elite's use of religion as a pacifier of the masses, and as a concealer of true human suffering. Their contribution helps contextualise the rise in superstition in Safavid Iran and its relation to mass mobilisation in the Islamic Republic and among Hizbullah's Shi'i support base in Lebanon.³

Similar to Spinoza, Marx, and Engels, Ibn Khaldun the renowned Moslem historian noted the usefulness of religion in providing continuity for delegitimised states. Prescribing to Shari'a law could be essential in preserving dynasties. Abun-Nasr provides a more detailed outline of Ibn Khaldun's theory of the rise and fall of states:

> According to this theory, new states appear through the conquest of the territory of a declining state by a tribal group still united by natural solidarity ('asabiyya) and characterised by the hardness and courage of the nomads. But after the establishment of the new state, the ruling tribal group succumbs to the luxury of town life, and its natural solidarity, hardiness, and courage weaken. The rulers consequently find themselves compelled to recruit mercenaries to defend their position. As the rulers' expenses increase on account of their luxurious style of life and the employment of mercenaries, they start imposing on their subjects heavy taxes and in this way alienate them. These developments will lead to the disintegration of the state and make it ripe for conquest by a new tribal group unless the rulers arrest them in time through strictly abiding by the prescriptions of the Shari'a in their conduct of government. (Abun-Nasr 1987, p. 13)

5.2 Islam and Supernatural Narratives

This section covers the contentious issue of supernatural narratives in Islam, and the reformists' conservative stance on rejecting such trends in the clerical establishment. This research helps contextualise the organisation's supernatural narratives within the wider scope of Islamic scholarship, especially the modern reformist institutions. The section contributes to the argument that Hizbullah's identity is modern by showing the novelty in such extensive deployment of supernatural narratives in a political context. The first part reviews the general Islamic reformist attitudes on supernatural narratives, based less on the miraculous prophethood of Mohamed and more on the Qur'an's textual superiority. The second part examines the phenomenon through a comparative perspective, looking at similar challenges facing Christian reformists. The third part examines the supernatural narratives in the work of Majlesi, and Shari'ati's critique of his role, both very relevant to Hizbullah's case.

In the sociology of religion, scholars such as Gellner and Nadia Abu Zahra differentiated "between an orthodox Islam of the Text of learned scholar, on the one hand, and the practices and traditions in the daily lives of Muslims, on the other" (Drieskens 2008, p. 8). Drieskens and Gilsenan coined the term "practical Islam" to denote popular practices (Drieskens 2008, p. 8). However, these practices were at the heart of Islamist reformist movements, curbing what was seen as the excesses of Sufi orders. Muslim reformers, centuries after the Prophet's death, struggled to bring about what they perceived as relatively sensible interpretations and jurisdictions, particularly due to the general, though not absolute, consensus that the religion's greatest miracle is the Qur'an, Islam's holy book. In the post-colonial period, this reform had a nationalist agenda, to unify the nation, as Lapidus notes:

> Islamic reformism also became the basis for anti-colonial movements and the formation of national states in Libya, Algeria, and Morocco. Muslim reformism helped create national political movements by calling for allegiance on the basis of Muslim principles which transcended purely local identifications. By turning Muslims from local sects, shrines, and mediators to the abstract principles of the faith, reformism set the foundations for the unification of large populations in national political struggles. Reformism provided the cultural standards and educational and egalitarian sentiments that served, like nationalism, as the basis of modern political regimes. (Lapidus 1988, p. 820)

"The failure" of Sufi orders, as noted by Gilsenan, was largely political, though noting the great effects of social changes in the twentieth century, such as mass urbanisation. Gilsenan explains:

> That the Orders did not survive to provide a refuge is I think particularly because of the redefinition of the arena of politics in Egypt and of the relations and bases of power… Once the Sheikhs lost their structural opportunities for the performance of the mediating function they were left without a social raison d'etre, or the means to assert their leadership. (Gilsenan 1973, p. 205)

The Qur'an has tackled the contentious issue of a miracle-free Prophet, in spite of the book's acknowledgement of the previous prophets' numerous miracles, including those of *Musa* (Moses) and ʿ*Issa* (Jesus).[11] Claiming miraculous status, the Qur'an challenged the Prophet's sceptical followers to compose a *sura*[12]: "If you have doubts about the revelation we have sent down to our servant, then produce a single *sura* like it—enlist whatever supporters you have other than God—if you truly [think you can]" (Yazicioglu 2011, p. 86). The Qurʾan even undermined the effect of miracles on disbelievers, claiming they would continue to doubt the Prophet's message, even if he had delivered the holy words with a strong miracle or proof, and not through revelation: "Even if we had sent down to you [the Prophet] a book inscribed on parchment, and they had touched it with their own hands, the disbelievers would still say, 'this is nothing but blatant sorcery'" (Yazicioglu 2011, p. 86).

The lack of miracles in Islam, explained by the Qurʾan's sufficiency for the Prophet's times and beyond, paved the way for a more reasoned interpretations. Abu Hamid Al-Ghazali (d. 1111 AD) argued that logic is far superior to miracles:

> I know very well that ten is more than three. If anyone tries to dissuade me by saying, "No, three is more than ten," and wants to prove it by changing in front of me this stick into a serpent, even if I saw him changing it, still this fact would engender no doubt about my knowledge. Certainly, I would be astonished at such a power, but I would not doubt my knowledge. (Yazicioglu 2011, p. 90)

Miracles, according to Al-Ghazali, are unreliable, open to ambiguity, and can simply be deceptive: "I believe in the veracity of Muhamed—peace be upon him—not by reason of the splitting of the moon, and he changing of the staff into serpent: for that way is open to ambiguity and one may not rely on it" (Yazicioglu 2011, p. 90). The basis for believing a Prophet lies in the consistency and truthfulness of the message, both of which render it a 'necessary knowledge'. The conviction in this knowledge is clearer than that of changing "a thousand sticks into snakes" (Yazicioglu 2011, p. 90).

Al-Ghazali was not alone in his suspicion of miracles, as Islamic clerics have generally placed more weight on *shariʿa* law, Islamic jurisdiction, and the Muslim's behaviour. Surpassing this clear line has been generally unacceptable, or could even lead to *gholow* or *reda* (exaggeration and apostasy, respectively). Miracles were the business of earlier times and are associated with experiencing prophethood (Terzic 2009, p. 15). Ibn Khaldun, the renowned Muslim scholar, tried to counter the rising literature on dreams, *jinn*, and astrology. *Jinn*, mentioned in the Qurʾan, were the "spirits with bodies of vapour or flame which could appear to the senses, often in the form of animals"; they were and often still are perceived as evil, prompting the faithful to seek help to control them (Hourani 1991, p. 204). Ibn Khaldun was mostly concerned with the rise of medical prescriptions and advice attributed to the Prophet; he criticised the then prevalent trend of alternative medicine, known as *al-tibb al-nabawi*, derived from *hadith*: "The Prophet (peace be upon him) was sent to teach us the religious law, not medicine or any other ordinary matter... None of the statements about medicine that occur in sound tradition should be considered to have the force of law" (Hourani 1991, p. 203). Ibn Khaldun's argument is relevant to Hizbullah's supernatural narratives, as it highlights the tension between the two camps, pertaining mostly to reformist worries over potential political manifestations.[13] While the practice dates back centuries and was abandoned in the reformist phase, dozens of books on medical advice and remedies presumably offered by the Prophet and the Twelve Imams, also belonging to *al-tibb al-nabawi*, could be found in Hizbullah-affiliated bookshops.

Islamic Shiʻi reforms bear similarities to later Christian attempts to eliminate the rivalry of magic and superstitious practices, as in the case of medieval England:

> The contemporary clergy saw the cunning folk and astrologers as their deadly rivals. They did so because they resented a competing pastoral agency, and because they were too anxious to replace a magical explanation of misfortune by a theological one. When plague, fire or some other disaster struck, they devoted much energy to refuting the theories of those who attributed the events to the stars, to magic, to fortune or bad luck. In their place they affirmed the sovereignty of God's providence and interpreted his judgments in accordance with the conception they had formed of his intentions. It was the sins of the people which were the cause of the fall of the commonwealths, declared a preacher at Paul's cross in 1609: neither the Fortune of the Epicureans, nor the Destiny of the Stoics, nor the mystical numbers of the Pythagoreans, nor the stars of the astrologers could provide a satisfactory alternative. (Thomas 1971, p. 762)

Although tensions persisted between the clergy and men of superstition, they were reconciled on the popular level, as magic and astrology "were seen as natural by contemporary intellectuals" (Thomas 1971, p. 763). Religion and magic mixed a great deal before the Reformation, but when the Reformation occurred it left a vacuum, which was filled by the astrologers and 'cunning men' (Thomas 1971, p. 763). Protestant sects "brought back much of the magic which their early Tudor predecessors had so energetically cast out" (Thomas 1971, p. 763). Their exploitation of healing practices was unprecedented, to an extent that to some, their lectures and teachings were synonymous with astrology: "During the interregnum, they exploited the possibilities of religion for healing and prophesying in a way unsurpassed in England since the days of the early Christian saints. The practical attraction of enthusiastic religion during these years closely matched those of magical arts" (Thomas 1971, p. 763).[14] The relationship between superstition or magic and religion was largely defined by or based on interest. The terms of this relationship were clear to the Catholic clergy in the Middle Ages:

> The leaders of the church thus abandoned the struggle against superstition whenever it seemed in their interest to do so. Throughout the Middle Ages their attitude to the credulities of their simpler followers was fundamentally ambivalent. They disliked them as gross and superstitious, but they had no wish to discourage attitudes which might foster popular devotion. (Thomas 1971, p. 56)

The Catholic Church only tolerated superstition when it fostered devotion to its institutions, given the latter's impact on the popular level. This form of informal exploitation existed among the Shiʿi clergy, specifically under the Safavid Empire (1501–1722).[15]

5.2.1 Majlesi: Reviving Superstition

In the 1960s and 1970s, Shariʿati, an anti-Shah intellectual who was dubbed the ideological father of the Islamic Revolution, was compelled to contest the writings and ideology of Mohammad Baqer Majlesi, a figure largely responsible for the dissemination of superstition in Shiʿi theology, interlinked with the clerical support for Iran's ruling dynasty.[16] Majlesi had revived superstitious texts in his collection of *hadith, Bihar Al-Anwar* (*The Seas of Light*), undoing the legacy of a Shiʿi reformist movement in the eleventh century. During that phase, senior Shiʿi clerics, among them the renowned Sheikh Mofid (d. 1022 AD) and Sharif Mortada (d. 1025), had sought to clear Shiʿi theology of reports attributing supernatural powers to the Shiʿi imams (Rahnema 2011, p. 184). Mortada and Mofid's rooted out *hadith* or reports "with a quite original metaphysical and mystical scope in Islam"; many of these *hadiths* attributed mystical and supernatural powers to the Twelve Imams (Rahnema 2011, p. 184).[17] The reports surfaced during the lifetime of the Imams, especially following the death of the Eighth Imam, Ali Ben Moussa Al-Reda, as a part of a "new extremist wing of the Imamate tradition" (Rahnema 2011, p. 185).

Centuries later, in the seventeenth century, Majlesi played a major role, through his *Bihar Al-Anwar* and numerous other works, in restoring superstitious reports and texts; a renowned contemporary Sunni cleric even described the extent of the former's influence by referring to Shiʻi religion as Majlesi's (Rahnema 2011, p. 186). Majlesi's effect on Shiʻi theology was enormous, according to contemporary figures; Rahnema notes: "What had come to be known as the Shi'i religion as propagated by Majlesi had overshadowed all previous readings of Shi'ism and that Majlesi's variant was dramatically different from that of the Shi'i luminaries such as Mofid, Sharif Morteza and Tusi" (Rahnema 2011, p. 187). Majlesi's *Behar Al-Anwar* included sections on miracles attributed to the Imams: for example, the 'miracles' chapter of the sixth Shiʻi Imam, Ja'far al-Sadeq, is 98 pages long and includes 227 traditions, only second to a chapter on Imam Ali Ben Abi Taleb, the first Shiʻi Imam (Loebenstein 2003, p. 200). Majlesi's work on documenting the supernatural occurrences in the lives of the Imams was pivotal for the reproduction of superstition in the post-Hizbullah era.[18]

5.2.2 *The Supernatural Imams: Political Consequences*

Parallel to his work of documenting and reviving superstition, Majlesi provided the same level of reverence and obedience to the Safavid ruler—the two were not separate. "The idea of proclaiming an imam to be God constituted the first half of a two-part claim," according to a senior Shiʻi cleric, "the second half was that the claimant himself was that God's messenger" (Rahnema 2011, p. 187). When the claims about the Imams are accepted, the claimant moves to solidify his position as a messenger of the holy dead Imam, "demanding respect and obedience from his followers" (Rahnema 2011, p. 187). They become "sub-Imams", whose new roles gain further holiness in the absence of the Twelfth Imam. Assuming, even indirectly, that these Shiʻi clerics or leaders (as in the case of the Safavid shahs) possess divine attributes only becomes possible if the followers accept the supernatural claims about the Imams.

When Ali Shariʻati decided to take on the clerical body supporting the Pahlawi dynasty, his critical work focussed on Majlesi considering the political implications of the latter's theology, which persisted for centuries after his death (Rahnema 2011, p. 19). Shariʻati coined the term 'Safavi

Shiism', as opposed to the genuine or original brand of Shiʿism (Ali's Shiʿism), arguing that the former lent legitimacy to the exploitation of the masses in order to guarantee the survival of the religious, political, and economic establishment in Iran (Rahnema 2011, p. 19). Shariʿati considers "Gandhi the fire worshipper more worthy of being a Shiʿi than Alameh Majlesi", sarcastically referring to the latter as "the thirteenth Shiʿi Imam" (Rahnema 2011, p. 19).

Parallel to the supernatural narratives in Majlesi's work were the politically motivated theological arguments he put forward to establish the divine right of the Safavid rulers, and to justify their war with the Ottoman Empire. In this, Shariʿati noticed two trends or deviations from what he deemed acceptable Shiʿi theology. The first was Majlesi's attempt to distinguish the Persian identity in Islamic texts, connecting Shiʿi theology with the contemporary rulers of Iran, the Safavid dynasty. Majlesi's work also demonised the second caliph, ʿOmar Bin al-Khattab, in order to solidify the rulers' position against the Ottoman Empire.[19] Shariʿati notes that Majlesi sought to blame ʿOmar for invading Iran, disregarding the connection between the military action and the advent of Islam (Shariʿati 2002, p. 135).[20] Majlesi's work portrays ʿOmar, a significant pillar of Sunni faith, as an enemy of the Prophet's family, *ahlul bait,* and of the Sassanids, the ancestors of the Safavids (Shariʿati 2002, p. 135). In addition to being motivated by the Ottoman–Safavid conflict, and not by religious necessity or the need to disperse information, this public attack on ʿOmar broke the Shiʿi tradition of *taqia*, dissimulation, in criticising Sunni doctrines.

Majlesi's *hadith* collection, often criticised by Shariʿati, included a story on the marriage of Imam Husayn, the third Shiʿi imam, to the daughter of Iran's last Sassanid ruling family, Yazdegerd III (632–651). The marriage is portrayed as between two victims of ʿOmar: the Prophet's household, and his legitimate heirs, and the Persian Empire. The marriage resulted in a son, the third Shiʿi Imam, Ali Ben Hussain, known as *Zainul Abedeen*.[21] The culmination of this marriage is in the twelfth Shiʿi Imam, *Al-Mahdi*, the saviour or Messiah of the end of times. Imam Mahdi, who bears exceptional importance in Shiʿi theology, is a combination of the Sassanid Empire and the Prophet's household, both of whom fell victim to ʿOmar, the second caliph. According to Shariʿati, "the Safavid movement and affiliated clerics had to do their best to reconcile Iranian nationalism and Islam, so that the former would appear in a green colour" (Shariʿati 2002, p. 140).[22] The tendency to raise the Imams to a godly level, Shariʿati notes, was often meant to gloss over 'knowledge', emptying Islamic teachings of their meaning, and thus carrying the risk of contesting contemporary authority (Shariʿati 2002, p. 140, 164). Shariʿati's connection between Majlesi's supernatural narratives and his ability to introduce such radically novel arguments for political reasons contributes to the understanding of the possible motivations for Hizbullah's adoption of supernatural elements of Shiʿa identity. When advocating a general supernatural approach, such politically motivated and often obvious connections between contemporary politics and the divine might seem acceptable, falling within the context of an accepted belief system.

Majlesi's overstated supernatural claims and stories could be put in better perspective if his political connections and statements are taken into consideration. In his introduction to the prayer book, *Zad Al-Ma'ad*, Majlesi writes the following on the incumbent Safavid ruler, Shah Sultan Hussein Al-Mussawi Bhader Khan: "The Supreme presence, the master of this age's Sultans… the cream of the Prophet's grandchildren. The water and greenery of the Prophet's garden, the eye and saddle of the Murtadawi (Alawi) house" (Shariʿati 2002, p. 204).[23] Majlesi's flowery praise for the Shah endows him with legitimacy, using similar language to that of other supernatural stories: the Shah is portrayed as a supernatural being in the introduction to a popular prayer book (Shariʿati 2002, p. 205). Angels are the Shah's 'attendants' and his sword creates "a running river of *kufar* [infidels'] heads", while Sufi masters pray for the immortality of his state, assisted by birds (Shariʿati 2002, p. 205). The Shah, according to Majlesi, is the manifestation of the Qurʾan, executing the holy book's verses in his actions. Angels, representatives of God, accompany him while his actions reflect the divine wishes and will. In his writings, Majlesi also referred to the first Safavid king as the "Shah of Shahs (Shahanshah) of an army of angels… the embodiment of all Divine graces… the shadow of God on earth"; the senior Shiʿi cleric sought to persuade people that their ruler possessed both "divine attributes and divine missions" (Rahnema 2011, p. 15). Majlesi's connection to the Safavid dynasty manifested itself in his appointment "to the prestigious and high profile religious position of *sheykholeslam* [the Shaykh of Islam] by Shah Soleyman" (Rahnema 2011, p. 192).

5.2.3 *Majlesi and Mainstream Shiʿism*

Majlesi lived under five Safavid shahs, and his political connection to them enabled him to institutionalise superstition, transforming it into both a popular belief and a state religion (Rahnema 2011, p. 16). Majlesi's popularity and influence, Rahnema argues, have roots in the limitations of Arabic Shiʿi books, the authors of which were scholars from Jabal ʿAmil, modern-day South Lebanon, brought in by the then Safavid ruler to spread Shiʿism in his predominantly Sunni empire. The Arabic Shiʿi books were unable to reach the Persian 'common folk', but Majlesi's simple language, by contrast, appealed to many, and "it can be strongly suggested that Persian Shi'i essentially learned their Shi'ism from Majlesi and his popularized work"[24] (Rahnema 2011, p. 190).

The popularity stems from the Shiʿi cleric's airing of often avoided topics pertaining to mundane day-to-day affairs. *Helyat Al-Motaqeen,* a very popular and accessible book of *hadith,* covers 14 aspects of daily life, even daring to venture into the subject of sexual relations, with tips from the Prophet and the Imams.[25] The book is a comprehensive guide to all forms of conduct, covering more than a dozen subjects, and delving many times into supernatural narratives (Rahnema 2011, p. 241). Majlesi's "concern with codifying the finest details of personal and social life was so pervasive that it hardly left any room for private initiative and reflection" (Rahnema 2011, p. 240). The dissemination of this book had political consequences, pertaining to its popularity and its pervasiveness: "Majlesi's command and almost monopoly over producing and propagating religious and ideological literature enabled him to move and mould the pious public as he and his so-called divinely guided kings wished" (Rahnema 2011, p. 240).

While it remains difficult to assess exactly to what extent Majlesi contributed to keeping the public resigned to authority or "docile and manageable", the popularity of his work and its influence on mainstream Shiʿism demonstrate it had a deep effect (Rahnema 2011, p. xi). Rahnema says Majlesism carried out 'mass brainwashing' of the public, and "through the dissemination and popularization of superstitious explanations or narration of events sought to foster an unquestioning and fatalistic community", facilitating control and domination (Rahnema 2011, p. 240). Majlesism in both its early and modern forms became a social engineering project:

> They [Majlesism and its clerical/non-clerical followers] arrogate the right to interpret and apply independent thought, which they label as dangerous to the common man, to themselves so as to impose their own manual of personal, social, political and religious behavior on society in order to engineer the lives of the common folk. (Rahnema 2011, p. xi)

Certain Safavid clerics, according to Rahnema, "maintained that the political rule and power of Shiʿi leaders was willed and approved by God, the prophet and the Imams" (Rahnema 2011, p. 16). Chardin, after visiting Safavid Iran three times, noted "the majority of Iranians believed that their kings were representatives of the imams and the deputy of the hidden imam during his occultation" (Rahnema 2011, p. 16). This goes against mainstream Islamic beliefs: "A politician laying claim to directly or indirectly possessing any of the powers that are in God's monopoly is an impostor hoping that the credulity of the common folk would allow him to realize his plans by abusing religiosity and faith" (Rahnema 2011, p. 14).

There are few established links in Iranian scholarship between the modern use of superstition, namely, by the former Iranian president, Mahmoud Ahmadinejad, and the late Iranian shah, Mohammad-Reza Pahlavi (called the 'Light of the Aryans'). The resurgence, however, suggests that Shi'i culture continues to be influenced by Majlesi's legacy (Rahnema 2011, p. 17), and certain 'Shi'i strands' even consider Majlesism to be the authentic reading of Shi'i Islam (Rahnema 2011, pp. 17–18). Majlesi's significance in the mainstream Shi'i faith can be established by the fact that Abbas Al-Qomi, the author of *Mafateeh al-Jenan*, the most popular prayer book, acknowledged Majlesi's influence (Rahnema 2011, p. 18). For at least 500 years, Rahnema says, "certain Iranian rulers have made explicit and implicit claims to being supernatural leaders, part human and part sacred, and some have believed, followed and staked their lives [on] them" (Rahnema 2011, p. 21).[26] In the early twentieth century, superstition was revived during the eras of the two absolute monarchs, Reza Shah and his son Mohamad Reza. Before his rise to power, Reza Shah had a dream about two lit candles in his room; his servant, Yadollah Ardel interpreted it as a sign of a double promotion. The dream "has been implicitly referred by some as proof of Reza Shah's spiritual dimension and supernatural agency" (Rahnema 2011, p. 114). Reza Shah's son and heir, Mohammed Reza, recounted experiencing three supernatural incidents during his childhood, implying a connection with an external force, in spite of his rule's secular nature and Western influences. In one of the supernatural occurrences, the seven-year-old heir saw an angelic man with a halo around his head, while walking in the Sa'dabad Palace (Rahnema 2011, p. 118). Mohammed Reza later claimed an "inspiration of a celestial origin" (*elham*) in which he realised that "the man whom he had met was none other than the Twelfth Imam" (Rahnema 2011, p. 118).

5.2.4 Majlesism in the Islamic Republic

Majlesism subsided with the rising role of the Shi'i centres in Najaf and Qom during the nineteenth and twentieth centuries. This retreat continued until the Islamic republic. Most recently, Majlesism, representing the supernatural trends in Shiʻi ideology, has resurfaced in the statements and policies of Ayatollah Mesbah Yazdi, the former head of the judiciary who was described as the spiritual father of Mahmoud Ahmadinejad. Yazdi claimed that "once the President is appointed and confirmed by the leader and becomes his agent, he will be exposed to the rays emanating from this source of light [Khamenei]", comparing obedience to the Iranian Supreme Leader to obedience to God (Rahnema 2011, p. 20).[27]

The advent of President Mahmoud Ahmadinejad marked a clear revival of superstitious ideology in Iran and Lebanon. Nearly two months after his speech at the United Nation's general assembly on the 17 September 2005, Ahmadinejad claimed, in a leaked video of a meeting with senior Iranian clerics, that a miracle occurred while he addressed the leaders of the world; the Iranian president said he was enveloped with a halo or a ray of light (Rahnema 2011, p. 38). During his speech to the world leaders at the UN annual summit in 2005, the Iranian president called upon God "to hasten the emergence" of Imam Mahdi, the Twelfth Imam of the Shiʻa and the saviour of the "end of times" (Rahnema 2011, p. 35). Ahmadinejad said that his assistant recorded the same experience, lending it credibility, and stated that he felt a hand had fixed the world leaders to their seats (Rahnema 2011, p. 38).

Ahmadinejad denied the episode during a televised presidential debate with Mahdi Karubi, a leading opposition candidate; however, senior clerics who attended the meeting, including Ayatollah Javadi Amoli, confirmed that he made these claims in the meeting (Rahnema 2011, p. 39). Gholam-Hossein Elham, the Iranian president's spokesman, when asked about the halo of light, claimed that the leaked video was 'doctored' (Rahnema 2011, p. 39). Regardless of the assumed political implications, the dissemination of the video in Iran, where a million copies were reportedly circulated, and its reported public screening in the presence of the Friday congregational prayer leaders, propagated the alleged connection between Ahmadinejad and the Twelfth Imam (Rahnema 2011, p. 42).

5.3 Supernatural Narratives in Hizbullah's Propaganda

Majlesi's work and its subsequent influence on supernatural narratives and politics in the Islamic Republic of Iran are linked to their emergence in Hizbullah's politics and discourse. There are two trends in the organisation's supernatural narratives the first relates to the Islamic Republic's own propaganda, translated into Arabic, and the second concerns the organisation's affiliated and sponsored supernatural literature on divine intervention during the conflict with Israeli occupiers, and the links between the leadership and the hidden Twelfth Imam, Allah's representative on earth.[28] This section argues that while the supernatural narratives constitute a part of these transnational links, the wider literature remains about the organisation itself. Although the translated transnational elements of Hizbullah's supernatural elements concern the experiences in the Islamic Revolution in Iran, they relate to the organisation's divine status, as *Wilayat al-Faqih* draws a strong connection between them. As with the book's main research question—how Hizbullah's identity is produced— the organisation's supernatural narratives draw on the Iranian experience but are directly associated with and serve the organisation's Lebanese (mostly ʿAmili) Shiʿi narratives.

Hizbullah's dissemination of superstition is often indirect, through affiliated publishers and clergy. Literature on meetings with the Imam is often related or connected to *Wilayat al-Faqih*, particularly linking the hierarchy to the divine, and to *jihad* (resistance), in which they take the form of miracles of combat. These combat miracles are not confined to Lebanon, but include the martyrs of the Islamic Republic's war with Iraq. In a copycat effort, mirroring Iran's official propaganda and discourse, *Al-Ma'aref*, a Hizbullah publishing house, printed a number of books on the martyrs of the Islamic Republic, some of which are discussed in the following section.

5.3.1 *Karamat: The Supernatural Agency*

Hizbullah literature on the Imams' supernatural happenings often uses the word *karamat*, usually meaning consideration or blessing, rather than miracles, *mu'jezat*, in Arabic. In *karamat*, the supernatural does not oblige divine proof, a requirement for messengers, or Prophets, or Imams, to encompass the largest mass of believers. A differentiation is clearly made between the two words; *al-karama* and the *mu'jeza* are both supernatural in nature, but the latter is reserved for Prophets to challenge their foes or disbelievers; while the former is still extraordinary, "Allah's gift to his special and pure worshippers", though neither challenging nor a signal of prophethood (Kourani 2000, p. 23). *Al-karama* happens to the pious as a result of the struggle against one's self (*jihad al nafs*) (Kourani 2000, p. 5–6). The work of Majlesi, discussed in the previous section, is significant to justify contemporary *karamat*, as the latter belongs to the former's theological approach. This explains Shariati's condemnation of Majlesi's legacy, in an attempt to deconstruct the theological foundation allowing the invention of a new *karamat* (prophecies or miracles) for political purposes.

The literature on *karamat* has been renewed in a number of contemporary books, with a special focus on the hidden Twelfth Imam, to whom modern links are created to establish divine legitimacy. The narrated miracles of Imam Mahdi commence with his birth: at his birth, the Twelfth Imam fell on his knees, raising his two index fingers (a sign of belief in the oneness of God), then 'sneezed, saying *alhamdulilah* (thank God) afterwards (Al-Bahraini 2005, p. 10). Shortly after his birth, the baby Imam was seen prostrating to Allah under a blanket, and uttered *al-shahadatain*— the Moslem confession of faith to one God and his prophet Mohammad— to his father, then greeted his mother (Al-Bahraini 2005, p. 9). Other stories in the same book claim he named the eleven imams after the Prophet, and when he reached himself, Imam Mahdi asked God to "accomplish what you promised me… and to fill earth with fairness and justice" (Al-Bahraini 2005, pp. 12–13). The miraculous stories of his birth include divine light emanating from his head to the skies, and the advent of angels in the form of birds that touched the newborn to receive his blessings (Al-Bahraini 2005, p. 23, 27). After his birth, the miracles attributed to the Imam are numerous, from his ability to predict the future and read minds, to supernatural powers like sitting on water to pray, or invisibility (Al-Bahraini 2005, pp. 44–47).

5.3.2 Types of Supernatural Sightings

Hizbullah's 'intellectual brokers'—a term coined by Smith in his work on nationalism and applicable in this case—publish their books in the organisation's subsidised printing houses, discussed in Chap. 4. Although many of these authors are officials or former officials in the organisation, it is difficult to identify their exact roles; however, the institutional link of the publishing house or sponsoring institution to Hizbullah remains more relevant, considering the organisation's centralised cultural policy, outlined in Chap. 2.

Fares Faqih, one of Hizbullah's intellectual brokers, argues in *Karamat Al-Imam Al-Mahdi*, a book on the contemporary miracles of the twelfth and last Shi'i Imam, that there are three types of sightings: sightings of the heart (non-physical but experienced when awake); sighting in dreams; and physical sightings. The non-physical sightings are a result of internal and external obedience (commitment to Islamic teachings), since "the Imam is the complete manifestation of God's name" (Faqih 2002, p. 11). Seeing the Imam in a believer's dreams "is true, as *al-Shaitan* [Satan] cannot play the role of *al-Awlia'* [saints or custodians] in the world of *ru'ia* [vision, as in dreams]" (Faqih 2002, p. 11). Literature about such visions in dreams is also common among Salafist organisations, such as the Taliban and Al-Qaeda, mostly to promote divine guidance. The Taliban's leader, Mullah Omar, and Osama Bin Laden both made such claims about their dreams; the former dreamt that he would establish control over Afghanistan, and the second dreamt of September 11 attacks in 2001 (Edgar 2006, pp. 206–207), although they remain suggestive and avoid the sort of direct links found in Hizbullah's literature.

5.3.3 Reinterpreting Hadith

In the third and most important type, the physical sighting, Faqih argues against a *hadith* (saying), attributed to the Twelfth Imam himself, in which he calls those who claim seeing him after his disappearance 'liars'. Far from the prevalent belief, Faqih reasons, the Twelfth Imam's *hadith* only had immediate effect during a critical transitional phase. In Twelver Shiʻi history, the last Imam's *ghaiba* (occultation) was transitional, starting with a shorter seven-decade-long disappearance, maintaining contact with followers through four ambassadors; the second phase, known as *al-ghaiba al-kubra*, the 'great occultation', extends till this day. Faqih argued that the Imam, by claiming that those who see him are liars, wanted to stop anyone from claiming to be his ambassador (Faqih 2002, p. 13). Faqih claims that the Imam's divine role requires such an intervention:

> The rule of divine kindness, dominant in the universe, imposes the intervention of God's greatest custodian (Imam Mahdi) on earth, to reform or protect humans, and this intervention does not exclude personal and physical intervention of *sahib al-zaman* [one of Imam Mahdi's names, translated as the 'proprietor of time']. (Faqih 2002, p. 13)

The same logic prevails over much of the literature on meeting the Imam. Al-Zubaidy, a major author on Hizbullah's supernatural narratives, argues that the same reasons for the Imam's contact with the outside world during *al-Ghaiba al-Sughra* persist after it:

5.3 SUPERNATURAL NARRATIVES IN HIZBULLAH'S PROPAGANDA 153

There is no doubt that Imam Mahdi might favour some trustworthy individuals with more than a meeting, and there is no doubt too that Islamic interests may require [the Imam's] appearance to the deviants if the results are guaranteed. One has to say that the same rate [of appearances] in *al-ghaiba al-sughra* reoccurs in one form or the other in *al-ghaiba al-kubra*. And all of this is, God willing, unquestionable. (Al-Zubaidy 2009, p. 32)[29]

Such direct statements justifying current supernatural narratives constitute an upgrade in the type provided by Majlesi. In fact, Majlesi's statements on the Safavid rulers rarely said clearly that such meetings take place, in the same way as the aforementioned *hadith*, attributed to the hidden Imam.

The literature on the *karamat* provides manuals for meeting Imam Mahdi, and covers both genders, as in Al-Nasseri's *Nisa' Talataqi Saheb Al-Zaman* (*Women meet Imam Mahdi*). This book was published in Dar Al-Mahaja al-Baida, a Hizbullah-affiliated printing house based in the southern suburbs of Beirut, the organisation's stronghold in the capital. Alongside the many miracles by the Imam, such as curing a paralysed child, the manual provides information on Imam Mahdi's regular sanctuaries, mostly located in Iran and Iraq: the Imams' graves, especially those of Imam Husayn, Jamkaran, and Kufa; *alsahla* mosques, Mecca during the pilgrimage season; places of worship carrying his name; and finally the 'Ashura' commemoration events (Al-Zubaidy 2009, pp. 65–69). The rituals or prayers in order to see the Imam are contentious; however, a 2009 book lists dozens of actions that a pregnant woman can undertake to ensure that her son becomes a soldier of Imam Mahdi. These rituals include prayers, readings of the Qur'an, tips such as "do not look in the mirror at night", alongside a month-by-month diet till birth: "First month, eat dates with *surat alqadr* daily, read *surat yasseen* on Thursdays and *surat alsafat* on Fridays... Fifth month, eat an egg with *surat al-hamd*... Eighth month, eat kebab with *surat yasseen*" (Al-Nasseri 2009, pp. 31–32). Al-Zubaidy also argues that the Imam changes his costumes, as "many times we see him wearing the Arab 'igal, the Bedouin outfit, or in a nice gracious costume, or in the clothes of a peasant " (Al-Zubaidy 2009, pp. 34–35). The Imam travels on a horse or a camel, or walks, while speaking in different languages and accents, showing his miracles when necessary; he avoids "any reference to his identity such as his address" or known name (Al-Zubaidy 2009, p. 35).

The Imam's reasons for meeting his followers are to save the Muslim populations from the injustices of deviant rulers and gangs, to return the

Black Rock to its rightful place in the Ka'ba (Mecca), and to notify his followers that the nation has not reached the rightful level for his appearance (Al-Zubaidy 2009, pp. 36–37). The Imam's appearances could also be for banal reasons, as, for example, "providing financial assistance to others", "curing of dangerous diseases … after doctors fail", teaching believers how to pray, emphasising respect for elderly parents, showing the way to those lost in the desert, or supporting "one side over the other in a debate if the interest requires its victory" (Al-Zubaidy 2009, p. 37).

Such books, according to vendors in the southern suburbs of Beirut, have proven very popular, leading to several editions in certain cases, including Al-Zubaidy's.[30]

5.3.4 Reaching Women

As in the case with Hizbullah's institutions, these supernatural narratives target different audiences, in order to ensure a wider reach. While in the institutions welfare is mixed with literature, the supernatural narratives are presented with contemporary miraculous occurrences, thus placing any such narratives in the political sphere, as normal occurrences are portrayed in the general context of miraculous happenings. In this context, al-Nasseri lists more than a 100 stories of women who allegedly saw Imam Mahdi; they were mostly patients with incurable diseases, who were cured after sighting him (al-Nasseri 2009, pp. 5–10). The women include non-Shi'i Muslims, whether in Egypt, Morocco, Turkey, or Tunisia, and a Christian lady, according to al-Nasseri, whose accounts bear many similarities to those of Christian sainthood and acts of healing.

As in different Islamic sects and various other religions, the appearance of the saviour, the hidden and alive Imam Mahdi in Shi'i texts, will signal the beginning of the end of times. There are similar narratives in the Sunni faith, with a major difference being that the Imam is yet to be born. In *Ista'idu fa Inna Al-Thuhor Qarib (Be Ready, the Appearance is Soon)*, Hijazi, a Lebanese Shi'i cleric, lists some of the signs that the resurrection is approaching, referring to stories of meetings between the faithful and the Imam throughout history, including one in which Imam Mahdi leaves a note (Hijazi 2006, p. 100). Among the signs was a contemporary one from the invasion of Iraq, quoted from an Iranian magazine called *Khorshid*:

> According to news from Iraq, quoting one of the Friday prayers' imams, who was arrested by the American forces; American officers considered their

work in Iraq was to arrest the promised Mahdi or kill him. According to this Iraqi clergyman, after his arrest and interrogation, several questions on the promised Mahdi were asked, including do you know the Promised Mahdi? Do you have any information about his residence or whereabouts? He added: when the Americans were desperate, and before releasing me, they proposed a reward for any information I provide on the promised Mahdi. It is worth mentioning that the extreme Christian Zionist movement held several activities during the past few years, that the resurrection of Waliy Al-ʿAsr [another name of Imam Mahdi] will constitute a threat to the security of the United States and Israel, and arrangements were made to face this danger. (Hijazi 2006, p. 52)

As with the transformation in ʿAshuraʾ rituals, discussed in Chap. 6, stories such as the aforementioned connect the divine, represented by the Imam Mahdi, to contemporary politics. The USA and Israel are not only enemies of the Iraqi resistance, but are also pursuing Imam Mahdi, who is presented in this suggestive manner as the mentor of the Shiʿi groups resisting foreign occupation.

5.3.5 Imam Khomeini's Karamat

Establishing the Imams' *karamat* as acceptable and believable occurrences paves the way for direct political links, starting with Ayatollah Khomeini, the leader of the Islamic Revolution of Iran and formulator of the *Wilayat al-Faqih* doctrine. Khomeini's miraculous happenings were in line with the stature bestowed upon him by his predecessor, Ali Khamenei, the current Supreme Leader of the Islamic Republic of Iran. While the argument for the Imams' miracles stands for certain selected individuals of high religious stature, such as Khomeini, Khamenei makes a subtle argument that places the former immediately after the Imams in standing. This stature reinforces the attempt to call the Supreme leader *Naʾeb Al-Imam*, Imam Mahdi's deputy. Khamenei says of Khomeini's 'exceptional' stature:

Imam Khomeini was a great personality that is difficult to find an equivalent—except for the Prophets and Infallibles [Imams]—in the history of great leaders throughout the ages and times… [H]e demonstrated to the world that human perfection and emulation of Imam Ali, and bordering on the line of infallibility are not impossible, they could be achieved and reached. (Kourani 2000, p. 20)

Khamenei indirectly links Khomeini to the legacy of the miraculous prophets such as Moses: "He who is armed by Moses's stick and white hand, Muhammad's strength is Ruhollah Khomeini who destroyed the edifice of Pharaohs, and lightened the hearts of *Mustaza'feen* [the oppressed]" (Kourani 2000, p. 21). Such stature for Khomeini justifies the *karamat* attributed to him. In a role similar to that of Prophets and Imams, writes Kourani, Khomeini bestowed dignity to humanity, gave the believer self-value, brought martyrdom to the *mujahedeen* (holy fighters), and "to Islam, [he brought] movement/mobility", and "added morals and values to the human being and materialistic life, as he broke statues and defeated atheist ideas" (Kourani 2000, p. 21). Ayatollah Sedouqi, quoted in the book, argues that the revolution's relatively low losses, "in comparison to other revolutions in the world", constitute a *karama*: "We consider this situation a karama and a connection to Imam Mahdi, and I am certain that Imam Khomeini enthuses his decisions and actions from the Imam (May Allah haste his Appearance)" (Kourani 2000, p. 82).

Khomeini's *karamat* is mostly based on his ability to predict the future, and his connection to the divine, which grants him the agency to ask for holy intervention, and strongly suggests communication with the Imams. Even when absent, Ayatollah Khomeini can still read his followers' minds:

> Seyyed Khalkhali printed a large number of Imam Khomeini's photos, in both large and small sizes, to be sent to Lebanon. And since the number of the photos was large, it was placed in an external warehouse at Imam Khomeini's house, and I do not know whether the Imam was notified of the photos' arrival. Anyways, my family was not at home that day, and the servant had gone home, so I decided to sleep in the external part of Imam Khomeini's house, known as the guests' underground section. Imam Khomeini lived in the internal section of the upper floor. At that night, I was alone, so the Imam asked me to bring him the photos from the warehouse. I told him "welcome", and as I entered the underground warehouse, disappearing from his sight, I looked at the photos, and I thought of keeping one as they were beautiful and attractive; then he shouted "and do not keep one". (Kourani 2000, p. 35)[31]

This story suggests that Khomeini possesses a direct link to the divine, whether through Imam Mahdi or Allah, enabling him to see through what is hidden to the ordinary human mind. The political consequences are an absolute and unquestionable belief in the leader's decisions and strategy.

Imam Khomeini's *karamat* encompasses the ability to communicate with the deceased Imams, such as this story narrated by a clergyman on the Ayatollah's connection with Musa Al-Kathem, the Seventh Shi'i Imam:

> The spiritual dimension of the Imam [Khomeini] is beyond our understanding and reach... and as a result of accompanying him for years, I saw from Imam Khomeini some occurrences that I could describe as *Karamat*. During his stay in Najaf, sending money to Iraq was extremely difficult. It happened that I arrived in Iraq from Syria with an amount of cash, and when I reached Baghdad's airport, security was heavily searching passengers, so I felt worried and anxious, so I asked Imam Musa Al-Kathem to help me: "My master, I carry this sum for your son, so help me." Then a security man came and allowed me to go through. When I reached Najaf, I went to Imam Khomeini, entered and greeted him. Upon seeing me, he smiled and said you faced a problem in the airport and asked Imam Musa Al-Kathem for help. I knew then that the Imam (Khomeini) was informed of this incident. (Kourani 2000, pp. 36–37)

Khomeini predicted the martyrdom of a clergyman's son in the Iran–Iraq War, even before the Islamic Revolution started, and when the Ayatollah was still in Najaf (Kourani 2000, p. 29). He also predicted the massacre of the Iranian pilgrims in Mecca, the right timing of military operations, and the actions of the Iraqi regime. The propagation of these books in Lebanon, although relating to Iran, could only be done through Hizbullah, the Lebanese network carrying Khomeini's legacy and representing his hierarchy.

While Kourani defines *almu'jiza* as prophetic, preferring otherwise to use the word *karamat,* his book is not restrictive. While the book narrates detailed stories on the Ayatollah's power of predictions and extraordinary knowledge, Kourani makes claims Khomeini possesses supernatural physical powers. These actions are dubbed "the manifestations of miracles (*I'jaz*)". Although the term *mu'jiza* (miracle) is reserved for prophets, it still manifests itself in Imam Khomeini's life.

In the manifestations of miracles, Ayatollah Khomeini, a contemporary twentieth-century character, is transformed into a mythical being, who miraculously disappears and reappears, first in prison, then in his own room (Kourani 2000, pp. 51–55). In explaining a disappearance, Kourani refers to precedence in Islamic history:

> This story [Khomeini's disappearance and reappearance in his room] in the lives of *Awlia'* [Muslim saints], is generally explained [by scholars] as the

extraordinary transfer to another place deep inside the earth for a mission he wants... and it could be explained by the ability to disappear for a meeting that should not be exposed. (Kourani 2000, p. 55)

Meetings between Supreme Leader and Imam Mahdi are only informally suggested in this passage and others, probably on account of being difficult to prove or sustain.[32] A story on Imam Khomeini's importance for Imam Mahdi, the hidden Twelfth Imam, presents the former as a commander or agent of the second, saying "yes, sir" and "I accomplished this work", or "I will accomplish it by the will of God" (Kourani 2000, p. 78).[33]

In the section on manifestations of miracles, Khomeini's miracles are similar to the pre-Muhamed prophets, such as Moses and Jesus. The Ayatollah stopped for night prayers on a desert road, where "there was no water, but suddenly, we noticed the flow of a water fountain, so the Imam raised his sleeves and washed for prayers [*wodo'*]" (Kourani 2000, pp. 56–57). In these stories, Khomeini cures terminal diseases and serious injuries—for example, he cures a man who has partially lost his sight after he was hit by shrapnel. Khomeini's presence, however, is not a prerequisite for miracles:

> One of my friends, loyal to Imam Khomeini, told me that a relative of his was suffering from an illness that doctors failed to treat. He succeeded, through a revolutionary guard whose mission was guarding the Imam's house, in getting a glass of water that Imam Khomeini partially drank from. After drinking the remaining water, the patient was cured in a miraculous way. (Kourani 2000, p. 96)[34]

The major political consequence of narrating and propagating stories of Khomeini's connection to the Twelfth Imam and his supernatural abilities is enforcing the belief in the *Walī al-Faqih* as a manifestation of divine authority. The authority and decisions of Khomeini, or his predecessors, are by default connected to Imam Mahdi's will. There are also subtle implications that Khomeini's successor, Ayatollah Khamenei, possesses similar powers pertaining to his role as the Twelfth Imam's deputy.[35]

5.3.6 The 'Miracles' of Iran's War

The propagation of the Twelfth Imam's 'miracles' included the endeavours of the 1980–1988 war between Iran and Iraq: the 'miracles' of the

Islamic Revolution in the Iran–Iraq War were simultaneously propagated in Lebanon and Iran. The stories of miracles during the war were disseminated simultaneously with those of Lebanon's 2006 War. The experience of the Iranian volunteers, *basij-e mustazefan,* and the Guardian Corps, *sepah-e pasdaran enqelab-e Eslami,* was rich with stories of "inexplicable mystical proximity" to both Allah and the Shiʿi Imams (Rahnema 2011, p. 47). In particular, numerous accounts circulated of the presence of the hidden Imam on the battlefield, dubbed the 'land of light' (Rahnema 2011, p. 47). Mesbah Yazdi, the former Iranian president's spiritual leader, demanded acknowledgement of miraculous happenings, such as those attributed to the battle of Khorramshahr during the Iran–Iraq War (Rahnema 2011, p. 49).

The martyrdom literature on the Iran–Iraq War was translated into Arabic and is still sold in Hizbullah-affiliated bookstores and publishing houses such as *Dar Al-Mahaja Al-Baidaʾ*.[36] The same publishing house, mentioned in the second chapter, among a number of other Hizbullah-subsidised publishing houses, printed accounts of the supernatural occurrences during the party's 2006 conflict with Israel. The stories of martyrs include either direct divine intervention or subtle hints at such happenings.

While there are indirect links between Hizbullah and Al-Zubaidy's books on the 2006 war with Israel, the literature on Iran's 'martyrs' is directly state-sponsored. The books, in a series called *Sadat Al-Qafila* (*Masters of the Caravan*), include statements by Ayatollahs Khamenei and Khomeini on the martyrs' qualities, and, in one instance, the former, current supreme leader of the Islamic republic of Iran, a war veteran himself, read the stories and wrote a short introduction to the book (ʿAkef et al. 2014, pp. 7–10). Khamenei draws a direct link between martyrdom and miracles:

> Peace be upon you, the guardians of Allah, and his beloved ones, peace be upon you the supporters of Allah's religion and the agents of his custodian… The verses of Allah, the miracles of faith, the evidence of the sublimity of the immortal human… the compelling proof against the short-sighted who consider that the divine ascension of humans is impossible in the age of dominant materialism. (ʿAkef et al. 2014, p. 9)

Martyrdom is eternal happiness, Khomeini writes in one of the series' books, using a quote by ʿAli Bin Abi Taleb, the first and most significant Imam in Shi'i theology, in which he compares his love for death to a baby's attachment to its mother's breast ('Akef et al. 2014, p. 13). As The Shi'a (followers) of Imam Ali, "if we fear death, this means we do not believe in the supernatural" ('Akef et al. 2014, p. 29). Thus, fear is not only a sign of disbelief, but also "the whispers of *Shaitan* [Satan]" ('Akef et al. 2014, p. 30). These whispers emerge in another context—that of questioning the result, and the price, of these sacrifices during war in a utilitarian or 'materialistic' fashion. These questions bear, either knowingly or unknowingly, an underlying "ignorance in the worlds of the unseen worlds (*'awalem al-ghayb*) and the philosophy of martyrdom, since the incidents of [the worldly] age—*al dahr*—cannot undermine the [martyr's] perpetuity, existence and his high stature" ('Akef et al. 2014, p. 43).

For Khomeini, the right perception of martyrdom, as a path to happiness and immortality, was the recipe for victory in the Iran–Iraq War:

> We contributed martyrs, but our martyrs are alive, alive and well, and immortal. We ask Allah to reward us with martyrdom, for it is the trouble of a moment and the happiness of an eternity, a momentary pain, followed by eternal happiness, absolute happiness… [O]ur youth considered martyrdom happiness, and there lied the secret of victory. ('Akef et al. 2014, p. 13)

The victory was also a result of an Islamic transformation from a 'carnal person' to one who 'adores love'; in an act of kindness and mercy, Islam, Khomeini writes, "created all this transformation" in this "oppressed people", so the "person who was used to frequenting places of fornication, was transformed into a *mujahid*" ('Akef et al. 2014, p. 42). The transformation itself is also a miracle, Khomeini notes, since "now many of our Revolutionary Guards and armed forces' young, even merchants and craftsmen, ask me to pray that they acquire martyrdom"; such a "revolutionary spirit" is a "divine miracle" simply because "humans are incapable of transforming a people in this form, and there must be supernatural factors" ('Akef et al. 2014, p. 45). These translated works entail two supernatural claims, relating firstly to the Supreme Leader's connection to the divine and his supernatural qualities and secondly to the belief that the ultimate sacrifice, in the form of martyrdom, paves the way for the faithful to experience such divine powers.

Khomeini's determinism concerning victory—that victory is inevitable for the faithful—is reminiscent of the concept of 'covenant' in nationalism, in which the community's members fulfil certain ritual and moral obligations that "define their sacred mission" in return for God's "special status, protection and privilege" (Smith 1996, p. 587). This covenant, in the case of the Islamic Republic and Hizbullah, entails an agreement to sacrifice oneself in holy wars, in return for eternal salvation; this "deep well-spring of energy" endows the community with the determination and moral fibre to endure hardships (Smith 1996, p. 587). Smith notes:

> In order to mobilize a large numbers of people, leaders and movements need to appeal to either material and status interests or promise individual salvation, or both. For many, status interests at least are served by a promise of individual and collective salvation. Now salvation in turn requires men and women to sanctify their lives and situations through correct belief and practice on the part of each member of a community of believers, and through the periodic ritual and moral renewal of that community. (Smith 1996, p. 586)

5.3.6.1 Martyrdom Is Victory

While Khomeini's theory of martyrdom leaves room for rebranding a military defeat as a spiritual triumph, a clear victory, such as the Islamic Revolution in 1979 and Iran's advance in 1982, could only be a result of divine intervention:

> We won with the strength of faith, since the call of all of our people's categories was the call of Islam, and we did not win with numbers and weapons since we had nothing, and they possessed everything. But we were armed with the weapon of *iman* [faith], and our people wished for martyrdom, just like the Prophet's companions during the early times of Islam. As they won against great empires with small numbers, we won also with small numbers and without weapons against a 2500-year-old titan empire, backed by the great powers, and we eliminated this great dam from our people's way. (*Akef et al.* 2014, p. 45)

Unlike ethnic and secular nationalism, where such unbalanced victories are often attributed to racial or genetic elements, Iran and Hizbullah's victories are a result of supernatural or unseen intervention, resulting from piousness and the longing for *shahada* (martyrdom). Khomeini explains that this piousness and willingness to sacrifice leads to victory, drawing subtle parallels to the Prophet's victory in *Badr*, where the Qur'an claims divine intervention through combatant angels.[37]

5.3.6.2 Extraordinary Beginnings

The story of a 'martyr' begins with signs of early piousness, and is accompanied by the parents' pride and sacrifice, making indirect references to the Qur'anic tale of Abraham and the sacrifice of Imam Husayn in the battle of Karbala. Martyrs are brave in the face of injustice, and their altruistic features are extraordinary.[38] The story of Abbass Karimi, the commander of the important Mohamad Rasoul-Allah division, who died during the Iran–Iraq War, begins with his father praying at Abul Fadl Al-Abbas's grave that his newborn will survive[39]:

> Abul Fadl Al'Abas! Please do not let this child die like his brother died before… My master, I came from a very faraway land, so that you answer my request, don't let me return home disappointed… If my newborn is a boy, I will call him after your blessed name: Abbas. ('Akef 2014, p. 11)

Months after his father's visit to Abul Fadl's grave, Abbas Karimi was born; his mother, without knowing of her husband's *neder* (religious pledge), suggested calling the boy Abbas, and the startled father accepted ('Akef 2014, p. 11). The story's narrator intervenes to state: "It is not nonsense to say that the biographies of the Earth's greatest humans are similar, in one way or the other" ('Akef 2014, p. 12).

5.3.6.3 Miracles on the Battlefield

The literature of the Iran–Iraq War is less direct and more suggestive when discussing miracles than the Hizbullah-affiliated literature on the 2006 conflict, which includes sightings of supernatural events and Imam Mahdi's interventions against aircraft and rockets.[40] In the story of Kawa, the young Iranian commander who miraculously survived numerous bullets fired at him from different angles, according to a fellow fighter:

> I thought I was in a dream, as Kawa ran fast on the road while enemies rained bullets on him… none reached him. I cannot say anything about that except that it was divine kindness and protection. At every moment, we waited for him to fall on the ground after receiving a bullet injury; it seemed to us that the enemy troops used all their weapons to stop him. (Sadouki and 'Akef 2012, p. 46)

In Karimi's story, a military incident is introduced as "one of the divine miracles that led to victory in the operations of *Al-Fath Al Mobeen*". In a reconnaissance mission, Karimi forgot cans of fruit and could not retrieve them, so "we counted on Allah". Hours later, a brigade was lost and found its way only by spotting the forgotten cans ('Akef and Fakour 2014, p. 145). The latter story is more typical of Iranian war tales, in which coincidence or good luck is attributed to divine or supernatural factors, rather than relating direct supernatural occurrences, such as Hizbullah's literature on its 2006 war, examined in the following section.

5.3.7 The 2006 War

Following the 2006 war in Lebanon, Hizbullah-affiliated publishing houses disseminated superstitious books, claiming miracles on the battlefield, and a connection between the party and the hidden Twelfth Imam. Ahmadinejad's own statements on miracles also spurred on the production of Lebanon-based superstitious literature, such as Shadi Fakih's *"Ahmadinejad wal-thawra al Moqbila"* (*Ahmadinejad and the Upcoming Global Revolution*). Majed Nasser Al-Zubaidi's book, *Karamat Al-Wa'd Al-Sadeq* (*Miracles of the True Promise*), published in 2008 by a Hizbullah-affiliated publishing house, serialises the miracles encountered by both Hizbullah's fighters and the Israeli occupation. The book was a bestseller, reaching its 12th edition in just a few years.[41] The author, Al-Zubaidi, claims that his superstitious account of the 2006 war between Hizbullah and Israel was a result of research and first-hand accounts:

> After a long research, reading newspapers, and meeting a number of the Islamic Resistance's *Mujahideen*, I realized that Allah, when he saw their faith in him and in their cause, has supported them against their enemy. Allah supplied them with his Angels and *Awlia* to tell the Israelis that Allah is the undefeatable, and that you're not the undefeatable army, as you claim. So take this Godly strike so that your faces are blackened in life and eternity. (Al-Zubaidy 2008, p. 8)

Al-Zubaidi's first chapter is a "comparison between Badr Al Kubra and Al Wa'd Al Sadeq", the first being Islam's first battle between Muslims, led by the Prophet Mohamed, and his 'apostate' foes from Mecca; the second is Hizbullah's 2006 conflict with Israel (Al-Zubaidy 2008, p. 11). In the ancient Islamic battle, according to the Qur'an and *hadith*, 'angels' fought alongside the Muslims, leading to the defeat of their enemies. A long and detailed comparative chart displays the many common features between the two battles, in spite of the 1,400-year difference (Al-Zubaidy 2008, p. 117). In 35 rows, the two-column chart traces the chronology of the Mohamed's battle and Hizbullah's 2006 conflict with Israel, in an attempt to prove the latter echoed the former—for instance, the first historical analogy in the chart lists the buildup to both battles: "*Almushrikoon* [the Apostates] acted immorally by torturing Moslems and the Prophet's companions before the battle of *Badr*. The Israeli enemy violated Lebanon's air sovereignty-these are considered immoral because they constitute a violation of people's rights—before *al-waʾd al-sadeq*" (Al-Zubaidy 2008, p. 117).

These sorts of analogies were sometimes direct, as in the ninth row. "The goal of Quraish was to kill the Prophet, and destroy Islam and Muslims", while "Israel's goal was to kill Seyyed Hassan Nasrallah, and destroy Hizbullah and its members" (Al-Zubaidy 2008, p. 118). In the 22nd row, superstition steps in: rather than present an obscure superstitious incident, with subtle references, as in the case of Ahmadinejad's halo of light, the book draws a direct analogy with divine intervention in the Prophet Mohamed's first victorious battle against the 'infidels', as recorded in the Qurʾan and widely accepted among Muslims from all sects. In the battle of Badr, "Muslims were supported by *Malaiʾka* (angels) to achieve victory", while in Hizbullah's 2006 battle, "Hizbullah's fighters were joined by *Malaiʾka* (angels) to achieve victory" (Al-Zubaidy 2008, p. 120). These 'warrior angels' in the battle of Badr were mentioned in the Qurʾan, and are widely acknowledged as a pillar of Muslim faith: "Remember when you sought help of your Lord and He answered you saying, 'I will help you with a thousand Angels each behind the other in succession'" (*Soorah Al-Anfal* (8) p. 9). The Prophet Mohamed and Nasrallah, Hizbullah's secretary general, are placed on a par, as a subtle hint that both have supernatural backing and authority as representatives of Allah (*Soorah al-Anfal* (8) pp. 120–121).

In another book, similar comparisons are drawn, albeit between the 'martyrs' of Hizbullah and the *Junud Allah* (soldiers of God) (Al-Zubaidy 2007, p. 15). *Junud Allah*, mentioned in verse in the Qurʾan's *Al-Fath sura*, are "angels, *jin*, human beings, and devils, as reported by Ibn Abass"[42] (Al-Zubaidy 2007, p. 9). Al Zubaidi described *al-jund* as a group of soldiers who follow their emir's orders: they are Allah's soldiers through whom He can realise his vengeance on the *kafereen* or infidels (Al-Zubaidy 2007, p. 10). After providing the religious framework to understanding the miracles of *Al Waʾd Al Sadeq*, the author narrates the book's stories, with little corroboration, even exceeding the supernatural incidents attributed to the battle of Badr. The documentation of these supernatural sightings during the battle mirrors the Qur'anic verse on Badr. The first story is about a group of Hizbullah fighters, one of whom is presented as the narrator, who went to an inhabited mountain cave, asking for water (Al-Zubaidy 2008, p. 125). The woman who lived there started bringing a large number of water jars and bottles, until a fighter asked her "for whom are you bringing all this water, *hajje*? This is too much, and may Allah reward you". The question startled her, and she "apologised for not having enough water to quench the thirst of the army behind us" (Al-Zubaidy 2008, p. 126). The unnamed Hizbullah fighter allegedly told the author: "This woman saw a large number of fatigued men behind us, they were Allah's angels sent to support us. We started looking both strangely and gladly at each other, while our bodies trembled, skin burned and eyes wept" (Al-Zubaidy 2008, p. 126).

Some stories are non-human, involving machines, which aid the warriors against their enemies, as in the story of a fighter in Bint Jbeil, who was surprised that his mortar continued to shell enemy position even after he left it unmanned:

> He [the Hizbullah fighter] left the area—after launching all the rockets in his possession against the Israelis—to preserve his life, and he had a communication device to contact his leadership… [A]fter leaving the area, his seniors called to bless and congratulate him over continuous mortar bombings against the enemy, and inflicting severe injuries or losses… He informed them the he left the area an hour ago without any direct hits, while running out of rockets. They told him: What are you saying? Rockets continue to strike the enemy. (Al-Zubaidy 2008, pp. 127–128)

The Hizbullah fighter, perplexed, returns to the area, only to find "the mortar launching rockets by itself, alongside 350 shells" (Al-Zubaidy 2008, p. 128).[43]

The book includes stories on primitive weapons and tools, such as white horses and swords, which usually evoke association with historic holy Islamic battles such as Badr and Ohod.[44] In one story, the author narrates in the first person:

> I asked one of the Islamic resistance fighters in Hizbullah in Lebanon about the strangest thing that occurred with him, or that he witnessed, and is eye-catching,[45] leads [one] to wonder and feel reassured. He told me: We were

in the Bint Jbeil area trying to hide ourselves from the Israeli bombing that was following us from one place to the other, so we entered some houses to hide from the Israeli landing, to be well prepared to meet it, so we saw numerous [riderless] white horses. I asked him: What were these horses doing, were they standing or running? He said: I saw them running continuously towards the Israeli enemy. (Al-Zubaidy 2008, p. 131)

The stories show a general lack of research, and, at times, basic understanding of South Lebanon's geography: for instance, Al-Zubaidi writes about a group of fighters who cannot swim, but were miraculously able to cross a deep river, "feeling carried by someone" (Al-Zubaidy 2008, p. 132). Rivers in South Lebanon are generally shallow, and do not feature such depth. These 2006 visions and miracles became a generally accepted phenomenon among many of Hizbullah's religious supporters.[46]

In his other book on Hizbullah's 2006 'divine victory', Al-Zubaidi divides the 2006 warring lines into *rejal Allah* (Men of God), referring to Hizbullah's fighters, and *rejal Iblis* (Men of Satan), the Israeli soldiers (Al-Zubaidy 2007, p. 7, 36). The men of Hizbullah, being *rejal Allah*, embody 'righteousness', while their enemies embody *albatel*, meaning falsehood or viciousness (Al-Zubaidi 2007, p. 27). Al-Zubaidi faces a crucial issue, namely, that the term *rejal Allah* was not mentioned in the Qurʾan, which uses instead the more inclusive term *junud Allah* (soldiers of God) (Al-Zubaidi 2007, p. 7). *Junud Allah*, according to the Qurʾan and *hadith*, includes non-human combatants, such as floods, frogs, lice, locusts, and blood (Al-Zubaidi 2007, pp. 20–21). Since Hizbullah resistance represents the different themes of combat from the Qurʾan, the organisation shares in the supernatural possibilities. In a deterministic approach, Al-Zubaidi explains why victory is the faithful's right, referring to the following Qurʾanic verse:

> And indeed we did send Messengers before you [Muhamed] to their own peoples. They came to them with clear proofs. Then, we took vengeance on those who committed crimes [of disbelief, sins, etc.], and [as for] the believers it was incumbent upon us to help [them]. (*alroom* 47)

Al-Zubaidi makes the case for the verse's application to the war with Israel, asking "where there is a more criminal entity than Israel that kills children, women, the elderly without a reason... so Allah avenged them in this battle, the battle of Wa'd Al-Sadeq" (Al-Zubaidi 2007, p. 95).

Superstitious belief in *Wilayat al-Faqih* is linked to its perceived connection to the Twelfth Imam, the heart of Shiʿi belief. While it relates to the Iranian leadership in its general concept, Hizbullah's hierarchy also benefits, as its leaders claim to represent the Supreme Leader's will, through their pronounced allegiance to the doctrine. This connection was reinforced either through the books of the ayatollahs, especially Khomeini and Mesbah Yazdi, or through informal indoctrination, through which the *Wālī al-Faqih* is referred to as *Nae'b al-Imam*, meaning the Twelfth Imam's deputy. Nasrallah makes a clear case for obeying the *Wālī al-Faqih* in a speech during the commemoration of '*Ashura*', in which a comparison is drawn with the imams and prophets:

> Brothers and Sisters, we and all Moslems have a *Waliy Amr* [Guardian], and if the majority of Moslems does not want to obey him, that would be their problem, and before many did not obey the Prophet or the infallible Imam, but this did not mean that the Imam was not an Imam or that the Prophet was not a Prophet. We have a *Waliy Amr* who is the deputy of Imam Mahdi, and his obedience is a requirement, and we experienced this *Waliy* and leader, in his purity, attributes, piety, and at the same time in his courage, providence, wisdom, consciousness. (Nasrallah 2000, p. 61)

In the same speech, Nasrallah attempts to make a case for Khamenei as a person, drawing on the Hizbullah leader's own experience and credibility:

> He [Khamenei] challenges the US, the European Union, and the fleets that fill the Gulf. Allah has blessed us with a *Waliy Amr* who is a unique man and exceptional personality. If we searched all of our Islamic countries and *hawzas* [clerical schools], we will not find a Shiʿi *faqih* [a senior cleric] who combines [addressing] the crowd and this level of sophistication as exists in the leader Imam Khamenei, May Allah protect him.

5.4 Conclusion

Hizbullah's production of supernatural narratives about its hierarchy and *jihad* or resistance is a process that deploys transnational links as leverage in establishing a direct connection with the divine. The translations of the Iranian accounts of the Iran–Iraq War, which describe supernatural occurrences and exemplary 'martyrs', paved the way for literature on miraculous happenings during Hizbullah's wars, based on Iranian precedent. In both cases, the revival of Majlesism as a theological tradition in the literature produced by Hizbullah-affiliated publishing houses has laid the ground for the production of supernatural narratives. Majlesi's supernatural stories purposefully sanctified the ruling Safavid Shahs and justified their war with the Ottoman Empire. Such uses of supernatural narratives to bestow legitimacy on rulers and their conflicts are an ancient practice. However, the current means of deploying these narratives in various forms, disseminating them on a mass scale and portraying them as a fundamental part of Shi'i identity, are modern.

Engaging an informal network of affiliated intellectual brokers in propagating these accounts helps distance the formal organisation from appearing in the cloak of self-promotion, which is condemned in Islam, where it is termed as the sin of *ria'*. However, Hizbullah's superstition is gradual, commencing with the *karamat* of the Imams, up to their legitimate representatives today as manifested in *Wilayat al-Faqih,* and the fighters under the hierarchy's command. The leadership has a special or hidden connection to the divine, while at the level of the lower ranks, warriors encounter selective sightings or miracles. Both the general and specific superstitions, whether propagating stories of Imam Mahdi's miracles and appearances, or miracles involving Hizbullah, play a complementary role. General superstition could arguably nurture a less questioning base of followers, while sanctifying Hizbullah's two ideological pillars: *Wilayat Al-Faqih* and *jihad* (resistance).

Notes

1. Reformists generally argue that Islam's major miracle lies within the Qur'an.
2. Mainstream religious institutions such as al-Azhar in Egypt or the Shi'i Najaf and Qum Hawzas, established clerical schools, tend to be conservative in dealing with supernatural beliefs.
3. In the Muslim *Shahadatain*, the basic tenet of Islam, the believer says: "I testify that none has the right to be worshipped but Allah, and I testify that Muhammad is The Messenger of Allah." Often, in the second part, Muslims add "and the Prophet is his worshipper and messenger (*'Abdaho Wa Rasulah*).
4. Miracles and supernatural occurrences are common beliefs in the Sufi tradition.
5. David Hume, the English philosopher, acknowledged the powerful effect of superstition. Superstition results "from weakness, fear, melancholy,

together with ignorance", enforcing "priestly powers" (Rahnema 2011, p. 31). On an individual level, psychoanalysis contributes to the understanding of the effects or consequences of faith in the supernatural. Freud, in agreement with Spinoza, considered belief in the supernatural a hindrance to freedom and obtaining knowledge. Religion, through indoctrinating people to believe in an illusion and prohibiting critical thinking, bears responsibility for the impoverishment of intelligence (Fromm 1950, p. 12). The belief in the illusion of a fatherly God hinders human development; avoiding reality is an infantile fixation: "Only the free man who has emancipated himself from authority –authority that threatens and protects—can make use of his power of reason and grasp the world and his role in it objectively, without illusion but also with the ability to develop and to make use of the capacities inherent to him" (Fromm 1950, p. 13).
6. Chakrabarty, writing on superstition and politics in India, considers its deployment effective among people due to the popular association between the supernatural and increasing 'life chances', pertaining to economic and living conditions: "They are always worldly: we expect miracle-making powers to intercede in the competition that is life, to enhance our chances for success or survival in whatever is the competitive exercise we are engaged in. The matter at hand could be related to politics, battles, jobs, games, fame and recognition, and so on" (Chakrabarty 2008, p. 17).
7. In another version of the letter's translation, by Donna Torr-International Publishers (1968), the last sentence fragment reads, "which is now very serviceable for making the masses stupid". The meaning remains equivalent as to numbing the masses.
8. Attempts to reconcile Marxist ideology with Shi'ite Islam resulted in the formation of Mojahedin-e-Khalq (The People's Mojahedin of Iran or MEK) in 1965. However, the group later witnessed the defections of those who believed Marxism could not be reconciled with Islam, and should be adopted separately.
9. Among the responses to the Marxist critique or rather condemnation of religion as a pacifying tool for the bourgeoisie, is the reference to the ideology's comprehensive worldview, and particularly its wish to replace religion. Schumpeter notes: "Marxism is a religion. To the believer it presents, first, a system of ultimate ends that embody the meaning of life and are absolute standards by which to judge events and actions; and secondly a guide to those ends which implies a plan of salvation and the indication of the evil from which mankind, or a chosen section of mankind, is to be saved" (McLellan 1987, p. 158).
10. Tensions arose between the reformed clerical establishment and superstition, regarding the lack of miracles by the Prophet. It is generally accepted that Mohamed's only public or witnessed miracle was the Qur'an, because of the fact that he was an illiterate orphan.

11. ʿIssa is the Arabic name for Jesus Christ.
12. The Qurʾan recorded another two un-witnessed miracles: the battle of Badr, in which unseen angels joined the fight, and the Prophet Mohammed's *buraq* (camel) flight from Mecca to Jerusalem, known in Islam as *al-Israʾ wa al-Miʾraj*. Both miracles were unseen, hidden, except from the Prophet himself.
13. Shariati highlights these concerns over the political consequences of supernatural narratives.
14. The Interregnum started with the execution of Charles I on 30 January 1649 and ended with the arrival of his son Charles II in London on 29 May 1660. The son's return marked the start of the Restoration.
15. The clergy's exploitation of popular superstition is similar to the Marxist theory on the deployment of religion and spirituality as an opiate for the masses in the class struggle. As soon as English and French materialists—bourgeois intellectuals—achieved dominance over the reactionary feudal and religious outlook, they "renounced their former free-thinking and began to make use of religion as an opiate for the popular masses" (Marx and Engels 1975, pp. 9–10). The belief that only Marxism can expose the essence of religion was at the heart of Marx's and Engel's critique of the French and English nineteenth-century atheists. Religion was merely "the fantastic reflection in men's minds of those external forces which control their daily life [pertaining to class relations], a reflection in which the terrestrial forces assume the form of supernatural forces" (Marx and Engels 1975, p. 128).
16. Shariʿati's main concern was not facing Majlesi's superstition, but his alleged legacy of utilising religion to fortify the ruler's position. By this token, the shah's supporters among the clerical class in Iran were Majlesi's heirs.
17. In Shiʿi Islam, *Hadith* is the body of sayings by the prophet and the Twelve Imams.
18. Books on the medicine of the Twelve Shiʿi Imams are available for sale on the shelves of Hizbullah-affiliated bookshops in the southern suburbs of Beirut, and in different Shiʿi areas across Lebanon.
19. The coupling of Shiʿi Islam and Persian identity is present in Hizbullah's informal indoctrination of its members.
20. Shariʾati wrote his book on Alawite Shiʿism and Safavid Shiʿism in 1971, but the Arabic translation was published in 2002.
21. *Zainul Abedeen* is Arabic for the 'Ornament of Worshippers'. He was ill when his father Imam Hussein, along with other members of the Prophet Mohamed's household, travelled to Iraq to revolt against Umayyad rule.
22. The colour green is generally favourable in Islam, and is mentioned many times in the Qurʾan, where it is associated with the inhabitants of *Janna* or Heaven.
23. 'Murtadawi' usually denotes the Shiʿite Twelve Imams, starting with the First Imam, Ali Ben Abi Taleb, the Prophet's cousin and son-in-law.

24. Majlesi's effect encompassed many parts of the Shi'i world, including Lebanon, where his books, especially *Helyat Al-Motaqeen,* are widespread.
25. *Helyat Al-Motaqeen* was available in every bookstore visited during fieldwork for this research in Beirut's southern suburbs, Hizbullah's stronghold.
26. In the case of Mohammad-Reza Pahlavi, the last Iranian shah, he continued to defend his divine claims to the very end, insisting after his toppling in 1979 that the revolutionaries, mostly Islamic, "were not real Shi'ite Moslems but a combination of black reactionary forces [his clerical opponents] and atheist foot soldiers of international communism" (Rahnema 2011, p. 23).
27. These divine rays are often used as a sign of the presence and approval of the Twelfth Imam, Mahdi Ben Al-Hassan, the Prophet's household descendent and 'saviour' of the end of times.
28. In the organisation's literature, the Twelfth Imam is referred to as *al-Hujja* and *Baqiatullah*. The first term is literally translated as 'argument'; however, it means more the proof or verification of Allah, while the second is the residue or remaining part of Allah on Earth.
29. The case for meetings with Imam Mahdi could have subtle references to *Welayat al-Faqih*. During my fieldwork, one interviewee, a Hizbullah student, recalled that the sheikh referred to meetings between the Imam and his deputy, *Waliy Al-Faqih*, Ayatollah Ali Khamenei, during which witnesses outside saw rays of light emanating from the door.
30. For instance, al-Zubaidy's book on the supernatural occurrences during the July 2006 War was the "best selling on record", according to the publishing house, Dar Al-Mahaja Al-Baida, reaching its 12th edition.
31. The story is narrated by one of Khomeini's companions, Hojatalislam Abdul Ali Qurhi, also a Shi'i clergyman.
32. The *karamat* miracles, as defined earlier, are random and unchallenging in their nature, relieving the claimant of demands for further proof.
33. The story is of a man who doubted Imam Khomeini, but then had a vision in his dream of a meeting between the Ayatollah and the Twelfth Shi'i Imam. The story sees him and his whole family crying over the vision, and he retracts his old position. Such a story is reminiscent of repentance stories—numerous in Islam—concerning the Prophet's doubters who change sides following a dramatic, often miraculous, experience.
34. The editor of Kourani's book wrote after this story that such an event "could not be ruled out" as the history of Imam Khomeini "is full of such things, and among his greatest *karamat* is his foretelling in the first years of the revolution's victory, of the future of the Iranian regime and the world surrounding it... and of course this news would only come out from a godly human (*insan rabani*) who would see with God's eyes" (Kourani 2000, p. 96).
35. Khomeini's pioneering role in the revolution, in addition to his prominent publications on Islam and politics, spirituality, and his *marje'* capacity, render him more significant than his successor and former subordinate.

36. *Dar Al-Mahaja Al-Baida'* publishing house is based in Beer El-Abed, the southern suburbs of Beirut.
37. Combatant angels also appear in the Spanish paintings of the imperial war against the Moors, the Muslims of Andalusia. This is typical of religiously inspired conflicts, including Sunni Islamists. Islamic State, for instance, placed extreme importance on the town of Dabiq in northern Syria, mentioned as significant to Doomsday in one of the Prophet's *Hadith*. The significance was clear in the way the organisation used the name for its English-language magazine. These indirect links are common.
38. The martyrs' cult is present in other contexts. In modern secular and ethnic nationalism, as in religious nationalism, the stories of martyrs are reproduced as exemplary models to emulate (Hung 2008, p. 280). In a policy similar to that adopted later in Iran's Islamic Republic and Lebanon's Hizbullah, the Chinese Communist Party systematically constructed martyrs' stories and images, years after the first commemoration of Chinese martyrs, "the exceptional descendants of China" (Hung 2008, p. 279). The government created the 'Cult of the Red Martyr', as Hung names it, through printed materials and mass-media propaganda. The influential *Biographies of the Chinese Communist Martyrs*, published two months after the founding of the PRC, bears similarities with the series of translated books on the martyrs of the Iran–Iraq War, namely, in the exceptional beginnings and ultimate sacrifice of these exemplary individuals. However, the Chinese approach lacks the subtle and direct superstitious elements of the Islamic martyrs.
39. Abul Fadl was Imam Hussein's half-brother.
40. One possible reason for the direct narratives in Hizbullah's literature is that the Iranian literature provided a precursor for such occurrences. Secondly, unlike the prolonged Iran–Iraq War, the organisation's resilience against Israeli aggression throughout the short war was surprising to many, providing a strong alibi for the emergence of such supernatural narratives.
41. Dar Al-Mahaja, the book's publishing house, is known to be affiliated with Hizbullah, and operates from Beirut's southern suburbs, the party's tightly controlled operational base.
42. The *jin* is a third type of conscious being, alongside humans and angels. They live in a third world, and are not visible to humans.
43. The book quotes the same fighter featured in the story, saying that a mortar "was seen launching rockets by itself in the area of Teir Harfa" (Al-Zubaidy 2008, p. 128).
44. Badr and Ohod are the two major battles of the Islamic army during the Prophet Mohamed's time; he won in the former and lost in the latter.
45. The literal translation is interesting, but 'eye-catching' better captures the meaning.
46. Among dozens of supporters and Hezbollah activists I have met, there has been a general acceptance of these miracles. The sightings of Imam Mahdi are the most common.

References

Books

Abun-Nasr, J. M. (1987). *A History of the Maghrib in the Islamic Period*. Cambridge: Cambridge University Press.

ʿAkef, S., & Fakour, A. (2014). *Hajar Tantather* (Hajar Waits). Beirut: Jamʿiat Al-Maʿaref Al-Islamiya Al-Thakafia.

Al-Nasseri, A. (2009). *Nisaʾ Taltaqi Saheb Al-Zaman* (Women Meet Imam Mahdi). Beirut: Dar Al-Mahaja Al-Baidaʾ.

Al-Zubaidy, M. N. (2007). *Rejal Allah Wal Nasr Al Ilahi* (The Men of God and the Divine Victory). Beirut: Muʾassasat Al-Huda Al-Islamiya.

Al-Zubaidy, M. N. (2008). *Karamat Al-Waʿd Al-Sadeq* (The Miracles of the Honest Promise). Beirut: Dar Al-Mahaja Al-Baidaʾ.

De Tollenaere, H. (1996). *The Politics of Divine Wisdom: Theosophy and Labour, National, and Women's Movements in Indonesia and South Asia 1875–1947*. Nijmegen, The Netherlands: Katholieke Universiteit Nijmegen.

Drieskens, B. (2008). *Living with Djinns: Understanding and Dealing with the Invisible in Cairo*. London: Saqi Books.

Faqih, F. (2002). *Karamat Al-Imam Al-Mahdi* (The Miracles of Imam Mahdi). Beirut: Dar al-Mahaja al-Baydaʾ.

Fromm, E. (1950). *Psychoanalysis and Religion*. New Haven, Connecticut: Yale University Press.

Gilsenan, M. (1973). *Saint and Sufi in Modern Egypt: An Essay in the Sociology of Religion*. Oxford: Clarendon Press.

Hijazi, H. (2006). *Istaʿidu fa Inn Al-Zuhor Qarib* (Be Ready, the Appearance Is Soon). Beirut: Dar Al-Mahaja Al-Baidaʾ.

Hodgson, M. G. S. (1974). *The Venture of Islam: The Gunpowder Empires and Modern Times*. Chicago: University of Chicago Press.

Holt, P. M. (1970). *The Mahdist State in the Sudan, 1881–1898: A Study of Its Origins, Development and Overthrow*. Oxford: Clarendon Press.

Hourani, A. (1991). *History of the Arab Peoples*. London: Faber and Faber.

Khomeini, R. (2011). *Al-Kalimat al-Qisar Lil Imam Al-Khomeini* (Imam Khomeini's Short Sayings). Beirut: Markaz Noon.

Kourani, H., & Al-Mahdi, M. M. (2000). *Al-Karamat Al-Ghaibiya Lil Imam Al-Khomeini* (The Unseen Miracles of Imam Khomeini). Beirut: Dar Al-Mahaja Al-Baidaʾ.

Lapidus, I. M. (1988). *A History of Islamic Societies*. Cambridge: Cambridge University Press.

Marx, K., & Engels, F. (1975). *On Religion*. Moscow: Progress Publishers.

McLellan, D. (1987). *Marxism and Religion*. London: Macmillan Press.

Moazzam, A. (1984). *Jamal ad-Din al-Afghani: A Muslim Intellectual*. New Delhi: Concept Publishing Company.

Nasrallah, H. (2000). *Khitab ʿAshuraʾ*. Beirut: Dar Al-Safwa.
Parish, H., & Naphy, W. (Eds.). (2002). *Religion and Superstition in Reformation Europe*. Manchester and New York: Manchester University Press.
Rahnema, A. (2011). *Superstition as Ideology in Iranian Politics: From Majlesi to Ahmadinejad*. Cambridge: Cambridge University Press.
Raines, J. (Ed.). (1998). *Marx on Religion*. Philadelphia: Temple University Press.
Sadouki, H., & ʿAkef, S. (2012). *Kawa, Muʿjizat Al Thawra*. Beirut: Jamʿiyat Al-Maʿaref Al-Islamiya Al-Thakafia.
Savory, R. (2007). *Iran Under the Safavids*. Cambridge: Cambridge University Press.
Thomas, K. (1971). *Religion and the Decline of Magic*. London: Penguin Books.

Journal Articles

Chakrabarty, D. (2008). The Power of Superstition in Public Life in India. *Economic and Political Weekly, 43*, 16–19.
Edgar, I. (2006). The 'True Dream' in Contemporary Islamic/Jihadist Dreamwork: A Case Study of the Dreams of Taliban Leader Mullah Omar. *Contemporary South Asia, 15*(3), 263–272.
Frankel, S. (1999). Politics and Rhetoric: The Intended Audience of Spinoza's "Tractatus Theologico-Politicus". *Review of Metaphysics, 52*(4), 897–924.
Hung, C.-t. (2008, April). The Cult of the Red Martyr: Politics of Commemoration in China. *Journal of Contemporary History, 43*(2), 279–304.
Loebenstein, J. (2003, April). Miracles in Šīʿī Thought: A Case-Study of the Miracles Attributed to Imām Ǧaʿfar al-Ṣādiq. *Arabica*, T. 50, Fasc. 2, 199–244.
Smith, A. (1996, December). The Resurgence of Nationalism? Myth and Memory in the Renewal of Nations. *The British Journal of Sociology, 47*(4), 575–598.
Terzić, F. (2009, Spring). The Problematic of Prophethood and Miracles: Muṣṭafā Ṣabrī's Response. *Islamic Studies, 48*(1), 5–33.
Yazicioglu, I. (2011). Redefining the Miraculous: Al-Ghazālī, Ibn Rushd and Said Nursi on Qur'anic Miracle Stories. *Journal of Qur'anic Studies., 13*(2), 86–108.

Links

Al-ʿAhd. (2013). Shaykh Qassem: Shuhada al-Wajeb al-Jihadi Hum Shuhada Almuqawama Dod Israel Wa Mashruʿaha (The Martyrs of the Jihadi Duty are Martyrs against Israel and its Project). *Al-ʿAhd News*, 21 May. Retrieved July 6, 2014, from https://goo.gl/PLAzsU
Engels, F. (1894). *On the History of Early Christianity*. Available at: https://www.marxists.org/archive/marx/works/1894/early-christianity/ (Accessed: 21 December, 2014)
Shariʿati, A. (1972). *Red Shiʿism: The Religion of Martyrdom; Black Shiʿism: The Religion of Mourning*. Retrieved May 4, 2015, from http://www.Shariati.com/english/redblack.html

CHAPTER 6

Transnational *Wilayat Al-Faqih*

This chapter explores the development of the *Wilayat al-Faqih* doctrine, transnational Shiʻi politics, and the export of the Islamic Revolution in Iran, and argues that this pillar of Hizbullah's identity is a modern development. To support this contention, the chapter demonstrates that the development of the Shiʻi clerical establishment into a powerful institution took place in the nineteenth century, when the advent of print technology helped consolidate its political power. This gradual process continued until Khomeini's formulation of *Wilayat al-Faqih* over two phases, under the influence of state reform. The chapter examines the transnational links shared by Hizbullah and Shiʻi groups in other countries in a comparative perspective, examining the tensions between the *Wilayat al-Faqih* and national politics, when and where it arises. Iranian national interests outplay the transnational links, especially in neighbouring countries, where a more inclusive approach is required, such as in the case of the Shiʻi Hazaras of Afghanistan. Such tensions between the national and transnational increase in Iran's neighbouring countries, where a foreign policy based on *realpolitik* outplays ideology, and transnational ideologies and doctrines take on national forms and identities, more suited for popular support.

The chapter argues that Hizbullah's leadership has been able to reconcile the tensions between the transnational and national, despite Tehran's considerable financial and political backing, as the relationship has not been put to a strong existential test, as it was in the case of the Hazaras. The organisation's lobbying efforts prove that its relationship with Iran is not as organic as it seems, since it needs to be nurtured. The clerical class in Iran, Iraq, and Lebanon faced very similar challenges throughout the 1950s and 1960s, ranging from the appeal of communist organisations to Shiʿi youth to the decomposition of the feudal system, a chief source of its revenues. While these simultaneous challenges in different national contexts require a coordinated transnational effort, the national conditions, discrepancies, and subsequent state response shaped Shiʿi ideology. The Lebanese consociational system, the weakness of the state, and the conflict with Israel added to the lack of need for Iranian *realpolitik* and set the ground for a relatively successful coexistence between the national and transnational.

6.1 The Clergy and the State

This section of the book traces the Shiʿi clerical establishment's development into its contemporary form, arguing that many of the traditions essential to the formulation of *Wilayat al-Faqih* were created in the nineteenth century, contrary to its adherents' claims of historical continuity. However, Twelver Shiʿism itself, in its current institutional form, *al—Marjaʿia*, is the product of a long historical process since the 'great occultation' of Imam Mahdi in 874 (Campo 2009, p. 72).[1] Originating from the great schism over appointing Prophet Mohamed's heir in 632, Shiʿism took the form of a 'legitimist' protest movement (Eickelman 2002, p. 256). Following the death of Ali, the fourth Muslim caliph, various protest movements were associated with Shiʿism, often termed proto-Shiʿism; some of these movements, like the Zaïdis, established sects separate from the mainstream Twelver Shiʿism, known in Arabic as ʾ*Ithna ʿAshari*. Here, however, the term Shiʿi will refer to the numerically dominant Twelver Shiʿism. The Shiʿa believe that ʿAli Ben Abi Taleb, the Prophet's cousin and son-in-law, was not only the legitimate heir, but also the first in the line of a dozen infallible Imams.[2] The Imams ʿAli and his eleven descendants are the legitimate leaders in their respective eras, and their sayings are equivalent to the Prophet's *hadith*.[3] Following the death of eleven Imams, and a seven-decade period of short occultation of the last Imam, jurisprudence started taking shape in mainstream Shiʿism. Although both continued to develop, often inspired by political changes and needs, Sunni jurisdiction preceded that of Shiʿism.

As charismatic holy headers, the 'infallible' Imams' presence rendered Shiʿi jurisprudence unnecessary; however, this changed drastically with the Twelfth Imam's greater occultation in 874, as the political upheavals of the time required leadership and guidance. In the smaller occultation, known as *al-Ghayba al-Soghra*, Imam Mohammad Ben al-Hassan al-ʿAskari, the Twelfth Shiʿi Imam, also known as *al-Mahdī al-Muntazar* and *al-Imam al-Hujja*, disappeared. According to Twelver Shiʿi belief, the last Imam maintained contact with his community of followers for nearly seven decades through four ambassadors. In the subsequent greater occultation, the Shiʿi community developed its rules of faith over centuries, leading to the establishment of *marjaʿiya* and *taqlid* in the nineteenth century. However, this developmental process was entangled with politics, as the early jurisprudents were "theoretically far more constricted than those of the Sunnis"; they favoured judgement through syllogism rather than analogy (Cole 1981, p. 36).

The rise of the Safavid Empire in the sixteenth century brought more power and independence to the Shiʿi clergy. To help spread this dissident faith among the Sunni majority in their realm, the Safavid shahs imported Shiʿi clergy from Jabal ʿAmil. However, the pact with the Safavid dynasty endowed the clerics with ample time and power to establish a semi-hierarchical institution:

> They developed Shia doctrine and ritual, while refining the process of recruitment to the clerical hierarchy which thus developed the critical mass. This era saw the first appearance of certain of the striking titles adopted by clerics still employed today, such as *hujjat al-islam* (Proof of Islam) or *ayatollah* (Sign of God), the appellation of the most advanced scholars. (Louër 2012, p. 7)

Taqlid, central to the nineteenth- and twentieth-century politics and structure, only became a mainstream practice in the eighteenth and nineteenth century, following the dominance of the *Usuli* school, which granted Shiʿi clergy, the *ulama*, a special status. The *ulama* had a following and were influential in their community; however, the system of *taqlid*, as now known in the Shiʿi community, is essentially modern. According to this system, Shiʿi followers are required to emulate a *mujtahid,* a senior cleric who has enough expertise to issue edicts, *fatwas,* or religious–legal judgements, through analogical reasoning based on the Qurʾan and the practice of the Prophets and Imams (Keddie 1983, p. 34).[4] A *mujtahid* resolves the problem of analogically applying ancient law on modern matters, such as banning drugs, deriving his judgement from the alcohol ban in the Quran. This system of jurisprudence laid the ground for Khomeini's later modern theory of *Wilayat al-Faqih.*

'Allama Hassan al-Hilli (d. 1326), from al-Hilla in southern Iraq, was the first to set the rules of *ijtihād* in his book, *Mabadi al-Wusul ila Ilm al-Usul* (*The Points of Departure from which Knowledge of the Principles is Attained*) (Janin and Kahlmeyer 2007, p. 75).[5] Al-Hilli defines *ijtihād* as "the utmost exertion of the faculties to speculate on those questions of law which are subject to conjecture"; the exercise is fallible, al-Hilli admits, and the result is sometimes wrong (Janin and Kahlmeyer 2007, p. 75). To practice *Ijtihād,* al-Hilli argues, the cleric should be exceptionally intelligent, well-trained and careful, and a master of the Arabic language, the 500 verses of law in the Qur'an, the appropriate *hadith,* and the prevailing consensus (*ijma*ᶜ) of his time (Janin and Kahlmeyer 2007, p. 75). The strict conditions for *ijtihād* mean only a few scholars would be able to practice it. The reason for this, al-Hilli argues, is "if the vast majority were burdened with *ijtihād* in questions, the world order would consequently be disturbed and everyone would be more concerned with discussing problems than with his livelihood" (Janin and Kahlmeyer 2007, p. 76). Al-Hilli set a few rules for the practice known later as *taqlid,* such as seeking the most knowledgeable opinion in case of conflict between two scholars. Prior to the Safavid era, Shi'i jurisprudence flourished briefly in Baghdad during the Buyid rule, only to end following their defeat by the Sunni Seljuq dynasty (Cole in Keddie 1983, p. 37).

Shi'i jurisprudence varied in forms well into the eighteenth century, as cautiousness prevailed over the clergy's role in the great occultation. However, the general consensus among these early Twelver thinkers was that they "would have considered the idea of a Shi'i state ruled by *ulama* in the absence of the Imam (*al-mahdī almuntazar*) as an unthinkable heresy" (Cole 1983, p. 37).[6] Juan Cole writes of one of the earliest mentions of Shi'i *Ijtihād*: "The eminent Shi'i jurisprudent Ibrahib Qatifi wrote in 1537 AD that ijtihād was not originally permitted in the Imami school and only became permissible because of the exigencies brought about by the occultation of the Imam" (Cole in Keddie 1983, p. 38).

The clerical theoretical scepticism over the clergy's ability to take on "the Imam's responsibilities", leadership, has persisted over the centuries. Mohamad Amin Astarabadi (d. 1624) founded the *al-Akhbari* school of jurisprudence to restore or "reassert the primacy of the infallible guidance of the imams over the interpretive role of the later *ulamas*" (Cole in Keddie 1983, p. 39). The *al-Akhbari* school dominated Shiʿism in the eighteenth century: "The Akhbari school flourished in Persia and the shrine cities of Iraq for almost two centuries, until the second half of the twelfth/eighteenth century …. The Akhbari doctrine and al-Astarabadi's criticism of the Usuli *mujtahids* were variously retained and propagated by other Twelver scholars in Persia, Iraq, Lebanon and Bahrayn, such as Abdullah Al-Samahiji al-Bahrani (d. 1135/1723) and Yusuf b. Ahmad al-Bahrani (d. 1186/1773)" (Daftary 2013, p. 55). The *al-Akhbari* school gained ground among the Shiʿa, following the Afghan conquest of the Safavids, which brought "ravaging Sunni tribesmen into Iran"; Nader Shah's "Sunni-Shiʿi ecumenism threatened to transform Shiʿism into little more than a fifth school of Sunni jurisprudence" (Cole in Keddie 1983, p. 39).

From Iraq's Shiʿi shrine cities, Mohammad Baqer Behbehani (1705–1791) and his students persuaded "a majority of their colleagues, both in Iraq and ultimately in Iran to forsake the *akhbari* school for their own", the *Usuli* school; lay Shiʿa, according to this prevalent trend, should emulate *mujtahids*, not only Imams (Cole in Keddie 1983, p. 40). Following the restoration of the *Usuli* school's dominance, Shiʿi *mujtahids* gradually developed a theory of emulation, that of following "the most knowledgeable", known in Arabic as *marjaʿiya*.[7] The first cleric to assume that role was Mohammad Hasan Najafi (c. 1788–1849); Najafi, the author of *Jawaher Al-Kalam*, a renowned legal text, established Najaf's predominance as a city of religious learning.[8] After building an expansive network of regional representatives, who distributed *fatwas* and collected *khums*, Najafi established the tenets of his religious administration (Louër 2012, p. 9). To consolidate this newly found institution, he appointed Mortaza Ansari to succeed him.[9] From his base in Iraq, Ansari further developed the institution of emulation, *taqlid*, following the religious rules or edicts formulated by a *mujtahid* deemed to be the most learned among the *ulama*. This senior cleric would be called *marjaʿ al-taqlid*, literally 'a reference of emulation', who would not only issue edicts for his followers to obey, but also collect taxes through his representatives (Walbridge 2001, p. 3–4). The *marjaʿ* is designated by his peers in an informal process, in which the assumed meritocracy is marred by the candidate's social influence or popularity (Louër 2012, p. 10). To consolidate this position as an institution in its own right, Ansari built on his wide recognition as a source of emulation in the Shiʿi world, as far as Turkey and India (Keddie 1983, p. 40).

Ansari introduced a new set of rules governing emulation. Emulation is a religious obligation, and rituals such as prayers are only valid if performed in accordance with a *mujtahid's* detailed judgement (Keddie 1983, p. 43). Emulation is so significant for Ansari that he urges Shi'i laymen to emigrate to consult a living exemplar (Keddie 1983, p. 43). It is forbidden for a Shi'i layman to continue emulating an exemplar once he is dead; he must emulate the most learned living *marja'* exemplar (Keddie 1983, p. 43). This approach drew a very sharp line between the clergy, especially the *mujtahids*, and laymen: they became leaders and followers, respectively (Keddie 1983, p.46). Ansari set the tradition of *resala,* a book of religious rules drawn up by the exemplar for lay followers. This tradition continues to this day. Ansari's legacy is significant as it laid the institutional and ideological foundations of *marja' al-taqlid al- ʾa'la,* the supreme exemplar in the mid-nineteenth century (Cole in Keddie 1983, p. 46). Yet, although some of his followers referred to him as 'caliph', Ansari made no political use of this powerful position; however, his successors did:

> The structure he [Ansari] helped erect had great potentialities for marshaling the Shi'i *ulama* and masses to support for a political cause. This was demonstrated very effectively by Hasan Shirazi, the supreme source for emulation who defied Naser ad-Din Shah and issued a ruling that the smoking of tobacco was forbidden after the shah had granted a Western tobacco concession. The idea that all Shi'i laymen owed allegiance to one Shi'i jurisprudent, and that the local *ulama* were to be judged on how faithful they were to the rulings of this supreme exemplar, provided an ideological underpinning for the social and political power of the ulama. (Cole in Keddie 1983, p. 46)

6.1.1 The Print Revolution

Ansari's successors combined institutional power and print culture, which "became a significant component of Iran' s intellectual and political landscape" only in the late nineteenth century (Balaghi 2001, p. 165). After the Qajar Shah Nasr al-Din granted the Imperial Tobacco Company of London "the entire tobacco concession from growing to packaging for £15,000 and 25 per cent of the annual profits", this sparked an outrage in Iran, and the emulators of the Shi'i marja' Hassan Shirazi urged him to intervene (Al-Wardi and Aboul-Enein 2012, p. 46).[10] After failing to convince the Shah, Shirazi issued a *fatwa* banning the use of tobacco. In a novel practice for the Shi'i establishment, Shirazi's *fatwa* was disseminated through wide-scale printing of 100,000 pamphlets, according to one estimate; some were read out in mosques, allowing unprecedented mass implementation[11]: "Amazingly, Persian (Iranian) and Iraqi Shiʿites within their communities left opium addicts alone, looked the other way when alcohol was sold or consumed, but enforced the Tanbak ban" (Al-Wardi and Aboul-Enein 2012, p. 46). In 1892, the Qajar Shah withdrew from the agreement, paying half a million pounds indemnity, while Shirazi's popularity became a landmark in the history of the Shiʿi establishment (Al-Wardi and Aboul-Enein 2012, p. 46).[12]

6.1.2 The Constitutional Movement

By the late nineteenth century and early twentieth century, the power of the Shiʿi clergy in Iran climaxed, encompassing institutions and an extensive social network among the mercantile classes and urban small traders (Tabari in Keddie 1983, p. 55). Iranian clerics dominated the educational system, and following the tobacco uprising, the clergy established themselves as a power not to be ignored. Shirazi died in 1895, three years after his political victory over the Qajar Shah, and three politically backed contenders for the *marjaʿ* seat emerged. In Iraq, meanwhile, the clergy faced a different set of challenges, as they clashed with repressive Ottoman authorities over the introduction of new taxes in 1908 (Al-Wardi and Aboul-Enein 2012, p. 47).

In Iran, however, the clergy's role in politics was evident in its publications and debates over the constitutional movement. Although they had emerged as a strong front following the tobacco uprising, the clergy were divided. Two trends emerged: the first led by Shaikh Fazlollah Nuri considered the constitutional revolution the 'great sedition', calling instead for a *Shari'a*-based Islamic parliament (Tabari in Keddie 1983, p. 58). For Nuri, drafting the constitution involved three interrelated innovations or *bedʿa* (acts forbidden in Islam): writing the un-Islamic constitution, enforcing it, and punishing those who do not obey it (Tabari in Keddie 1983, p. 58). The tumultuous nature of the constitutional phase, which ended with Reza Shah's coup, marked the failure of the pro-constitutional clergy, paving the way for a pure Islamic vision cemented by Ayatollah Khomeini. For a decade following the constitutionalists' military victory in July 1909, and the ensuing election of a second parliament, weak and incompetent governments fed "the disillusionment with the utopian promise of constitutionalism" (Tabari in Keddie 1983, p. 58). The pro-constitutionalist clergy were particularly affected as "reforms were at the expense of their traditional functions". The 1921 establishment of the Reza Shah military dictatorship required a different kind of religious response.

6.1.3 Najaf's 1920 Revolution

Only a year prior to the rise of Reza Shah, Najaf was at the centre of an *ulama*-led revolution against the British mandate in Iraq; even though they inflicted high losses on the foreign invaders, the revolutionaries were eventually defeated. As a result, the British pursued a sectarian policy of punishment and exclusion:

> When the revolution ended and, consequently, the framework of a national government was being contemplated, the bases of alliances shifted from mainly economic and ideological grounds to sectarian ones. The Shi'a allies of yesteryear were cast aside by the emerging Sunni political elite, merely because the Shi'a fell on the other side of the sectarian line of division. The British institutionalized this political exclusion, in keeping with their often-expressed anti-Shi'a sentiment. And in the aftermath of the revolution, its fervent supporters retained nothing but their wounds while its cynical detractors collected the spoils. (Kadhim 2012, p. 6)

Conversely, the Shi'i *mujtahids*, according to Kadhim, failed "to appreciate the new political reality associated with the creation of a nation-state in Iraq". These senior clerics lacked the ability or know-how to partake in the political manoeuvering, and as they were mostly Iranian citizens, the government had the power to deport them after terminating their contracts. The *mujtahids* "continued to play by the old rules" (Kadhim 2012, pp. 154–155). As a result, many clerics moved from Najaf to the Iranian city of Qom, facilitating its "re-emergence as a religious centre of first importance" (Louër 2012, pp. 10–11).

In Iran, however, the clerical establishment's power and even financial viability were threatened. Reza Shah embarked on reforms, many of which had been originally requested by the constitutionalists, and diminished the clergy's power. Establishing modern schools and universities provided the state with secular bureaucrats and reduced the reach of the clergy's *madrasa* system; most importantly, he gradually abolished the religious courts' jurisdiction (Tabari in Keddie 1983, p. 58).[13] Under Reza Shah, the Ministry of Endowments granted the state control over *vaqf* properties, including mosques and *hussayniya*s.[14] The state's gradual encroachment on the clergy's power continued, forcing "the clergy in many areas to sanction counting tax payments (like tea and sugar) as part of *khums* and *zakat*" (Keddie 1983, p. 58). In 1936, the state banned wearing the veil in public and the practice of cutting foreheads during *'Ashura'*, the Shi'i commemoration of Imam Husayn's martyrdom (Tabari in Keddie 1983, p. 61).

6.1.4 Khomeini's 'Islamic Parliament'

The widespread support for Reza Shah's reforms meant that the clergy's response could rarely exceed "unhappy silence" (Tabari in Keddie 1983, p. 62). Under this "unhappy silence", exacerbated by the perceived public support for the reforms, Ayatollah Ruhollah Khomeini began developing his theory of 'Islamist government'. Still, Khomeini's vision of government was less direct than *Wilayat al-Faqih*: the proposed system was composed of a clerical assembly (*mujtahid* members), which would elect a sultan "who would not disobey divine law nor practice oppression nor transgress against people's property, life and honour" (Tabari in Keddie 1983, p. 62). Khomeini later wrote that the *Wilayat al-Faqih* is reserved for those who attained the *mujtahid* level in the clerical establishment. In this statement, Khomeini stipulates that the sultan, a religious layman, not a cleric, "would not disobey divine law"; however, the council *majles* should be "composed of pious *faqihs* or be placed under their supervision". The remaining leaders should simply obey the "divine law": "When we say government (*Hokumat* and *Velayat*) in our time belongs to the *faqihs*, we do not mean to say that the shah, the ministers, the soldiers, and the dustmen should all be *faqih*" (Tabari in Keddie 1983, p. 62). The effect of Reza Shah's reforms could be clearly traced in Khomeini's thinking, especially when he highlights the significance of Islamic law over other forms of government:

> Clearly, even the mujtahids do not have the right to allow anyone to rule. Even the prophet and the Imams were not allowed by God to do this. They can only confer authority upon someone who does not violate God's laws –these being founded on reason and justice—and who accepts the formal law of the country to be the divine laws of heaven, and not European laws or worse. (Tabari in Keddie 1983, p. 62)

While in Iran, Khomeini saw himself as part of the general body of clergy, joining their condemnation of the 'moral degradation' under Reza Shah, from the unveiling of women to drinking and selling wine

(Tabari in Keddie 1983, p. 63).[15] Khomeini's criticism went beyond Reza Shah's European-inspired modernisation to cover less controversial aspects such as modern medicine and surgery, emphasising instead the usefulness of traditional methods and practices (Tabari in Keddie 1983, p. 64).

Khomeini's ideas, however, remained isolated, while the majority of the clergy grew increasingly aloof from politics, as the political scene in the post-war era was dominated by the Communist Party (*Tudeh*) and the National Front (Tabari in Keddie 1983, p. 64). As part of the quietest body of clergy, Khomeini was close to Ayatollah Burujerdi, a figure seen as 'hostile' to religious activism (Louër 2012, p. 20).[16] Khomeini, like many students of senior clerics in Iran and Iraq, was a 'career cleric' in an institution where only the death of a *marjaʿ* would pave the way for the rise of another, usually his student.

The CIA-backed 1953 coup against Mohamad Mosaddeq's government left the nationalist camp in crisis, chiefly since "important figures from the National Front, like Bazargan and Taleqani, broke away and founded the Freedom movement"; their goal was to act "as a bridge between the universities and the theological circles… since the entry of the religious leaders into the struggle was the need of the time and desire of the people" (Tabari in Keddie 1983, p. 64). Following the coup, the clergy met in Qom and Tehran to discuss their future role in politics and reforms in the hierarchy, with many of the current regime's clergy participating in these proceedings (Tabari in Keddie 1983, p. 65). These discussions covered many aspects of religion and politics, such as "the idea that no Shiʿi society is possible without the delegation of the Imam's authority", "the development of *ijtihād* as a powerful instrument for the adaptation of Islam to changing circumstances", and "the interpretation of Islam as a total way of life, therefore incorporating social economic and political issues into the religious ones" (Tabari in Keddie 1983, p. 65). Khomeini led weekly discussions of the clergy's response or stance towards the Shah's policies. These discussions were driven by two trends in Iranian governmental politics: the first was the influx of American advisors, who steered the capitalist policies and reforms in the coup's aftermath, and the second was that Jewish and Baha'i Iranians were profiting from these government policies, exacerbating Khomeini's "fears over the future of Islam" in Iran, as is clear in this message:

> It is incumbent upon me, according to my religious duties, to warn the Iranian people and the Muslims of the world that Islam and the Qurʾan are

in danger; that the independence of the country and its economy are about to be taken over by Zionists, who in Iran appear as the party of Baha'is, and if this deadly silence of Muslims continues, they will soon take over the entire economy of the country and drive it to complete bankruptcy. Iranian television is a Jewish spy base, the government sees this and approves of it. (Tabari in Keddie 1983, pp. 65–66)

The death of Ayatollah Borujerdi, the chief Shi'i *marja'*, paved the way to Khomeini's rise in the clerical establishment; Borujerdi, although identified as a non-political cleric, strengthened the financial structure of the clerical school, *al-hawza al'ilmiya* (in Arabic) *or Hauza-yi Ilmiya* (in Persian), led by the supreme *marja'*, through a network that collects the followers' *khums* and *zakat* contributions (Tabari in Keddie 1983, p. 66). In spite of his popular appeal and stronger position, Khomeini's stance remained limited to reforming the Shah's government, pushing it into adopting Islamic policies and aligning itself with the clergy. This was clear in a speech Khomeini made following the government's annulment of a local election bill after mass protests:

Why are they (the government) trying, by every means, to alienate and break the support of the clergy? ... Why don't they instead rely on the clergy? ... [I]f the people see that the government protects the interests and welfare of Islam and Muslims, and that it serves the nation, then they will support the government ... But, alas, the government cannot comprehend these facts, it refuses to understand that without the clergy the country has no backbone ... I advise the shah not to lose this force! ... To give such advice is incumbent... it is the duty of the 'ulama' and the clergy to advice and to show the way to everyone, from the shah down to the most minor officials. (Tabari in Keddie 1983, p. 68)

However, the clerical response to governmental policies escalated as the Shah's regime embarked on a reform programme intended to appease the working class and peasantry; the clergy interpreted these new government policies as "a rejection of its demand for greater influence in the government and a further attempt to curb its social influence and political role" (Tabari in Keddie 1983, p. 68). The 26 January 1963 referendum on the Shah's six-point programme further exacerbated tensions between the Khomeini-led clergy and the government; the programme included policies such as women's suffrage and a profit-sharing scheme for workers (Tabari 1981, p. 68). The clerical growing unease culminated in Khomeini's public denunciation of the Shah's regime in the ʿAshuraʾ speech of 3 June 1963, leading to his arrest two days later, which sparked wide protests.

6.1.5 Facing the Communist Challenge

In Iraq, the rising influence of the Communist Party, especially among Shiʿi youth and the intelligentsia, alarmed the clerical establishment in Najaf. The communist-backed Abdul Karim Qassem coup in 1958 dealt a significant blow to the clerical establishment. The new regime passed two laws, which would directly affect the powerful clergy. These were "a new family law, which deprived the clergy of much of its judicial privilege, and also a new agrarian law that would over time eliminate the class of great landowners, who had traditionally financed clerical institutions" (Louër 2012, p. 15). The traditional Iranian and Iraqi clerics were the feudal lords' allies, allowing their foes, whether Communists in Iraq or the shah's regime in Iran, to associate them with reactionary politics. The shah, for example, equated feudal lords with clergymen, as defenders of the status quo. The communist encroachment even reached the clerical school itself, with seminary students, such as the Lebanese Hussein Mroueh, converting to Marxism.[17] To counter this expansion, junior clerics, religious intellectuals, and merchants established the Islamic Daʿwa Party ('Islamic Call') in 1958 (Mockaitis 2013, p. 222). The role of Najaf's Grand Ayatollah, Mohsin al-Hakim, was substantial, as two of his sons, Mohammad Mahdi and Mohammad Baqer, were founding members of the new party, which signalled it had their father's all-important blessing.[18]

In his capacity as the grand Shiʿi *marjaʿ*, al-Hakim's concern over the spread of communism among the Shiʿa was not confined to Iraq. In Lebanon, the Communist Party's appeal to Shiʿi youth increased substantially after a wave of Shiʿi migration from the countryside to Beirut's suburbs, due to dispossessions and poverty in the rural 'misery belts' (Abisaab and Abisaab 2014, p.107). To counter this effect, al-Hakim sent his student, Musa al-Sadr, to the city of Tyr in South Lebanon, after the death of a local *marjaʿ*. Al-Sadr competed with the communists in attracting the Shiʿa, calling for social equality and a fairer distribution of political and economic power among Lebanon's confessional groups. His campaign drew US attention: "As early as 1966, the reports of the US Embassy in Beirut described al-Sadr as a bulwark against the influence of 'Abd al-Nasir on the Shiʿi masses. In 1974, Sadr confessed to the US Ambassador Godley that his main concern was to counter communist influence among Shi'i youth" (Traboulsi 2007, p. 178). Al-Sadr battle against communism and the Lebanese confessional system brought about a different set of alliances to his counterparts. The Iranian cleric, who was granted Lebanese citizenship after his arrival in Lebanon, maintained "close and even cordial" ties with the Shah's regime till 1973 (Norton 1987, p. 41). Norton argues that Al-Sadr received considerable funding from the Shah[19]; however, his relations with Shari'ati and the Liberation Movement of Iran (LMI) were also strengthened (Norton 1987, p. 41).[20]

In Afghanistan, communist movements challenged the alliance of Shi'i Hazara clerics and powerful feudal lords, known as *khans*. However, unlike in the Arab and Iranian cases, the Hazara's overlapping ethnic and sectarian identities reproduced tensions with transnational ideologies.[21] The Hazaras, the Persian-speaking Shi'a of Afghanistan, racially identified as Mongols, are both an ethnic and religious minority in a predominantly Sunni nation-state (Thesiger 1955, p. 313; Mervin 2010, p. 45).[22] Severe repression, genocide, active discrimination, and marginalisation have defined this minority's relations with the Afghan state, reflecting overlapping ethnic and class grievances.[23] Until the late 1970s, feudal lords dominated the politics of the mountainous Hazarajat in central Afghanistan. The *khans* were traditional allies of the *sayyids*, who claim to descend from the prophet's bloodline; the latter's claim to status allowed them to prosper as a class, as they received half of the Shi'i *khums* tax.[24] Due to the region's rugged geography and the lack of access to the mountainous regions, Kabul often relied on the *khans* to collect taxes in return for a semi-autonomous status (Ibrahimi 2006, p. 7). In the 1950s and 1960s, thousands of Hazaras, however, moved into Kabul, especially its western district; this movement was paralleled by a further migration to Iran and Pakistan in search of jobs. They were associated with low-pay jobs, as one Hazara puts it: "For much of this country's history, the Hazara were typically servants, cleaners, porters and little else, a largely Shi'i minority sidelined for generations, and in some instances massacred, by Pashtun rulers" (Oppel 2010).[25]

During the 1950s and 1960s, many Hazaras joined diverse Marxist groups. However, the larger segment of Hazara youth, including the children of *khans*, were not attracted to, or affiliated with, the ruling pro-Soviet People's Democratic Party of Afghanistan (PDPA), a Marxist-Leninist Party established in 1965, but filled the ranks of Sazman-e Jawanan-e Mutaraqqi (Progressive Youth Organisation), an offshoot of the main Afghan Maoist group, Shula-e Javid. Its leader Akram

Yari was an ethnic Hazara (Ibrahimi 2006, p. 8).[26] In the late 1960s and early 1970s, Mutaraqqi's party eclipsed the PDPA's two factions, Khalq and Parcham, and took control of the Kabul University students' organisation (Bradsher 1999, p. 13).[27] The rise of Mutaraqqi's faction, particularly in Kabul, was fuelled by Hazara support; they were the poorest labourers in the Afghan capital, and the group's leader was an ethnic brother. The Hazaras, facing longstanding economic oppression and ethnic discrimination, were less keen to join the two branches of the PDPA, which had upper middle-class and ethnic components:

> The Parcham faction was oriented toward urbanized, westernized members of the upper middle class from a number of ethnic groups, especially Tajiks and detribalized Pashtuns. Khalq was predominantly Pashtun and embraced a wider economic and social cross-section of the population with a more diverse background. (Bradsher 1999, p. 12)

Nevertheless, the PDPA regime broke ranks with the State's history of Hazara under-representation. Under the communist regime, the first Hazara Prime Minister Sultan Ali Keshtmand, a Kabul-educated economist, was appointed (Bradsher 1999, p. 130).[28] However, the organisation's Khalq faction, once in power, imprisoned Akram Yari and hundreds of Hazara Maoists, where many disappeared; this policy alienated thousands of Hazara communists (Ibrahimi 2006, p. 8). Islamist movements, led by Najaf-educated clerics and influenced by Shariʿati, began to organise, establishing networks that were mobilised in 1979, following the Islamic Revolution in Iran. They organised a failed uprising in west Kabul, the former popular base of the Maoist *shola*.

6.2 Internal Shiʿi Tensions

6.2.1 *Karbala Versus Najaf*

Although Iraq's Shiʿi clergy establishment faced grave challenges from the government and Communist Party, internal competition and rifts persisted. Karbala, home to the most significant Shiʿi shrines, retained a leading clerical role until an Ottoman attack in the mid-nineteenth century when thousands were killed, and scholars moved en masse to nearby Najaf (Louër 2012, p. 17). The Karbala and Najaf rivalry persisted. In this context, two years after the establishment of Da'wa, Mohammed al-Shirazi, a young cleric, declared himself a marja‛; his followers launched a campaign to promote his controversial marja‛ia (Louër 2012, p. 17). Al-Shirazi's ambitions were political, and his followers were soon organised as a transnational network, competing with Da'wa: "Anticipating Khomeini, he formulated a doctrine proposing government of the state by the clergy, a system he later categorized as shurat al-fuqaha (the council of the scholars). The Islamic state, in his view, should be governed by a collegiate institution that would bring together all the maraji'" (Louër 2012, p. 18). The network, which took form in the mid-1960s, was always a family affair; Mohammad Taqi al-Mudarresi, al-Shirazi's nephew, established the Message movement, which later became known as Munazzamat al-'Amal al-Islami (the Islamic Action Organisation) (Louër 2012, p. 18). Since al-Shirazi criticised the Western-style organisation of Da'wa, independent from the *marja‛ia*, his network remained connected to his leadership, even in its transnational branches (Louër 2012, p. 18).

The Karbala–Najaf rivalry, in its Shirazi-Da'wa form, was evident in these two groups' relations with the shah's regime during the tumultuous decade leading to the Islamic Revolution. The regime supported the Islamic Da'wa Party, in order to forestall the Iranian clergy's development as a powerful opposition force and to destabilise the Iraqi government (Louër 2012, p. 21). According to Louër, Khomeini was a 'heavy guest' in Najaf, where many clerics considered the shah's support essential. Shirazists, on the other hand, had no reservations about condemning the shah and backing Khomeini; they even organised a formal welcoming ceremony when the Iranian ayatollah arrived in Iraq, and provided his associates with counterfeit passports (Louër 2012, p. 21). In return, Khomeini used his connections with the PLO to provide military training for the Shirazists in militant camps in Lebanon, where they posed as Iranian Arabs from the Khuzistan region (Louër 2012, p. 22).[29]

6.2.2 Clergy Versus Laity

While Khomeini found little support in Najaf, his Iraqi sojourn was vital to the formulation of his theory of 'Islamic government', based on *Wilayat al-Faqih* (Guardianship of the Jurist); he laid out the argument in speeches given between 21 January and 8 February 1970 (Khomeini 1995, p. 1). Arguing that "there is not a single topic in human life for which Islam has not provided instructions and established a norm", Khomeini retreated on his earlier demand for a 'religious shah; rather, now he stipulated that the ruler should be a *faqih*, who is most knowledgeable in Islamic law:

> Thus, the view of the Shi'ah concerning government and the nature of the persons who should assume rule was clear from the time following the death of the Prophet down to the beginning of the Occultation. It is specified that the ruler should be foremost in knowledge of the laws and ordinances of Islam, and just in their implementation... the two qualities of knowledge of the law and justice are present in countless fuqaha of the present age. If they come together, they could establish a government of universal justice in the world. If a worthy individual possessing these two qualities arises and establishes a government, he will possess the same authority as the Most Noble Messenger in the administration of society, and it will be the duty of all people to obey him. (Khomeini 1995, pp. 33–34)

Khomeini here grants the *faqih* an authority equal to that of the Prophet and the Imams, though this does not elevate the former to the infallibles' status. The *faqih* is the worldly manifestation of the divine law, and though not a prophet or an infallible imam, he acts in the same capacity as if they were present. The relation between the ruler and the people is that of absolute obedience, as in the case of the guardian and minor:

> When we say that after the Occultation, the just faqih has the same authority that the Most Noble Messenger and the Imams had, [but] do not imagine that the status of the faqih is identical to that of the Imams and the Prophet. For here we are not speaking of status, but rather of function. By 'authority', we mean government, the administration of the country, and the implementation of the sacred laws of the shariah. These constitute a serious, difficult duty but do not earn anyone extraordinary status or raise him above the level of common humanity. In other words, authority here has the meaning of government, administration, and execution of law; contrary to what many people believe, it is not a privilege, but a grave responsibility. The governance of the faqih is a rational and extrinsic matter; it exists only as a type of appointment, like the appointment of a guardian to a minor. With respect to duty and position, there is indeed no difference between the guardian of a nation and the guardian of a minor, to the governorship of a province, or to some other post. In cases like these, it is not reasonable that there would be a difference between the Prophet and the Imams, on the one hand, and the just faqih, on the other. (Khomeini 1995, p. 34)

This theory, published later under the title of 'Islamic Government', contradicted the leading Islamist laymen intellectuals, particularly Ali Shariʿati. Shariʿati, later known as the Islamic Revolution's chief ideologue because of his books' popularity among the youth and student movements, emphasised the sovereignty of the people in Islamic form of government. The leader should be accountable to both the people who directly elect him and the Twelfth Imam:

> As opposed to [when] those four individuals were appointed [to be] representatives, the Imam does not appoint [any representatives during the greater occultation]; the followers of the Imam themselves must choose them. How do they choose them? By looking at the qualification and conditions that Imam himself determined... You choose the most pious, most learned individuals among you . A special [type of] electoral system comes into being during the greater occultation. These elected officials are chosen by the people, but have a responsibility toward the Imam, as opposed to [Western] democracy, where the official is elected by the people and is responsible [only] toward those who elected him and made him reach [that post]. (Shariʿati 2015)[30]

Khomeini's theory, by contrast, was top-down, as became clear later in the Islamic Republic's constitution: the leader would be selected by senior clerics, rather than by popular vote. While Shariʿati stressed the significance of accountability to the people and the Imam, Khomeini granted the leader near-absolute immunity in both theory and practice.

The difference in approach between Shariʿati and Khomeini was rooted in the former's animosity towards clerics. A Paris-educated lay intellectual, influenced by Marxist and anti-colonial intellectuals, Shariʿati blamed the clerical establishment for the shortcomings and dominant quietism of Islam, rendering it less popular among the youth. Khomeini held a totally different stance. While critical of certain traditional segments of the clerical class, Khomeini's own political experience took form out of the tensions between the clergy and the Shah's increasingly antagonistic policies. This placed the two men at odds; unlike Khomeini, Shariʿati was an advocate of Mossaddeq and Kashani. As to the Shah's land reform programme, Shariʿati and Khomeini were theoretically at odds:

> Khomeini opposed the land reform incorporated into the Shah's White Revolution—indeed, he was one of the foremost opponents of the measure. There were religious thinkers at the time, such as Ali Shariʿati, who,

while they opposed land reform, nonetheless tried to accommodate the principle of equitable distribution into a reform program of their own. Khomeini did not do this—he condemned the idea as anti-Islamic, a position that placed him at odds with the mass of Iran's landless peasants. (Pelletiere 1992, p. 54)

These lay-clergy differences, though subtle in the pre-revolution phase when the shah's repression overshadowed differences, became more apparent after Khomeini's return to Iran. The tensions surfaced more clearly during the years 1979–1982, both internally and in the transnational networks vying for Iranian support.[31]

In Lebanon, Musa al-Sadr established Amal (the Movement of the Deprived); lay figures, such as Nabih Berri and Hussein al-Husseini, both lawyers, dominated the movement, especially after al-Sadr's disappearance in Libya in 1978. Amal's close relation with the Freedom Movement of Iran (FMI), and its lay structure, set it apart from the Islamic Republic, and it remains closely aligned to the Syrian regime.[32]

6.2.2.1 The Islamic Republic and Transnational Shi'i Movements

The Islamic Revolution's victory in Iran reinvigorated transnational Shi'i networks; with this refreshed revolutionary vigour, new tensions emerged, while old ones intensified. In the first few years of the Islamic Republic, different Islamic factions, sometimes ideologically at odds, competed in policy-making. The newly found republic's external influence, or the export of the revolution, was exploited for internal purposes, often to undermine pragmatists. Moreover, tensions emerged between the *realpolitik* required in foreign policy and the Islamic Republic's ideology. The Islamic Republic established a dichotomy in foreign policy between neighbouring countries, like Afghanistan and Iraq, where *realpolitik* reigned, and farther realms, as in the case of Lebanon, where a more ideologically consistent policy was possible. Additionally, the Islamic Republic's full adoption of *Wilayat al-Faqih* gradually stirred up tensions between the sceptical older, more traditional clerics and their juniors; Tehran often empowered the younger clerics, more prone to accept the *Wilayat* doctrine. Following Khomeini's death, and the rise of Ali Khamenei, the tensions revived, and Khamenei backed a younger generation of clerics. However, with the revolution's success, Shi'i Islam changed drastically, both in public perception and in its rituals such as the 'Ashura'.

6.3 The Invention of Tradition: 'Two Images of Husayn'

In Iran, as in Lebanon, before and after the revolution, the commemoration of *'Ashura'* transformed from a passive to a politically charged, active ritual.[33] It was a layman, not a cleric, who first made the argument for a paradigm shift in commemorating *'Ashura'*; Ali Shari'ati wrote extensively on the political and social lessons from the battle of Karbala, and condemned the conventional quietist 'Ashura' practices and perceptions, blaming them on the Safavid rulers who required them to ensure subservience. A more active revolutionary approach was needed, Shari'ati wrote, a return to the genuine "Red Shi'ism", the "Religion of Martyrdom", rather than the "Black Shi'ism" or the "Religion of Mourning":

> Shi'a do not accept the path chosen by history. They negate the leadership which ruled over history and deceived the majority of the people through its succession to the Prophet, and then, supposed support of Islam and fight against paganism. Shi'a turn their backs on the opulent mosques and magnificent palaces of the caliphs of Islam and turn to the lonely, mud house of Fatima. Shi'a, who represent the oppressed, justice-seeking class in the caliphate system… 'Ashura' recalls the teaching of this continuing fact that the present Islam, is a criminal Islam in the dress of 'tradition' and that the real Islam is the hidden Islam, hidden in the red cloak of martyrdom. (Shari'ati 1972)

The changing rituals morphed out of Islamist activism and a print revolution, in which Shari'ati played a crucial role. Part of the Islamist campaign to counter the communists' appeal among the Shi'i youth since the 1950s, newly established Islamist publishing houses actively disseminated books and pamphlets throughout Iran. This contributed to altering the public perception of Shi'ism, as religious books topped the bestseller list in Iran during the early 1970s (Boroujerdi 1996, p. 89). The religious books' share of the print market more than tripled during the period from April 1963 to May 1974, from 10.1 to 33.5 per cent, respectively (Boroujerdi 1996, p. 90). Among the various publications, Shari'ati, due to his wide appeal among the educated young, was highly influential, on an equal footing as Khomeini (Hanson 1983, p. 1).

In 1981, Mary Hegland observed the *'Ashura'* ceremonies in Aliabad, an Iranian town, before and after the 1979 Islamic Revolution; she witnessed the change of Imam Husayn's image from an 'intercessor' into an 'example' to be emulated. In the first instance, Imam Husayn's martyrdom in Karbala enabled him to play the role of the mediator between Allah and believers; thus, martyrdom transforms the Imam into a legal mediator of life-related requests from believers to the divine:

> According to this view of Shi'i Islam, Imam Hussain, because he was martyred and therefore beloved of God, is able to serve as an intercessor of forgiving sins and granting entrance to Paradise as well as fulfilling more mundane wishes and requests. Weeping and mourning for Hussain is supposed to be especially effective in gaining his favour and thereby also assuring the fulfillment of one's desires. (Hegland in Keddie 1983, p. 221)

Such a relationship takes the form of a transaction, though without ruling out the laymen's respect or adulation for the Imam; the Shi'i makes a vow, *nezer*, to the Imam, that an act of charity or prayers/pilgrimage will be undertaken, in case his material wish is fulfilled. According to Hegland, the intercessor ritual removes any potential political connotations from the Imam's rebellious story:

> In this interpretation of Islam, the behavior of Imam Husain and his accomplishments, ideals, and values are far less important than his connection with God and the resulting power at his disposal. In making this assertion, I am not denying the very real love and devotion that many Iranians hold for Hussain. But it does seem that for many, Imam Hussain was loved more for his position—beloved of God and thus able to grant requests—than for his personal qualities. Personal acquaintance with the imam as a person is not relevant, because a true admiration and respect are not most requirements for the relationship between him and believers. In the end, the relationship is an instrumental one and requires only outward, public deference and honor. In the eyes of the believer, the main aim is to get on good terms with imams or *imamzadehs* so as to increase the chances of receiving assistance from them when is needed. (Hegland in Keddie 1983, p. 222)

Hegland notes that such an approach carries an underlying political statement—that is, commending the connection to the powerful, accepting the status quo and that "you [the believer] are dependent upon the powerful and the hope of their assistance" (Hegland in Keddie 1983, p. 222). While Hegland suggests that this traditional relation with '*Ashura*' amounts to 'taught acquiescence', there is no evidence that the modern, politically hyped approach has any roots, as certain rituals and tradition associated with it are completely modern. Most importantly, religion in its traditional form, while it might have served the status quo, never presented itself as holding an independent worldview, let alone being a political alternative, such as Marxism. The rise of Marxist ideology in the town and elsewhere in Iran posed a challenge to the clerical establishment and religious leaders, such as Ali Shariʿati, paving the way to a more active ideology. The ʿAshuraʾ rituals were therefore revolutionised: Husayn's martyrdom was no longer a passive story of sacrifice for the divine. Husayn knew of his imminent death, and just like the story of Jesus Christ, the third Shiʿi Imam faced his death. Unlike the intercessor role and more in line with mainstream Christian faith, Imam Husayn "knew that his martyrdom would set an example for all ages, calling Muslims of successive generations to rise up and fight against tyranny and godlessness" (Hegland in Keddie 1983, p. 226).

In these rituals, taking Husayn as an 'example', marches and self-flagellation are politically charged; rather than treating the martyrdom as a historical matter, the participants replace *Yazid*, Imam Husayn's enemy whose mightier army won in Karbala, with a contemporary enemy, whose character is set by Islamist politics. In the pre-revolutionary case, the enemy was the shah and his allies, the USA and Israel. Hegland notes:

> In years preceding the revolution, participants in the mourning rituals of ʿAshuraʾ had struck their chests and beat their backs with chains while chanting mourning couplets and crying in unison, 'Hussain, Hussain, Hussain'. In contrast, during the revolutionary processions of ʿAshuraʾ 1978, marchers raised their fists to beat the air, marking the rhythm of the phrase '*Marg bar shah*' ('Down with the Shah'). (Hegland in Keddie 1983, p. 232)

Such rituals entail a duty to emulate Imam Husayn's story, through facing tyranny and injustice in the modern world; the Islamist leadership sets the parameters of this conflict.

6.4 Transnational and National Shiʿi Tensions

The export of the model of the Iranian Islamic Revolution, based on the *Wilayat al-Faqih* theory, to the Shiʿi minorities in the Persian Gulf faced resistance from two groups: traditional clerics and older Shiʿi movements, such as Amal in Lebanon and the Islamic Daʾwa Party in Iraq.[34] Younger clerics, generally more radical than their seniors, were less reluctant to adopt the Iranian model, and "have often been instrumentalised by Iran to the detriment of their local implantation" (Roy 2010, p. 34). In the case of Lebanon, where the Amal movement had been established by a senior cleric, al-Sadr, the Iranian Revolutionary Guards established Hizbullah in 1982. Simultaneously, in Iraq, where the Islamic Daʿwa Party was established in the 1950s, Tehran founded another umbrella group to contain the former's resistance to Iranian influence:

> In the eyes of Tehran it presented the double inconvenience of being too autonomous and rejecting *Velayat* [*Wilayat al-Faqih*]. Iranian leaders therefore encouraged the development of the Supreme Council of the Islamic Revolution, directed by Muhammad Baqir al-Hakim, a former member of al-Da'wa and the son of Grand Ayatollah [Mohsin] al-Hakim. (Roy 2010, p. 37)

Following the Islamic revolution, Shiʿi mobilisation in the Gulf was shaped by the various local grievances and politics. In eastern Saudi Arabia and Bahrain, the Shiʿa had territorial claims to the region, which was previously united; they perceived themselves as natives, and the Islamic revolution in Iran was a call for mobilisation:

> In November 1979 the ʿAshuraʾ rituals gave rise to large popular demonstrations in both countries, with the masses carrying portraits of Imam Khomeini and shouting slogans hostile to the regimes. In both countries, the demonstrations were violently repressed, resulting in the deaths of dozens of youths and the arrests of hundreds more. In Saudi Arabia, this event, which was the culmination—up to now—of popular mobilization, is remembered as the intifada of muharram 1400. (Louër 2008, pp. 68–69)

The Islamic revolution in Iran exacerbated both sectarian and regime-Shiʿi tensions in the Gulf, specifically in Saudi Arabia and Bahrain. In Saudi Arabia, Shiʿa rarely viewed themselves as a minority, since the prevalent belief or perception is that their region was united with Bahrain centuries before the rise of the Saudi dynasty.

In Kuwait, Qatar, the United Arab Emirates, and Oman, the Shiʿi relations with the regimes were less conflictual. The Shiʿi minorities in these Gulf countries had no territorial claims and were ethnically diverse, divided into social groups, rather than forming a cohesive community with common grievances. With the date of their arrival defining the community's internal divisions, the royal family played a role in defining its relation with various segments of the Shiʻi minority:

> The important Shi'a merchant families arrived simultaneously with the ruling al-Sabah family, in the first half of the eighteenth century. They originated mostly from Iran, Bahrain and Hasa (*al-ehsa*), although some also came from Jabal ʻAmil, or even from Iraq. They fall within the category of so-called original Kuwaitis (*asli*), those who arrived before 1920 and enjoy all social and political rights including the right to vote in national elections. Another part of the Shi'a population arrived from Iran more recently, in the late nineteenth and early twentieth centuries, and is made up of poor families attracted by the economic boom by Kuwait in the wake of the development of the pearl trade and later the oil industry. Some hold Kuwaiti nationality, but their naturalization does not entitle them to all political rights; specifically, they do not have the right to vote… others are *bedun* (stateless) and while enjoying some social rights are deprived of any political rights. (Louër 2008, p. 69)

Due to the lack of a native language and the good relations between *asli* families and the al-Sabah royal family, the political Shiʻi history in Kuwait has always been defined by an alliance with the regime, often against Sunni Arab nationalists and Islamist blocs (Louër 2008, p. 70). These positive relations with the government meant that Shiʻi political violence in Kuwait was confined to small groups, although the state responded with deportations, mostly to Iran, and sectarian purges of sensitive positions (Louër 2008, p. 70).

Tehran's influence among the Shiʻia of the Gulf was rarely channelled through those of Iranian descent. Contrary to this faulty premise, compared to the Arab Shiʻia of Bahrain, the '*ajam* (the Arab word for Shiʻia of Iranians descent), "were relatively indifferent to the Iranian revolution"; while the Arab Shiʻa feel resentment over this until today, many of them were convinced that the *ʻAjam* seized the opportunity offered by the revolutionary enthusiasm of the Baharna to forge closer ties to the authorities. While the Arab Shi'a were marching in the streets carrying portraits of Imam Khomeini, the Iranian Shi'a kept a low profile, reasserting their allegiance to the ruling Al-Khalifa family. (Louër 2008, p. 71)

Regardless of Shiʻi Arab perceptions, Shiʻia of Iranian descent must not be necessarily seen as political opportunists, as they are much more susceptible to deportation, Louër argues. This threat materialised in Iraq, where Saddam Hussein expelled 30,000 Iraqi citizens of Iranian origin in the

1970s on the eve of the war against Iran in 1980, many of whom had been living in the country for generations (Cockburn and Cockburn 2000, p. 80).

6.4.1   The Rise and Fall of the Shura[35]

Directly after the Islamic Revolution in Iran, Afghan Hazaras, still bitter from the PDPA repression of *Shola*, launched an uprising in west Kabul and the mountainous Hazarajat region. Initially, the militarily superior government forces crushed the uprising; however, large areas of Hazarajat fell out of government control.[36] The Najaf-educated clerics, mostly followers of al-Khoei, allied with the *khans*, local militias, and *sayyids* to establish a coalition government to fill the region's power vacuum. Ayatollah Sayyid Beheshti led the new government, known as the Shura-yi Inqilab-i Ittifaq-i Islami-yi Afghanistan (Council of the Islamic Revolutionary Alliance) in the summer of 1979.[37] The coalition of *sayyids* and *khans*, the two traditional forces in the Hazara minority, reintroduced the government's administrative policies based on seven districts. In its central committee, the *shura* established *jihadi*, judicial, financial, and cultural and public relations commissions (Ibrahimi 2006, p. 10). Due to the little financial help received from Pakistan, where the main Hazara group was ethno-nationalist, the *shura* had to rely heavily on local taxation, a policy which depreciated their local support and capacity for mobilisation.[38] Three major elements eroded Beheshti's authority: the alliance with the *khans*, his belonging to a class of traditional clergy who followed Ayatollah al-Khoei rather than Ayatollah Khomeini, and, finally, the fact that local military commanders consolidated their individual power in their respective districts.[39]

The *shura* failed to establish a strong relationship with neighbouring Iran, as Beheshti refused "to recognize Khomeini as the supreme religious leader". This rejection was obvious in the *shura* slogan: '*Allah Akbar, Khomeini Rahbar, Beheshti Rahbar*' ('God is great, Khomeini is leader, and Beheshti is leader') (Ibrahimi 2006, p. 14). Beheshti presented himself at par with Khomeini. Tehran stipulated that the *shura* leaders, seeking Iranian financing and military support, switch from Kho'i to Khomeini.[40] The Iranian stance forced the desperate *shura's* Iraqi-trained clerics to seek assistance again in Pakistan; however, their attempts "were not very successful" (Ibrahimi 2006, p. 16).[41]

6.4.2 Factionalism: Iranian Internal Politics and Transnational Networks

Attempts to export the Islamic Revolution commenced early. In the spring of 1979, Ayatollah Montazeri's son, Mohamad, and Mehdi Hashemi set up Satja, an organisation which established links with Islamist networks in the Arab world. The unofficial work and links of this organisation with Arab Shi'i networks angered the Islamic Republican Army and the provisional government, which was still not under the full control of Khomeinists.[42] Satja was disbanded, and Montazeri rebuked his son publicly. However, Montazeri and Hashemi established the Office of Liberation Movements, through the Revolutionary Guards, to export the Islamic revolution (IBP 2012, p. 126). Mohammad Montazeri's death in the 1981 bombing of the Islamic Republican Party paved the way for Hashemi's emergence as the champion of the radical export of the revolution (IBP 2012, p. 127).

The first three years of the Islamic Republic witnessed critical political upheavals and manoeuvres. After removing Abol Hassan Bani Sadr from office in 1981 and executing thousands of members of Mujaheddin-e Khalq, a militant opposition group, Khomeinist clerics consolidated their domination of political life (Spellman 2004, p. 25). The year 1982 was a pivotal year on different levels, as the Iranian forces gained the upper hand in the Iraq–Iran War, while Khomeinists completed the institutionalisation of the Islamic Republic. The Khomeinists built a parallel state, directly connected to the leader. The foundations or *Bonyads* would play a pivotal role in the export of the revolution through their international offices, alongside the Revolutionary Guards (*Pasdaran*), the Sâzmân-e Basij-e Mostaz' afin (The Organisation for Mobilisation of the Oppressed). The *Bonyads*, responsible, according to some estimates, for 58 per cent of state budgets, the *Pasdaran*, and the *Basij* constitute a state within a state, which, while undermining the authority of elected presidents, grants the Supreme Leader's office sufficient capabilities to manoeuvre in foreign policy (Keshavarzian 2007, p. 127). In 1982, the consolidated Iranian regime pursued an active policy of exporting the revolution, with a particular emphasis on *Wilayat al-Faqih*.

In 1982, Tehran hosted the first Conference for the Downtrodden (*mustad'afin*), during which Khomeini urged attending Lebanese clerics to mobilise their population against Israeli occupation (Hamzeh 2004, p. 20). Among these clerics were Sayyid Abbas al-Musawi, Shaykh Subhi al-Tufayli, Shaykh Muhammad Yazbak, Shaykh Na'im Qasim, Sayyid

Ibrahim Amin al-Sayyid, and the young Sayyid Hassan Nasrallah (Hamzeh 2004, p. 19).[43] Iran was directly involved in Hizbullah's establishment, to the extent that Khomeini himself suggested its name, derived from the Qur'an (Hamzeh 2004, p. 24).[44] Ali Akbar Mohtashami-pur, a Najaf-educated cleric and the Iranian ambassador to Damascus, played the chief role. Hundreds of Revolutionary Guards set up the first training camp (Louër 2012, p. 58). The organisation was modelled on the Islamic Revolution's institutions—Hizbullah's institutions are basically extensions of the Iranian mother foundations, bearing the same names and often drawing on the same funds.

6.4.2.1 Khomeinist Factionalism

During the second half of the 1980s, factionalism peaked within the Islamic Republic; Ali Akbar Rafsanjani led the pragmatic camp against Montazeri and Mohtashami-Pur radicals. Rafsanjani wanted to end the war with Iraq, decrease regional and international tensions, and settle the Iran-affiliated hostage crisis in Lebanon. The radicals employed their Lebanon connections as a spoiler against Rafsanjani's efforts:

> Using his links to al-Tufayli, Mohtashami-pur apparently ordered kidnappings; on January 24, 1987, three American professors—Alann Steen, Jesse Turner and Robert Polhill—were kidnapped; six days later, Terry Waite, a self-appointed British hostage negotiator, disappeared. In a further challenge to Rafsanjani, Mohtashemi-Pur and Brigadier General Ali Reza Asgari, the Revolutionary Guard's commander in Lebanon, apparently ordered the abduction, on February 17, 1988, of Lt. Col. William Higgins, an observer with the United Nations Trust and Support Organization. Higgins was considered a high-value target likely to complicate Rafsanjani's efforts to put the hostage issue to rest. Two days later, Ali Khamenei indirectly rebuked the kidnappers by stating the only Iranian progress would pave the way for the export of the revolution. (Seliktar 2012, pp. 65–66)

Seliktar connects factional conflicts within the Iranian regime with major Hizbullah operations against foreign targets. Mohtashemi-Pur and Hassan Karroubi exploited their links to Hizbullah to support the Maktabis (Leftists) campaign, a radical Islamic group and Rafsanjani's foes, for the third Majlis elections.[45] Khomeini kept both sides at bay, balancing their acts with his wide powers. After supporting the Maktibis by calling for a "vote for candidates who work for the barefooted and not those adhering to capitalism", the leftists won a majority in the Majles. A day after the election results were made public, Khomeini appointed Rafsanjani as commander-in-chief of the armed forces.[46] Meanwhile, the Lebanese organisation hijacked a Kuwaiti flight to Bangkok on 5 April 1988, diverting it to Algeria. Eleven days later, and after the killing of two US passengers, the Algerian authorities agreed to release the Hizbullah militants who were on the hijacked plane in exchange for the remaining passengers (Seliktar 2012, p. 66).

Hizbullah internalised Iranian factionalism, where Nasrallah and 'Abbas al-Musawi teamed up against al-Tufayli and Hussein al-Musawi's hardline bloc. The organisation's revolutionary and ideological fervour created tensions with the rise of Rafsanjani-masterminded *realpolitik* in the Iranian regime. However, the degree to which Nasrallah and al-Musawi were acting on Rafsanjani's behalf is difficult to determine. The 1991 replacement of al-Tufayli with al-Musawi, which amounted to a coup, and Nasrallah's connections with Ali Khamenei, were both suggestive of direct intervention. Unlike in other contexts, the pragmatic Syrian regime was more favourable to Rafsanjani's stance. The 1989 Ta'if agreement provided regional and international cover for the Assad regime's dominant role in Lebanon; this new order rendered al-Tufayli's renegade policies incompatible.[47]

6.4.2.2 The Hazara Civil War

In 1982 Khomeinist groups launched a campaign to end the *shura* rule in the Hazarajat. The Islamic Republic's regime oversaw the establishment of Pasdaran-e Jihad Islami (Guardians of the Islamic Jihad of Afghanistan) and the Sazaman-e Nasr Inqilab-e Islami Afghanistan (Victory Organisation for Islamic Revolution in Afghanistan). The *shura* authority, already riddled with internal rifts, was eroded when senior members such as Sadeqi Nili defected to the Pasdaran (Ibrahimi 2006, pp. 16–17). The Khomeinist groups, with Iranian financial and military backing, were building sophisticated organisations, drawing on support from the Hazara refugees in Iran.[48] In 1982, Sadeq Nili returned from Iran with substantial military assistance but refused to share it with the *shura* forces, and then killed a Beheshti emissary. This incident sparked a full-scale conflict. By 1984, the *shura* forces were defeated on all fronts and retreated to the district of Nawur, their last stronghold (Ibrahimi 2006, p. 17). The Iran-backed Khomeinists emerged victorious, building on resentment of the *shura* among the population due to religious taxes, and on the support of a local, non-traditional, younger generation of clergy. Following the fall of *shura* rule, more infighting occurred among the various Islamist groups, "eroding the credibility of their ideologies and leaderships" (Ibrahimi 2009, p. 1).

6.4.2.3 Rafsanjani's Realpolitik[49]

After years of infighting, news of the imminent Soviet withdrawal and the exclusion of Hazaras from Pakistan-sponsored negotiations pressured Hazara factions to unite.[50] Hezb-e Wahdat-e Islami Afghanistan (The Islamic Unity Party of Afghanistan) was established in 1989, combining nine groups. Abdul Ali Mazari, a cleric educated in Qom and Najaf, emerged as a leader. Although a former cadre of *Sazaman,* Mazari adopted an ethno-nationalist approach, focussing on the Hazara people's grievances and drifting away from Iranian influence. Iran's pragmatist foreign policy in Afghanistan, a neighbouring and strategically significant country, further alienated Mazari. Iran was seen as the main hindrance to the unification of Hazara political parties, given its significant leverage during the past decade of divisive politics.[51] Secondly, Iran backed certain Sunni factions, especially the Sunni Uzbek leader Abdul Rashid Dostum, a former communist general, and Burhanuddin Rabbani (Maley 1998, p. 125). Unlike the Pasdaran, which was a mere Afghan branch of the Iranian Revolutionary Guards, Sazman, to which Mazari belonged, had a more balanced relation with Iran. The relation oscillated between the Iranian foreign ministry and Montazeri, a controversial figure in Iran's internal politics, which left some elements of the regime unhappy (Rubin 1995, p. 223; Ibrahimi 2006, p. 17).[52] Sazman, the most popular in the 1980s, took on ethno-nationalist elements in its ideology and rhetoric, and tried to balance Iran's influence through inching close towards Peshawar parties (Rubin 1995, p. 223). What tipped ethno-nationalism against the transnational Islamist elements was the "distinctive ethnic character" of postcommunist civil war fighting, namely, in Kabul (Harpviken 1997, p. 280). The Iranian openness to new alliances outside the Hazara community was not overlooked by Ali Mazari, the new leader.

Another visible sign of Wahdat's apparent ethnic leanings was the rejection of Harakat-e Islami, an Islamic movement dominated by non-Hazara Shiʿa. Shaykh Asif Mohsini, the group's leader, objected to the dominant "Hazara grievances and political aspirations"; Harakat's Hazara followers later flocked to Wahdat (Ibrahimi 2009 4). Rahmat Foulad, an educated Hazara, left Harakat's ranks to join Mazari's Wahdat; his rationale for defection was Mohsini's preference for his ethnic brethren, the

Pashtuns (Foulad 2015).[53] Mazari's inclusive ethnic approach meant reaching out to non-Khomeinist and traditional elements, namely, the remnants of Beheshti's *shura*; in 1992, the party's doors were open to Kabul's educated Hazara elite, many of whom were former leftists (Ibrahimi 2009, pp. 4–5).[54] While this urban elite lacked official representation within the party's leadership, their influence on Mazari angered Wahdat's conservative figures (Ibrahimi 2009 6).[55] According to Foulad, who knew Mazari from the early years of Wahdat till his death a few years later, claims that the Hazara leader realised early on the Iranian *realpolitik* approach (Foulad 2015).

The more hostile turn in the Hazaras' relations with Iran came with the defeat of Wahdat in Afshar, a district in west Kabul, in 1993. Iran backed the Tajik-dominated Islamic Republic of Afghanistan's government, and failed to persuade Mazari to support it.[56] Tehran had cultural ties with Persian-speaking Sunni Tajik, who are ethnically identified as 'Iranians'. The forces of Rabbani, Ahmad Shah Massoud (Tajik), and Abdul Rasul Sayyaf attacked the western Kabul stronghold of Wahdat. After Wahdat retreated, Sayyaf's forces committed a massacre, and human rights organisations reported widespread rape and looting[57]:

> Although Rabbani's government did condemn the massacre as one of his government's "mistakes", the tragedy was blamed on his soldiers... today, Afshar remains a ghost district, its surviving inhabitants having fled in the aftermath of the massacre. Its legacy, however, remains very much in the hearts and minds of the Shia and Hazara population. (Mousavi 1998, p. 199)

Rahmad Foulad and his two sons were fighting in the battle of Afshar, and he recalls the anger among *Wahdat* fighters as "Iranians sent us biscuits and photos of Imam Khomeini", while supporting "their Aryan brethren Rabbani".[58] The Hazara disappointment reflected on those who still believed in *Wilayat al-Faqih,* according to Foulad:

> Iran is not interested in safeguarding Shi'as in Afghanistan; their approach is political. During the battle in Kabul, Iran supported Sayyaf, a Wahhabi, and Rabbani against the Hazaras. They continued to send us photos and speeches of Khomeini, until Baba Mazari refused to receive them, after learning of the Iranian support to his enemies... I used to believe in Wilayat al-Faqih, but I do not now. I am not stupid. It is about ethnicity, not religion. (Foulad 2015)

The Afshar massacre had been carved in the Hazaras' collective memory, commemorated annually ever since.[59] Mazari's call for a federal solution may have alarmed the Iranian leadership, weary of its own ethnic problems and emerging separatist movements. The ethnic bitterness after Afshar, the Taliban's advances, and Mazari's seemingly cold relations with Iran led many to believe in a possible Iranian role in the Hazara leader's capture and killing by the Taliban in 1995[60] (Habib and Mohammadi 2012).[61]

The Taliban victory in Kabul, Mazar-e Sharif, and Bamyan drove remaining Wahdat forces further into the north. Khalili, Wahdat's leader, fled to Iran, as his party suffered massive losses in its rank and file. Only Mohaqiq remained in Afghanistan to fight the Taliban from the north; however, the party, although widely acknowledged to politically represent the Hazaras, never recovered its pre-Taliban invasion capacity. The Wahdat participation in the Northern Alliance, led by Ahmad Shah Massoud and backed by Iran, was sufficient to grant Wahdat a role in the 2001 post-Taliban political process.

6.4.3 *Wilayat Al-Faqih in the Post-Khomeini Era*

For many Shi'i clerics, *Wilayat al-Faqih* undermined the *marja'iya*, an institution largely perceived as a meritocracy where religious knowledge and learning define the ascent to power. During the reign of Khomeini, a grand ayatollah and a *marja'*, the tension between his religious status and political position was less apparent; however, a year before his death, he asserted *Wilayat's* dominance over *marja'iya*. Khomeini's successor, former Iranian President Ali Khamenei, prematurely claimed the Grand Ayatollah title, exacerbating tensions with senior clerics. According to Roy:

> In the Iranian constitution, the Guide is not necessarily the highest representative of the religious hierarchy, but the one who is agah be zaman ("conscious of his time"), which marks his participation in history and politics. Khomeini explicitly reiterated this primacy of politics over religious law in his letter of February 1988 to president Khamenei, in which he states that it is legitimate to suspend a religious obligation (in this case the pilgrimage) if a compelling reason of (the Islamic) state demands it. At the time of Khomeini's death, when a new Guide had to be elected, a political successor—Khamenei, who was not even an ayatollah—was preferred to the grand ayatollahs. When in an effort to harmonize political and religious orders,

Islamists tried to bestow upon him the religious titles that the political leader of the revolution lacked, this was rejected by all the grand ayatollahs, including those favorably disposed towards the regime. (Roy 2010, p. 39)

Khamenei's claim to *Wilayat al-Faqih* and *marja'iya* alienated the senior clerics in Iran and abroad. Even senior clergy who were loyal to Khomeini's ideology found it difficult to accept a former president as both a religious and political leader. Four years after Khamenei's appointment, the death of Grand Ayatollah Golpaygani brought the issue of *marja'iya* to the forefront. Golpaygani's family did not allow Khamenei to lead the funeral prayers, "thus denying him the opportunity to choose the deceased's successor" (Ehteshami 1995, p. 53).[62] The family's decision was symbolic, since Golpaygani led the prayers at Khomeini's funeral, signalling the former's seniority as a Shi'i *marja'*. In Iran, Khamenei succumbed to pressure and chose to press for the ascension of Grand Ayatollah Araki, a proponent of *Wilayat al-Faqih* (Ehteshami 1995, p. 54). However, he sought to assert his *marja'* status abroad, splitting Iran's support base and pitting the younger clerics over the Islamic Republic's historical allies: "Shaykh Fadlallah chose to back Ayatollah Mirza Ali Sistani of Najaf (a former student of Ayatollah Khoei) in the succession struggle, while the Lebanese movement's political leader, Hassan Nasrallah, gave his support to Ayatollah Khamenei" (Ehteshami 1995, p. 53).[63] Khomeinist clerics, such as Iraq's Mohammad Baqer al-Hakim who had ironically defied the traditional clergy class at a younger age, adopted their stance a decade later: "Fadlallah, along with Baqer Al-Hakim and Mohammad Shamsiddin, signed the petition asking Khamenei to support Sistani's candidacy" (Ehteshami 1995, p. 54).[64]

In a sign of the clerical rift, Khamenei's book of *fatwas*, known in Shi'i terminology as *Resala*, was only published outside Iran. The recent institutionalisation of Hizbullah and the rise of Nasrallah, a junior cleric in his early 30s, to lead the organisation in 1992, helped Khamenei in his controversial claim to *Marja'iyya* in Lebanon.[65] On the other hand, Fadlallah's rejection of Khamenei's claim created tensions with Hizbullah (Luts 2010). After declaring his own *marja'iyya* in 1995, and growing financially and institutionally independent from the Iran-backed party, Fadlallah was subjected to an indirect campaign of harassment (Abisaab et al. 2004, p. 200).

Although the public discourse and *Wilayat al-Faqih* could present the relation between Iran and Hizbullah as one-sided, with latter on the receiving end, the reality is that the Lebanese Shiʻi organisation promotes itself as crucial to Iranian interests. The Iranian–Hizbullah differences, when they exist, remain reconcilable, given the geographical distance and common interests. This approach contributes to the general argument of this book on the significance to Hizbullah's internal project of levying transnational links in order to achieve its national goal.

While Iran's leverage given financing and ideology remains immense, Hizbullah's relations with the Islamic Republic are two-way, with the organisation's lobbying efforts factoring in Iran's continued interest in supporting the group financially, politically, and militarily.[66] While ideologically committed to *Wilayat al-Faqih*, Hizbullah is aware of the need to constantly market itself as vital for Iranian interests. The organisation's top brass, fluent in Persian, engage annually in self-promotion events and discussions, while building relations across the spectrum in Iran. To avoid a backlash, Hizbullah, though continuously affirming its commitment to, and belief in, *Wilayat al-Faqih*, does not endorse or publicly support any individual presidential candidate in Iran.[67] Among the various factions in the Islamic Republic, there is a relative consensus on Hizbullah's usefulness and success:

> Although its relationship with Hizbullah has evolved over the past three decades, from Tehran's perspective, Hizbullah is still considered a success. As a result, support for the Lebanese group is one of the only foreign-policy issues accepted by all factions. For reformists, backing Hizbullah also offers a way to mitigate pressure emanating from the conservative establishment that demands a more "Islamic" foreign policy. Likewise, the Islamic government is not immune to lobbying, and because of longstanding religious, cultural, political, military, and financial links between Iranian and Lebanese Shia, there is a powerful pro-Hizbullah Lobby in Tehran. (Juneau and Razavi 2013, p. 126)

Recent events and networks suggest that the Iranian regime considers Hizbullah part of its own structure or realm. This approach became public following the assassination of ʻImad Moghnieh, a senior Hizbullah commander, in 2008. Iran treated Moghnieh as one of its symbolic martyrs, and erected a tombstone in Behesht-e-Zahra:

> Iran's relationship with "Hajj Imad" was no brief affair. The Islamic Republic had denied that until the day he was martyred where it paid tribute to the fallen leader at his funeral. The Iranian delegation was led by Ali

Akbar Velayati, representative of the supreme leader, Ayatollah Ali Khamenei, and by then Foreign Minister Manushehr Mottaki on behalf of President Mahmoud Ahmadinejad. A symbolic tombstone was also erected at Behesht-e-Zahra, graveyard of Iran's own martyrs in Tehran. (Chalhoub 2012)

Fluent in Persian, "with a distinct Tehran accent", Moghnieh organised tours for Iranian officials over Hizbullah positions in South Lebanon (Chalhoub 2012). Iran channels a substantial part of its regional influence through Hizbullah: for example, Iranian-funded Iraqi, Saudi, Bahraini, and Yemeni media organisations are based in Hizbullah-controlled areas in Beirut (Hage Ali 2012).[68] Hizbullah manages Iranian support to Hamas, Islamic Jihad Movement, and other Palestinian military movements (Afrasiabi and Entessar 2014).

Attempts to export Hizbullah's model, however, have remained limited, partially due to Lebanon's singularity. In 1998, the National Islamic Alliance in Kuwait, which adopts the *Wilayat al-Faqih* concept, was established (Louër 62–3). While the organisation includes senior figures, such as 'Adnan 'Abd al-Samad and 'Abd al-Muhsin Jamal, both former members of a local al-Da'wa branch during the 1970s, the leadership went to Hussein al-Ma'tuk, a young cleric educated in Qom, who is referred to as the *wakeel* (representative) of Ali Khamenei. The title '*wakeel*' in Shi'i terminology often refers to representatives of the *marja'*. In 2008, however, the National Islamic Alliance suffered a blow after organising a rally to commemorate the death of Imad Moghnieh, a Hizbullah figure "deemed responsible for at least one attack in Kuwait"; the group's leaders were arrested for several days; "the episode seriously undermined their credibility among the Kuwaiti Shi'as, many of whom considered that they had contributed to spreading an incorrect image of Shi'as as disloyal citizens" (Louër 2012, p. 63).

In Afghanistan, the Hazara fortunes drastically changed after the Taliban regime was toppled in October 2001. The US-sponsored political process saw Khalili's appointment in the Vice President position, while Mohaqiq became a minister of planning. However, Mohaqiq withdrew from the cabinet as the powers of his department were transferred to the powerful finance minister, Ashraf Ghani (Ibrahimi 2009, p. 10). Since then, Mohaqiq and Khalili engaged in fierce competition, with each claiming representation of the 'real' *wahdat*. Effectively, the party's unity ended along with claims of exclusive ethnic representation;

a large independent bloc of Hazara MPs emerged. Mohaqiq retained the largest share of the vote in both the parliamentary and presidential elections, partly due to his criticism of President Hamid Karzai, who was open to negotiating with the Taliban.[69] Khalili, Karzai's deputy and ally, was associated with widespread corruption and more pragmatic policies: "Many of Hizb-e Wahdat top-level officials have transformed from politicians into big businessmen and entrepreneurs. This has contributed to the widening gap between the leaders and their constituencies" (Ibrahimi 2009, p. 14).

Mohaqiq and Khalili's parties, due to the lack of party elections and internal structure, are based on networks of clerics and followers who have a client-based relationship with their leadership. After decades of Islamic and Khomeinist domination of Hazara politics, the younger generation seem less inclined to this ideology, especially *wahdat*:

> Many appear to be resistant to the Islamic Republic's revolutionary ideology and model of *velayat-e faghih*. Young Hazaras, in particular, are more likely to be drawn to Iran's youth culture, which is often at variance with the Islamic Republic's strict social and religious norms. The Hazara, a relatively well-educated population, may be under no illusion as to the popularity and even viability of the Islamic Republic. (Nader et al. 2014, p. 16)

Wahdat's 1980s institutions and continued Iranian investment in promoting *Wilayat al-Faqih* among Hazaras and in Hazarajat largely failed to achieve its goals (Nader et al. 2014, p. 17). In addition to the cultural factor, Iranian pragmatic foreign policy alienated Hazaras. Iran's financial support to Karzai, who admitted receiving 'bags of cash' from Tehran, could be seen a factor in this increasing anti-Iranian sentiment (Boonen 2010). The Iranian regime has been accused of aiding certain elements within the Taliban; in particular, the Quds Force, the external operations arm of the Iranian Revolutionary Guard, allegedly provides training for the Taliban (Harrison 2013). The formerly 'discrete' relations became public after a Taliban delegation visited Tehran in what was described as a "meeting of two governments", according to the group's spokesman; the semi-official *Fars* news agency was the first to announce the visit (Harrison 2013). Tehran's *realpolitik* in Afghanistan is at odds with Hazara ethno-nationalist aspirations. Iran supports Pashtun, Tajik, and Uzbek groups and politicians, and is blamed for fomenting internal divisions among Hazara factions, opposing a federal or separatist solution in Afghanistan.[70]

Similarly, in Iraq, Iran supports various Shi'a groups, thus preventing any single player from claiming sole representation of Iraqi Shi'i majority, steering them away from Tehran's influence.[71] In a similar fashion to Afghanistan, Iran maintains strong relations with other ethnic and religious groups in Iraq, such as Jalal Talabani's Patriotic Union of Kurdistan. Unlike in Lebanon, where Iran unified various groups under Hizbullah's leadership, Tehran supports many smaller organisations and militias in Iraq, and has played a role in splitting larger groups, such as the Supreme Council of the Islamic Revolution in Iraq, now known simply as the Supreme Islamic Council.[72]

In March 2012, Hadi Al-Ameri, the leader of the Badr Organisation, officially split ways with SCIRI (the Supreme Council for the Islamic Revolution in Iraq). Al-Ameri's close ties to the Revolutionary Guards' Al-Quds Force and its leader General Qassem Suleimani, although previously known, became public, as both men appeared in photos at the front line. In an interview with the *New Yorker*, Al-Ameri declared: "I love Qassem Suleimani! He is my dearest friend" (Filkins 2013). Ammar al-Hakim, who took over the leadership of SCIRI from his father, declared in the organisation's new charter his commitment to the democratic process, breaking with *Wilayat al-Faqih*: "The active projects... commence with the development of the citizen, both practically and intellectually, and so the organization becomes a tool in the Ummah's (nation) hand, not a baton to fulfill the sovereigns' whims. The people are the source of decision-making" (Al-Hakim 2015, pp. 14–15). On the other hand, Badr's commitment to *Wilayat al-Faqih* is clear. The organisation's armed wing, now called the Islamic Resistance, declared the following in a statement on the 18 August 2014:

> We, from the start, headed to the military fronts after a taklif shar'i [a religious order] from Ayatollah Ali Khamenei, the leader of the Islamic Revolution, before the religious marje' Seyyed Ali Sistani's fatwa. We were fighting on the Syria and al-Anbar fronts... Now, we see that the government is in the Americans' hands ... and America entered the front needlessly, as the Iraqi forces own the initiative on the ground and all fronts....
> So we, today ... are under the Wilayat al-Faqih's orders, and we will definitely not participate in an alliance with America. (Badr 2014)

6.5 Conclusion

Shaped by both the clerical establishment's political experiences and print technology in the nineteenth and twentieth centuries, the development of Shiʿi Islam from a quietist religion to its current Khomeinist form is a modern phenomenon. While clerics such as al-Hilli argued for *ijtihād* in the fifteenth century, the *al-marjaʿiyya*'s capacity for mass mobilisation emerged with the advent of print in the late nineteenth century. The effect of print manifested in al-Shirazi's *fatwa* to boycott tobacco, forcing Iran's ruler to change course. Similarly, Shiʿi rituals witnessed a paradigm change, specifically in public perception, as they inched into activism and became politically charged. Shariʿati's writings and lectures were the main driver behind the change of the 'Ashura' rituals.

Since the early twentieth century, the reform movement in Iran, in opposition and in government, radicalised the clerical establishment, creating the current that culminated in Khomeini's *Wilayat al-Faqih* theory, a basic tenet of Hizbullah's identity. This process is clear in Khomeini's ideological radicalisation. His theory of Islamic government transformed from a hybrid clerical–shah rule to an absolute clerical leadership from the mid-twentieth century during his exile in Najaf, where his theory of *Wilayat al-Faqih* or Islamic government was postulated. Simultaneously, the decade prior to the revolution witnessed an Islamic print revolution, tripling the output as Shiʿi intellectuals and clerics in Iran and abroad rushed to provide an Islamic alternative to the increasing popularity of communism. These changes contributed to Khomeini's *Wilayat al-Faqih*, rendering it a modern doctrine, rooted in the nineteenth century.

On the transnational level, four factors defined the export of *Wilayat al-Faqih* and demonstrate the dominance of internal politics and individual groups' interests over transnational ideology. First, the established senior clerics resisted the transnational encroachment on their traditional power sphere, while the younger clergy were more prone to join the Khomeinist movements. Secondly, Iranian factionalism, whether during the early years of the revolution, or throughout the pragmatist-leftist divide, utilised transnational networks for internal purposes. Thirdly, Iranian foreign policy tipped *realpolitik* over ideology in neighbouring countries, while furthering ideological ties in the more distant realms such as Lebanon, where Hizbullah's perceived successes were useful to Iran internally. Finally, tensions emerged between ideology and the necessary pragmatism in the nation-state. After setbacks in the relations with Iran and falling out with its anti-irredentist policy, Khomeinist Hazara organisations adopted the ethno-nationalist politics in Afghanistan. Adapting to the post-Saddam Hussein era, SCIRI departed from the *Wilayat al-Faqih* doctrine, and reconciled its Islamic ideology with electoral democracy.

In Lebanon, a non-neighbouring country, Hizbullah's internal goals can be accommodated with Iran's agenda. In fact, the organisation's lobbying efforts suggests a certain extent of influence on Hizbullah's part within Iranian circles, in relation to preserving a consensus among various political factions. The transnational links, with their relatively vast financial, material, and political resources, serve the organisation's internal purposes well. However, as the various other Shiʿi experiences highlight, the transnational link or the commitment to *the Wilayat al-Faqih* doctrine does not necessarily hinder the possibility of a break in relations if the gap between Iranian interests and those of Hizbullah seems irreconcilable.

Notes

1. Shiʿism is inclusive of groups such as the Ismaili and Zaidi sects; however, Twelver Shiʿism is the numerically dominant group.
2. This belief, in its entirety, is restricted to the Twelver Imami Shiʿis, also known simply as the Twelvers or *ithna ʿashari*.
3. Unlike in the Sunni case, where the Prophet's companions played the major role in recording his sayings, the Twelve Imams are central in Shiʿi *hadith* volumes.
4. The practice is known as *ijtihād*, or individual endeavour.
5. According to Juan Cole, Al-Hilli was "perhaps the first Shiʿi thinker to use the word *ijtihād* in a positive sense to mean the application of individual effort to the derivation of a judgement on the basis of technical expertise" (Cole 1981, p. 36).
6. Unlike in Sunni Islam, Friday prayers are not obligatory in Shiʿi Islam; they only become so after *al-mahdi's* appearance.
7. Najafi's emulation structure was based on al-Hilli's theory.
8. *Jawaher al-Kalam* is literally translated from the Arabic as the 'jewels of speech'.
9. Ansari discontinued this tradition. Najafi's step was seen as emanating from his interest in continuing his legacy.
10. Another political advantage added to the advent of print is that Shirazi wrote in Persian, while Ansari's mother language was Arabic. This is particularly significant, as there were limitations to Shiʿi political influence in Ottoman-controlled Shiʿi territory.

11. The 'tobacco revolt' came at a time when inter-city transportation increased, allowing communication to reach further.
12. Shirazi's followers bestowed on him the title *al-Imam al-Mujadid* (the Imam of Renewal).
13. The religious courts in Lebanon, for instance, provided the clerical establishment with much of its power, although in this case, it is restricted to personal affairs, known as *ahwal shakhsia*, which includes cases of marriage, divorce, and inheritance.
14. Shiʿis religious ceremonies usually take place in *hussayniyas*, named after the third Shiʿi imam, Hussein Ben Ali, whose death is commemorated annually.
15. During the confrontational phase with the shah, Khomeini became critical of traditional clerics, the older and more institutionalised members of the clergy, for their quietist approach.
16. Burujerdi was specifically hostile towards Abu al-Qasim Kashani (1882–1962) who was politically active since the 1920 revolution against the British army in Iraq. Kashani moved to Iran, where his political activism aligned him with Mosaddeq's National Front, and he served as the speaker of parliament, representing the movement's religious wing (Louër 2012, p. 20).
17. Mroueh wrote about his intellectual journey from clerical school to communist, using the title *From Najaf, Marx Entered my Life*.
18. Al-Hakim was the senior *marjaʿ* in Najaf for 15 years, from 1955 to 1970, and his religious authority was widely acknowledged, significantly more than his two heirs: Abo Al-Qassem al-Khoei and Ruhollah Khomeini. This stature makes his discrete endorsement of Da'wa highly significant.
19. Norton claims that al-Sadr, after falling out with the shah, may have received funding from the Baʿthist regime in Iraq.
20. Al-Sadr organised Shariʿati's funeral in Damascus, a move that angered the regime, which protested to the Lebanese government through their Beirut embassy.
21. This overlapping identity produced ethnically distinct communism and Islamism, in a fashion similar to Iraqi Kurdistan. In the Kurdish region, the Iraqi Communist Party maintained a separate Kurdish branch, while both Sunni and Shiʿi Islamists formed independent Kurdish branches.
22. While the Hazaras are the largest ethnic group, the Shiʿi of Afghanistan are more ethnically diverse, and include, for instance, the Persians who inhabit western border areas near Iran, and the Qizilbash and Bayat, both of whom have Turkish origins; by the same token, the Hazaras are not all Twelver Shiʿis, as they include Ismaʿili and Sunni elements.
23. Central to the Hazaras' nationalist persecution narrative is the vilification of Afghanistan's founder, Abdul Rahman; this juxtaposes the Hazaras with

the Pachtun-dominated state. In 1892, Abdul Rahman, the then prince of Kabul, launched a campaign to enforce his rule after a territorial agreement with the Russians and the British, repressing a Hazara uprising, and expropriating land and expelling thousands (Semple 2012, p. 3; Canfield 2004, p. 243). Abdul Rahman's army comprised 100,000 soldiers, and they were sent on a 'religious crusade' against the 'godless' Shiʻi Hazaras (Williams 2011, p. 183). In Hazara literature, 60 per cent of their population was killed in the campaign, while a large segment of Quetta's Hazaras trace their origins back to Abul Rahman's expulsions or forced migration (Interview with Liaqat Ali Hazara 2015).
24. *Khums*, an obligatory religious tax for Shiʻa, is a fifth of overall profits. Half of *khums* is the Imam's *sahm* (share), and the other half is *Sahm al-sāda* (the share of the Prophets' descendants).
25. Similar portrayals of the Hazara are found in Afghan literary works, such as *The Kite Runner* by Khaled Hosseini. The servants in the main character's house are a Hazara family, whose son Hassan is the narrator's best friend: "They called him 'flat-nosed' because of Ali and Hassan' s characteristic Hazara Mongoloid features. For years, that was all I knew about the Hazaras, that they were Mongul descendants, and that they looked a little like Chinese people. School textbooks barely mentioned them and referred to their ancestry only in passing. Then one day, I was in Baba's study, looking through his stuff, when I found one of my mother' s old history books. It was written by an Iranian named Khorami. I blew the dust off it, sneaked it into bed with me that night, and was stunned to find an entire chapter on Hazara history. An entire chapter dedicated to Hassan's people! In it, I read that my people, the Pashtuns, had persecuted and oppressed the Hazaras. It said the Hazaras had tried to rise against the Pashtuns in the nineteenth century, but the Pashtuns had 'quelled them with unspeakable violence'. The book said that my people had killed the Hazaras, driven them from their lands, burned their homes, and sold their women. The book said part of the reason Pashtuns had oppressed the Hazaras was that Pashtuns were Sunni Muslims, while Hazaras were Shiʻa. The book said a lot of things I didn't know, things my teachers hadn't mentioned. Things Baba hadn't mentioned either. It also said some things I did know, like that people called Hazaras mice-eating, flat-nosed, load-carrying donkeys. I had heard some of the kids in the neighborhood yell those names to Hassan" (Hosseini 2003, p. 23).
26. The same trend of ethnic following occurred elsewhere, as Hazaras flocked into organisations led by their ethnic brethren.
27. Both PDPA factions took their names from the two newspapers they ran, *Parcham* and *Khalq*. Even Yari's group was referred to as *Shola*, the name of its publication.

28. Keshtmand served as prime minister from 1981 to 1988, and then briefly from 1989 to 1990. He resides in London after receiving asylum from John Major's government.
29. The PLO maintained good relations with the Iraqi regime, which funded various Palestinian groups. The PLO support for Khomeini's movement was out of antagonism towards the shah, an ally of Israel and its chief patron, the USA.
30. Shariati made this speech during the early 1970s. The recording is available online and cited in the bibliography.
31. Khomeini's contempt for the electorate, or the democratic process, was clear in his statements. The establishment of revolutionary institutions, parallel to the classic state ones, was vital for this vision. Khomeini stressed that the elected institutions were to address "matters beneath the dignity of Islam to concern itself with" (Tayekh 2009, p. 25).
32. To this day, the Amal movement reveres Mostafa Chamran, one of the Freedom Movement of Iran's founders, for his role in organising its militia's resistance activities against the Israeli occupation.
33. Check Chap. 2, pp. 33–36.
34. Khomeini's religious credentials and charismatic leadership eclipsed some of the reluctance to fully accept *Welayat al-Faqih*. However, following his death in 1989, the same clergy who had accepted Khomeini's leadership role were more resistant to the rise of Ali Khamenei, his successor as Supreme Leader. This was evident in the case of Lebanon's Mohamad Hussein Fadlallah and Afghanistan's Mazari.
35. The Afghan Hazaras' case, a minority in a multi-ethnic, weak state in recurrent conflict, bears similarities to Lebanon's Hizbullah.
36. The uprising's failure in west Kabul became a part of the general Hazara grievances towards other ethnic groups, as they lent it little if any support. However, considering the Soviet-backed government's military strength and Kabul's significance, the chances of the uprising's success, even if aided by other ethnic groups, appeared slim; nevertheless, the Hazara perception of the event fits in their overall narrative of exclusion.
37. The *Shura* was declared after the government forces crushed an uprising in the Bamian province.
38. In Quetta, where there is a substantial Hazara minority, the nationalist sentiments outflanked Islamism. As in the Diasporas' nationalist fervour elsewhere, Quetta's Hazaras have been more inclined into a separatist and idealistic view of establishing Hazaristan, claiming pre-Abdul Rahman territories and focussing on the myth of ancestry from Genghis Khan, the Moghul Emperor. In the 1960s, they established the Tanzim-e Nasle Naq-e Hazara Moghul (Organization of the New Generation of the Moghul Hazaras); many Tanzim members joined the more inclusive

nationalist group, Ittehadiah Islami-e Mujahedin Afghanistan (Islamic Association of the Mujahedin of Afghanistan), which had an ethnic ideology at odds with Islamist and leftist dominant parties (Ibrahimi 2006, pp. 9–10). *Shura* forces took over Ittehadiah's single military base in the winter of 1980, while their activities were banned throughout the region (Ibrahimi 2006, p. 10).

39. The Jihadi commission, while significant for coordination, remained a loose coalition, given the strength of the local leaders (Ibrahimi 2006, p. 12).
40. Kho's stance towards Islamic government is unclear, favouring a more traditional view of clerical role. It is ironic that his followers ran this supposedly clerical government in Hazarajat, declaring *jihad* against its enemies.
41. The Iraqi-trained clerics resisted the new generation of radical Khomeinist clergy, even at the high cost of losing Iranian support.
42. Satja was established in the spring of 1979, weeks after the revolution's success.
43. Clerics from al-Da'wah and Amal joined forces with Shi'i cadres from the Fatah movement and the Lebanese Communist Party (Hamzeh 2004, p. 24).
44. Surat al-Ma'ida no. 5 p. 26
45. *Maktabis* were named after a leftist newsletter published by the Islamic Republican Party. Baktiari says the following on the name and group: "The name *maktabi* came from a newsletter called *Insan-c Maktabi*, which was edited by Hassan Ayat and circulated among party cadres. The newsletter, which sought to steer the IRP toward a more radical position, appealed to the younger, non-clerical members of the IRP. Those who called themselves *maktabi* wanted to emphasize that they were the 'followers of the Holy Book', and they categorically rejected the argument that the clergy should not directly involve itself in the affairs of the state. They advocated a strongly centralized economy, the total nationalization of major industries, and a comprehensive land reform, and they viewed the Islamic revolution as a movement geared to benefit the *mostaz'afin* (downtrodden)" (Baktiari 1996. 81).
46. The appointment was symbolic as Mohtashemi-Pur declared the vote was a clear mandate to continue the war.
47. After removing al-Tufayli, the Syrian regime excluded Hizbullah from the disarmament of militias, allowing the Shi'i organisation to resist Israeli occupation (Chalcraft; 2009: 137).
48. The Hazara refugees of Iran were and remain a significant factor in Afghan politics. The Iranian authorities strongly recruited Hazara fighters for its Iran–Iraq War and later to fight alongside the Syrian regime's forces.

49. Following Khomeini's death, Rafsanjani was elected president for two consecutive terms (1989–1997).
50. The fall of Bamyan, the provincial centre, to the Hazara factions in August 1988, facilitated the unification process, especially that of *Sazman-e Nasr* (Ibrahimi 2009, p. 2).
51. A former Wahdat official alleged that Husain Ibrahimi, the representative of the Iranian Supreme Leader Ali Khamenei in Afghanistan, "tried to prevent" the formation of the party to maintain Tehran's influence; however, "the Iranians decided to work with it and supported it in the early days of its existence" (Ibrahimi 2009, p. 3).
52. Montazeri remained a controversial figure until Khomeini sidelined him before his death.
53. Foulad stresses that contradictions between Mohsini's transnational ideology and his ethnically driven actions drove Hazaras out of the party, more than their attraction to Mazari (Interview with Rahmat Foulad. 5 May, 2015, London).
54. This inclusive approach is typical of nationalism, specifically in a multiethnic context.
55. As a result of such influences, Mazari, perhaps less concerned about his organisation's unity in light of his wide popularity and iconic status, was growing more pragmatic, forging alliances outside the Islamic sphere. Such a policy left the Iranian regime more wary of Mazari's intentions, and the fact that unity stands to threaten Tehran's leverage over the Hazara community.
56. Mazari's main issue with Rabbani's government was its exclusion of the Hazaras.
57. Human Rights Watch also reported Hazara atrocities against other minorities.
58. Foulad claims that Iranian officials told Mazari that while he is a Shi'i 'brother, Rabbani is 'one of us' (Foulad uses the words 'White Aryan'). The Iranian meeting with Mazari was held to persuade him to support Rabbani's government, according to Foulad. (Interview with Rahmad Foulad. 5 May 2015, London).
59. Since Wahdat's breakup in 2009, Khalili and Mohaqiq have been using the annual commemoration to separately address their Hazara followers, and individually claim to represent the continuity of Mazari's legacy.
60. The claims revolve around the notion that Mazari would not have gone to the Taliban-held territories without guarantees to his own safety.
61. Interview with Marzuq Ali (a Hazara village elder). 5 May 2015. Marzuq communicated with Mazari.
62. Golpaygani had led the prayers in Khomeini's funeral. The funeral prayer is a reference to the successor of the deceased *marja'*.
63. Fadlallah is a *sayyid*, not a Shaykh, as Ehteshami wrote.

64. Ehteshami's analysis has two factual errors. The first is that Fadlallah, while described as the 'spiritual leader', had no organisational role in Hizbullah. However, he played a supportive role, and was considered a Khomeinist and radical figure in Lebanon, in comparison to Sayyid Musa al-Sadr, the leader of the Amal movement. The second error was considering Ayatollah Sistani, an Iranian citizen, an 'Arab *marja*' (Ehteshami 1995, pp. 53–54).
65. Nasrallah is 20 years younger than Khamenei, and was selected secretary general more than two years after the new Supreme Leader assumed office.
66. A Hizbullah official, fluent in Persian, told me of his visit to a university in Tehran, where students asked why Iran spends money on an organisation thousands of miles away, while its own people are suffering from poverty. The official responded by asking why the USA has a base in Guam.
67. During my visit to Iran, secular activists associated Hizbullah with the regime, due to its allegiance to Khamenei, a partisan figure in Iranian politics. However, on the political level, Hizbullah remains open to engaging with any Iranian administration.
68. The Bahraini authorities accuse Hizbullah of training Shiʻi activists; however, the accusations remain unsubstantiated. On the Yemen front, Hizbullah has channelled Iranian support to the former president of South Yemen, Ali Salem al-Beidh. During my fieldwork in Lebanon, I visited his office in the southern suburbs of Beirut.
69. The return of the Taliban, or elements of the group, to the Afghan government, remains a frightening thought to many Hazaras. The Hazaras I interviewed were highly critical of Wahdat's decision to hand in the organisation's arms, since the remaining ethnic militias kept their weapons and organisational structure.
70. Mazari's call for a federal solution in Afghanistan is continuously reiterated in the annual commemorations of his death.
71. Iran was accused of adopting a 'divide and conquer' strategy to maintain control over various Iraqi groups.
72. Hizbullah Iraq, Badr, SCIRI, ʻAsaeb al-Haq, branches of al-Daʻwa Party, Ahmad Chalabi's group, and Sadrist movements are all recipients of Iranian funds and support.

REFERENCES

BOOKS

Abisaab, R., & Abisaab, M. (2014). *The Shiʻites of Lebanon: Modernism, Communism, and Hizbullah's Islamists*. Syracuse: Syracuse University Press.

Al-Hakim, A. (2015). *Ruʾyatuna Al-Tanzimiya* (Our Organizational Vision). Retrieved from http://www.almejlis.org/assets/files/5843_1_1425213297.pdf

Al-Wardi, A., & Aboul-Enein, Y. (2012). *Iraq in Turmoil: Historical Perspectives of Dr. Ali al-Wardi, From the Ottoman Empire to King Faisal.* Annapolis: Naval Institute Press.

Baktiari, B. (1996). *Parliamentary Politics in Revolutionary Iran: The Institutionalization of Factional Politics.* Gainesville: University Press of Florida.

Boroujerdi, M. (1996). *Iranian Intellectuals and the West: The Tormented Triumph of Nativism.* Syracuse: Syracuse University Press.

Bradsher, H. (1999). *Afghan Communism and Soviet Intervention.* Oxford: Oxford University Press.

Campo, J. (2009). *Encyclopedia of Islam.* New York: Infobase Publishing.

Chalcraft, J. (2009). *The Invisible Cage: Syrian Migrant Workers in Lebanon.* Stanford, CA: Stanford University Press.

Cockburn, A., & Cockburn, P. (2000). *Saddam Hussein, an American Obsession.* London: Verso.

Daftary, F. (2013). *A History of Shi'i Islam.* London: I.B. Tauris.

Ehteshami, A. (1995). *After Khomeini: The Iranian Second Republic.* New York: Routledge.

Eickelman, D. (2002). *The Middle East and Central Asia: An Anthropological Approach.* New Jersey: Prentice Hall.

Hamzeh, A. N. (2004). *In the Path of Hizbullah.* Syracuse: Syracuse University Press.

Hosseini, K. (2003). *The Kite Runner.* New York: Riverhead Books.

International Business Publications, USA. (2012, September 1). *Iran Country Study Guide, Vol. 1. Strategic Information and Daaaevelopments.* Washington, DC: International Business Publications, USA.

Janin, H., & Kahlmeyer, A. (2007). *Islamic Law: The Sharia from Muhammad's Time to the Present.* Jefferson, NC: McFarland & Co.

Juneau, T., & Razavi, S. (Eds.). (2013). *Iranian Foreign Policy Since 2001: Alone in the World.* London: Routledge.

Kadhim, A. (2012). *Reclaiming Iraq: The 1920 Revolution and the Founding of the Modern State.* Austin, TX: University of Texas Press.

Keddie, N. (Ed.). (1983). *Religion and Politics in Iran. Shi'ism from Quietism to Revolution.* New Haven, CT: Yale University Press.

Keshavarzian, A. (2007). *Bazaar and State in Iran: The Politics of the Tehran Marketplace.* Cambridge: Cambridge University Press.

Khomeini, R. (1995). *Islamic Government.* Tehran: The Institute for Compilation and Publication of Imam Khomeini's Works. Retrieved from http://www.iran-chamber.com/history/rkhomeini/books/velayat_faqeeh.pdf

Louër, L. (2008). *Transnational Shia Politics: Religious and Political Networks in the Gulf.* New York: Columbia University Press.

Louër, L. (2012). *Shi'ism and Politics in the Middle East.* London: C. Hurst & Co. (Publishers) Ltd.

Maley, W. (Ed.). (1998). *Fundamentalism Reborn? Afghanistan and the Taliban.* New York: New York University Press.

Mervin, S. (Ed.). (2010). *The Shi'a Worlds and Iran*. London: Saqi Books.
Mockaitis, T. (Ed.). (2013). *The Iraq War Encyclopedia*. Santa Barbara: ABC-Clio.
Mousavi, S. A. (1998). *The Hazaras of Afghanistan: An Historical, Cultural, Economic and Political Study*. Richmond, Surry: Curzon Press.
Nader, A., et al. (2014). *Iran's Influence in Afghanistan: Implications for the U.S. Drawdown*. Santa Monica: Rand.
Norton, A. R. (1987). *Amal and the Shi'a: Struggle for the Soul of Lebanon*. Austin: University of Texas Press.
Pelletiere, S. (1992). *The Iran-Iraq War: Chaos in a Vacuum*. New York: Praeger.
Roy, O. (2010). The Impact of the Iranian Revolution on the Middle East. In S. Mervin (Ed.), *The Shi'a Worlds and Iran* (pp. 29–44). London: Saqi Books.
Rubin, B. (1995). *The Fragmentation of Afghanistan: State Formation and Collapse in the International System*. New Haven, CT: Yale University Press.
Seliktar, O. (2012). *Navigating Iran: From Carter to Obama*. New York: Palgrave Macmillan.
Semple, M. (2012). *The Rise of the Hazaras and the Challenge of Pluralism in Afghanistan 1978–2011*. Cambridge, MA: Harvard Center for Islamic Studies.
Spellman, K. (2004). *Religion and Nation: Iranian Local and Transnational Networks in Britain*. New York: Berghahn Books.
Tayekh, R. (2009). *Guardians of the Revolution: Iran and the World in the Age of the Ayatollahs*. New York: Oxford University Press.
Traboulsi, F. (2007). *A History of Modern Lebanon*. London: Pluto Press.
Walbridge, L. S. (Ed.). (2001). *The Most Learned of the Shi'a: The Institution of the Marja' Taqlid*. Oxford: Oxford University Press.
Williams, B. G. (2011). Afghanistan, Hazaras. In A. Moghadam (Ed.), *Militancy and Political Violence in Shi'ism: Trends and Patterns* (pp. 181–200). New York: Routledge.

Journal Articles

Balaghi, S. (2001). Print Culture in Late Qajar Iran: The Cartoons of "Kashkūl". *Iranian Studies*, 34(1/4) [Special Issue: Qajar Art and Society], 165–181.
Canfield, R. L. (2004). New Trends Among the Hazaras: From "the Amity of Wolves" to "The Practice of Brotherhood". *Iranian Studies*, 37(2), 241–262.
Hanson, B. (1983). The 'Westoxication' of Iran: Depictions and Reactions of Behrangi, al-e Ahmad, and Shari'ati. *International Journal of Middle East Studies*, 15(1), 1–23.
Harpviken, K. B. (1997). Transcending Traditionalism: The Emergence of Non-State Military Formations in Afghanistan. *Journal of Peace Research*, 34(3), 271–287.
Thesiger, W. (1955). The Hazaras of Central Afghanistan. *Geographic Journal*, 121(3), 312–319.

Reports

Ibrahimi, N. (2006). *The Failure of a Clerical Proto-State: Hazarajat, 1979–1984* [Online]. London: Crisis States Research Centre, LSE. Retrieved May 8, 2015, from http://r4d.dfid.gov.uk/PDF/Outputs/CrisisStates/wp6.2.pdf

Ibrahimi, N. (2009). *The Dissipation of Political Capital Among Afghanistan's Hazaras: 2001–2009* [Online]. London: Crisis States Research Centre, LSE. Retrieved May 8, 2015, from http://eprints.lse.ac.uk/28493/1/WP51.2.pdf

News Articles

Afrasiabi, K., & Entessar, N. (2014, August 12). *Iran Uses Hamas for Leverage in Nuclear Negotiations*. Retrieved from http://america.aljazeera.com/opinions/2014/8/iran-hamas-palestinenuclearnegotiations.html

Badrpress. (2014, August 18). *Badr, Al-Janah Al'askari Li Monazamat Badr: Lasna Militia Wa Lan Nusharek Behelf Ma' Amrika* (The Badr Organization's Military Branch: We Are Not a Militia and Will Not Participate in an Alliance with the U.S.). Retrieved from http://badrpress.com/badr/feeds.php?lang=ar&page_name=politic&id=26461

Boonen J. (2010, October 25). *Hamid Karzai Admits Office Gets 'Bags of Money' from Iran*. Retrieved from http://www.theguardian.com/world/2010/oct/25/hamid-karzai-office-cash-iran

Chalhoub, E. (2012, February 14). *Imad Mughniyeh in Iran: The Stuff of Legends*. Retrieved from http://english.al-akhbar.com/node/4198

Filkins, D. (2013, September 30). *The Shadow Commander*. Retrieved from http://www.newyorker.com/magazine/2013/09/30/the-shadow-commander

Habib, S., & Mohammadi, I. (2012). *Role of Iran in Assassination of Baba Mazari*. Retrieved July 20, 2014, from www.hazarapeople.com/2012/04/24/iran-and-hizbe-wahdat-e-islami/

Hage Ali, M. (2012, July 3). *Iraqi Intrigue in Lebanon*. Retrieved from http://www.executive-magazine.com/business-finance/finance/iraqi-intrigue-in-lebanon

Harrison, E. (2013, June 3). *Afghan Taliban Send Delegation to Iran*. Retrieved from http://www.theguardian.com/world/2013/jun/03/afghan-taliban-send-delegation-iran

Luts, M. (2010, July 6). *Shiite Muslim Cleric Mourned in Lebanon*. Retrieved from http://articles.latimes.com/2010/jul/06/world/la-fg-fadlallah-funeral-20100707

Shari'ati, A. (2015, May 4). *"Red Shi'ism: The Religion of Martyrdom; Black Shi'ism: The Religion of Mourning"*. Retrieved from http://www.Shariati.com/english/redblack.html

Interviews

Rahmat Foulad, interview by Mohanad Hage Ali, London, May 5, 2015.

CHAPTER 7

Conclusion

This book set out to answer the question: how is Hizbullah's identity produced and how modern is it? In so doing, it has drawn on the debates around nationalism, mainly the modernist versus perennial and ethnosymbolist arguments. It appears that Hizbullah consciously emulated the Islamic Republic of Iran in its efforts to create a sense of sectarian cultural identity among its population. The organisation embarked on the similar construction of a new Lebanese Shiʻi identity, using the building blocks of earlier attempts. The study of nationalism has for the most part focussed on secular and ethnic movements in Europe and in anti-colonial contexts in other regions; however, research on the rise of sectarian and Islamist identities in Lebanon has concluded that these confessional sub-identities are significant enough to be considered a sectarian form of nationalism. In this regard, the Druze and Christian identities in Lebanon have been more pivotal to the definition of the country's politics and its various forms of nationalism than has the formation of an inclusive Lebanese identity. Makdisi's research on the development of 'sectarian nationalism'—he rightly differentiates between historical manifestations of religious violence and current forms of sectarian identity and conflict—and Gellner's contention that Islam performs the political functions of nationalism are both examples of this approach towards the study of confessional identities and their political manifestations in the Levant.

However, the Lebanese Shiʻi sectarian identity arrived later than that of the Maronites and Druze. Despite this, its advent has had a greater impact.

The insertion of the Shiʿa into Lebanon's sectarian politics took a more organised and institutionalised form, modelled on the Islamic Republic of Iran, and enlisting its help. Hizbullah, which declared its arrival in its first open letter in 1985, rapidly expanded its organisational and institutional network throughout the 1990s to cover welfare, scouts, national syndicates, and education, from elementary schools to graduate studies. This expansion was simultaneously supported by the spread of dedicated media outlets and a booming publications list, with regular journals numbering in the dozens. Its central magazine, *Baqiatullah*, claims to have a circulation of 30,000, making it the biggest publication in Lebanon. Hizbullah's autonomous status within Lebanon (established by the Syrian regime following the Lebanese civil war), coupled with its vast institutional network, has enabled it to act in the capacity of a 'state within a state'.

As is the case with nationalism, such institutions produce and to a large extent impose a specific identity, which is "learned and internalized through socialization" (Ozkirimli 2005, p. 33). The process itself is modern in that it recreates this identity in different forms for its respective audiences. Chapter 2, for example, illustrated how Shiʿi identity has metamorphosed through Hizbullah's various institutions, highlighting the creative way the organisation has reappropriated and transformed traditional Shiʿi forms and rituals. By studying these institutions, this book has demonstrated how Hizbullah has tailored its message to suit its various followers, reinventing the identity it has created in different forms that will resonate more strongly with a specific community. For instance, the Muʾassasat al-Jareeh (the Foundation for the Wounded) focuses on the injuries Ayatollah Khamenei sustained in the Iran–Iraq War when delivering its message of the centrality of the concept of *Wilayat al-Faqih*, and it highlights the story of the last fight of Abu al-Fadl al-ʿAbbas, Imam Husayn's half-brother, who lost both his arms, to stress the essential importance resistance has to the Shiʿi sense of identity. Hizbullah's claims to historical continuity are similarly manifest in its emphasis on the leadership of the *ulama* throughout Shiʿi history, as produced in various contexts.

The organisation's claims to historical continuity and its revival of the past include the integration into its internal structure of concepts it alleges existed in early Islamic times, such as that of the *altaʿbiʾa* (the mobilisation forces). Ayatollah Khamenei, Iran's Supreme Leader, attributes the concept's 'revival' to Imam Khomeini. However, as Chap. 2 detailed, one of Hizbullah's founding members acknowledges that they studied the internal structures of Marxist–Leninist organisations when establishing the party: Hizbullah emulates the Leninist concept of the 'vanguard party' and its emphasis on the centrality of the party newspaper. Indeed, its publications are a crucial element in the organisation's strategy, as each institution now issues its own magazine, adapting Hizbullah's sectarian Shi'i message to its specific audience. At the same time as the organisation has grown to encompass several institutions, it has centralised the dissemination of a specific Shi'i identity. The CCU, one of Hizbullah's largest institutions, oversees this process, training each of the institutions' clerical teams, vetting the different magazines, and providing expertise in ideological matters. This now deeply centralised and bureaucratic process has inevitably resulted in complaints, but balancing this centralisation to a certain extent is another similarity to the Marxist–Leninist model at the level of local organisation: every town and neighbourhood retains its own structure, ensuring mass participation. These branches have a certain degree of autonomy in local decision-making and the implementation of major decisions.

The volume of Hizbullah's publication is such that the organisation as a whole is the largest single publisher nationwide; *Baqiatullah*, its principal magazine, claims to be the largest publication in the country. The scale of its print publishing is more than matched by the organisation's enormous online capacity, under the supervision of a smaller institution called the Central Electronic Unit, which oversees the organisation's many websites and supervises its technical and online security. For instance, Al-Manar Television's website is the country's number one online news source, according to the Alexa online popularity rankings; it runs Arabic, English, French, and Spanish news services. Every Hizbullah institution maintains a website, some of which, like Al-Ta'bi'a, have continuously updated news sections. On the social media level, each institution also maintains an interactive Facebook and Twitter presence—interactive in the sense that they engage with their specific audience. Hizbullah's social media presence suggests a strong understanding of agenda-setting: for example, the organisation's Twitter front, led by the central account of Jabha Majazye (a metaphorical front), has managed to impose a nationwide hashtag trend pertaining to party policies and events through a swarm-like effect, which sees hundreds of people tweeting simultaneously. Every Jabha Majazye tweet starts a hashtag, which is displayed in a professionally designed photo, coordinating the stream of tweets from individual accounts and sparking a reaction from the public, thus setting a trend.

Such a wide reach, whether through television productions, radio, online, or print, or directly through the various institutions' and local branches' interpersonal contacts, is comprehensive enough to capture a significant audience within Lebanon's Shiʻi population. One plausible explanation of Hizbullah's aggressive print strategy is the communist influence: Lenin discussed in detail the benefit of the party publication at an organisational level, stressing in particular that, in addition to its propaganda benefits, its interactive aspect means it creates a community of engaged contributors and readers, as well as networks of distributors.

The importance of a historical lineage underpins all the messages carried by Hizbullah's media. The early twentieth-century nationalist histories of Lebanon constructed symbols and narrated events with the presumption that the residents of modern South Lebanon constituted a distinct people with a common history and a collective memory. The justification for the lack of sufficient sources to back the extraordinary claims made in these histories fits into the general theme of victimisation and conspiracy. Jaber, for example, blamed the persecution the *ulama* of Jabal ʻAmil suffered for the destruction and loss of many documents. These justifications are based on the underlying assumption that the lack of source material to establish the veracity of the history is of less importance than the effect produced by the narration of a historical sequence of events. It is left to the ʻAmili imagination to supply the missing links. Jaber weaves a history of the 'ʻAmili people', marked by piety, resistance against invaders, zealousness for just causes, and the wise leadership of the *ulama*. His history is best viewed within the larger context of Lebanon's sectarian narratives, as the Shiʻa sect is a constituent element of the country's political system. Jaber's work, with his extensive use of the terms the 'ʻAmili people' and 'ʻAmili resistance', and his references to the authority of the *ulama*, played a significant role in Hizbullah's later recreation of a Shiʻi historical identity.

A further echo of nineteenth- and twentieth-century ideas is evident in the importance of institutions to the development of a Shiʻi sectarian consciousness The same factors pertaining to the rise of nationalism, especially the advent of print capitalism and the post-industrial context, apply to sectarian nationalism. According to researchers on the subject, Shiʻi sectarianism resulted from French colonial institutionalisation in the twentieth century, while Christian and Druze sectarianism is rooted in the nineteenth-century Ottoman reforms. Makdisi's study on the rise of sectarianism in Mount Lebanon, and Weiss's research on the French colonial institutional basis for Shiʻi sectarianism, are further evidence of the modernity of what the former calls 'sectarian nationalism'. Sectarian nationalism, as Makdisi argues, is "the deployment of religious heritage as a primary marker of modern political identity"; he states that this function differentiates it from the religious violence of the ancient past (Makdisi 2000, p. 7). In the Lebanese consociational system, the religious sect constitutes the primary identity for Lebanon's citizens, defining their relationship with the state. As such, creating a powerful sect is a prerequisite for acquiring more power in the state—or in parallel to the state—as in the case of Hizbullah.

Jaber's historical narrative, although it laid the foundations for Hizbullah's subsequent reconstructed narratives, displays some discrepancies with the latter. His narrative acknowledged—though to a lesser extent than more neutral observers—the feudal system that dominated Shi'i history, and despite praising it at times, described its often detrimental effects, such as infighting. Another difference with Hizbullah lies in Jaber's Arab nationalist agenda, which asserted itself in the significant role he gave Sunni leaders, such as Thaher al-Omar and Reda Bey al-Solh, in his history. These two elements are largely absent, or are far weaker, in Hizbullah's historical account. Chapter 3 highlighted Jaber's constructs and their relationship to his political ideology, and in so doing suggests that Islamic movements such as Hizbullah are not simply a reversion to an early Islamic era but, rather, a reconstruction of a modern construct. Hizbullah's historical material glosses over these elements in Jaber's history and provides a more polished version, in line with its reconstructed Shi'i identity. The pre-Hizbullah histories were intended to serve a local political project under the banner of pan-Arab nationalism—a project that never saw the light in Lebanon. However, the examination of this early constructed history highlights the invented concepts upon which Hizbullah based its later narrative. Jaber's creation of the notions of the ''Amili people' and the 'Amili ethos of resistance and commitment to Shi'i Islam were based on the so-called oral accounts. After considering Jaber's historical narrative, Hizbullah also used 'oral sources' to remodel Shi'i history into a narrative that suggests the organisation's contemporary struggles and mode of politics have a historical continuity.

Hizbullah's historical narrative is therefore a reconstruction of an already constructed history. An examination of the organisation's dominant narratives reveals the extent of their construction. Hizbullah, in a process similar to that of nationalism, wove these narratives into a so-called historical process, sanctifying them with a sense of historical continuity. While Jaber constructed a historical narrative, introducing novel concepts such as the ''Amili people', Kourani reconstructed his predecessor's narrative so that it expressed a sectarian political identification: the ''Amili people' have turned into the 'Islamic 'Amili resistance'. The collective 'Amili identity assumed by Jaber's account thus becomes a prototype of the contemporary movement: all those who resisted the Ottomans, the French colonial authorities, and the early Zionist settlers have become Shi'i 'Amilis, holding the same Islamic ideals as Hizbullah and belonging to an early *ulama*-led movement.

The construction process proceeds in reverse, so that the basic elements of Hizbullah's sectarian identity manifest themselves throughout the various historical phases in such a way that the organisation appears to be the culmination of a natural historical process. *Wilayat al-Faqih*, although a modern concept, is apparently manifest in what is interpreted as the historical leadership of the *ulama*, especially that of the Shi'i 'ālim (cleric) 'Abd al-Hussein Sharafeddine. Sharafeddine is portrayed as the leader of Jabal 'Amil's Islamic resistance. The armed bands, as Traboulsi (2007) calls them, were transformed in Hizbullah accounts into Islamic resistance fighters, whose major figures, especially Adham Khanjar and Sadeq al-Hamza, are portrayed as pious men, just like Hizbullah's warriors—Al-Hamze and Khanjar are both portrayed as studying the Qur'an and listening to the instructions of the *ulama*. Their movement, and their subsequent treatment by the unjust system which emerged from the colonial era, are said to hold crucial lessons for Lebanese Shi'a today.

Hizbullah's discourse draws on these past lessons when justifying its current policies, regardless of whether the enemy is Israel, opposition factions inside Lebanon, or Syrian rebels, as has been the case since 2011. The sanctity of resistance is a constant, unaffected by the identity of the enemy. This reversal in direction when constructing Hizbullah's history is not absolute in the sense that it does not exclude borrowing symbols and names from the past to define contemporary politics—this explains why Nasrallah is dubbed 'al-Tha'er al-'Amili' (the 'Amili Rebel') in a Hizbullah-commissioned biographical work. The organisation's discourse on and accounts of contemporary events pursue a similar approach: for example, the Al-Manar television production, *Al-Ghalibun* (*The Victorious*), portraying the growth of Islamic resistance against Israeli occupation in the late 1970s and early 1980s, provides a narrative in line with Kourani's historical overview and overlooks the part played in the resistance by communist, Syrian nationalist, and Amal forces. Hizbullah's Al-Manar TV has played an active role in the dissemination of the organisation's historical narrative. Two major series proved very popular: the first was the aforementioned *Al-Ghalibun*, while the second series, *Qiyamat al-Banadeq* (*The Rise of the Rifles*), told the story of the resistance to the French and Ottoman occupations. *Qiyamat al-Banadeq* took Kourani's history to another level, justifying the portrayal of Islamic resistance with 'oral testimony' derived from interviews with witnesses from that era. The series portrayed the *ulama* as insightful leaders, identifying them with the leaders of the contemporary Hizbullah resistance movement. In 2015, the organisation further augmented its efforts on the historical front: Jabal ʿAmil's literary society was launched with a speech by Hizbullah's secretary general, which linked Jabal ʿAmil's supposed historical leadership by the *ulama* to today's Islamic resistance, replicating the circumstances in which it was said to operate.

Discussing Hizbullah's attempts at identity construction brings us to the question of what kind of nation the organisation aspires to build. The answer, however, is less than straightforward, particularly if we subject its political alliances within Lebanon to analysis. Through allying itself with Christian, secular, and certain traditional groups, Hizbullah has managed to build a coalition on the basis of a common acceptance of its superior status in the Lebanese state. The organisation maintains a military force and a relatively formidable arsenal, and therefore holds the upper hand when the political process results in unfavourable decisions, such as the events that took place on 7 May 2008, when it used military force to impose a political solution. The anti-Hizbullah coalition, formed after the demonstrations on 14 March 2005, held a majority of seats in parliament, and it decided to limit the organisation's influence in the security sphere by removing the head of airport security, a Shiʿi officer, and to launch an investigation into Hizbullah's private (landline) telephone network in Beirut's southern suburbs. In response, the organisation's armed forces, with its allies, took over west Beirut and attacked the Mount Lebanon strongholds of Walid Jumblatt, the Druze leader and a major partner in the coalition. Jumblatt's surrender and Hizbullah's rapid victory in west Beirut resulted in a political agreement and a new coalition government. Given this sort of scenario, any project promoting full Shiʿi nationhood would reduce Hizbullah's current political sway in Lebanon; however, if the balance of power between the Lebanese sects were to be altered to Hizbullah's detriment, the organisation might well transform into an irredentist movement. The Christian Nationalist Phalanges Party and Lebanese Forces militia are good examples of this sort of metamorphosis. When the balance of power augmented the Christian domination of Lebanon, both organisations maintained an inclusive national discourse, but as the Christian militia lost its battle for control of the Muslim-majority parts of Lebanon, its strategy and consequently its discourse shifted into a separatist mode.

While religion has been part of the region's politics throughout much of its recorded history, the supernatural elements in Hizbullah-sponsored propaganda and literature are modern in their scale and associations. The organisation's supernatural narratives are based on a revival of an ancient Shi'i tradition, represented by the works of Ayatollah Mohamad Baqer Majlesi, a seventeenth-century cleric. Majlesi, according to Ali Rahnema, an Iranian scholar, revived these tendencies for political reasons, preparing the ground for the establishment of an indirect link between the Safavid shah and the divine (Rahnema 2011, p. 15). The Shi'i cleric's main work, *Bihar al-Anwar*, focussed on stories of the Imams' spiritual powers, and this helped in later efforts to establish the shah's divine associations. Although Majlesi showered the shah with praise, he did not engage in a systematic effort to document or propagate spiritually inflected stories of the shah's actions.

While more systematic than Majlesi's attempts, due to its access to print and online technology, Hizbullah has produced similar narratives of the organisation's wars, which more openly associate its leadership with divinity. There are two trends in its supernatural propaganda: the first is rooted in the association between the party's hierarchy, based on *Wilayat al-Faqih*, and the hidden Twelfth Imam; the second trend draws on the first's underlying assumptions about divinity, weaving a rich narrative of supernatural tales about miracles occurring either during Hizbullah's war against the Israeli occupiers or in relation to its leaders' connection to the divine. The use of religion and these sorts of supernatural narratives could hardly be called modern, considering their recurrent use throughout Islamic history; however, their mass deployment by Hizbullah is modern, especially in terms of their widespread propagation in both its online and print media. The revival of this tradition in a contemporary context invites questions on the possibility of the transformation in beliefs, whether amongst the Shi'a or other confessional groups, especially in relation to its influence on political mobilisation. The association of a political and military group with the divine could have implications for the nature of its popular support. As discussed in Chap. 5, the literature on the relationship between supernatural narratives and politics aims to create a less questioning, more amenable popular base, although it remains difficult to assess whether this result has been achieved in practice. Such an association, on the other hand, could create higher expectations, leading to frustration with the ruling elite. This could be one of the reasons why Hizbullah has not publicly endorsed such accounts of its conflicts, although it continues to subtly intimate indirect and direct associations with the divine.

This leads to the question of whether Hizbullah's identity is invented or is based on ancient symbols and rituals, reviving an old identity through modern means. This question taps into the ethnosymbolist–modernist debate and the argument over whether the concept of the 'nation' is itself entirely modern. The research for this book has found, however, that the deployment of the Khomeinist doctrine as part of Shi'i identity has no precedent, at least within the Lebanese context. This assertion is partly based on Makdisi's analysis that shows that sectarian nationalism, particularly in its Maronite and Druze forms, is a nineteenth-century phenomenon. This finds equivalence in the later birth of Shi'i sectarianism, which, as Weiss argues, is a product of French colonial policy in the early twentieth century. The development of the 'Ashura' ritual from an annual event into a set of politically charged rituals encapsulates the difference between the ancient and the modern, as Chap. 2 illustrates. The older forms of 'Ashura' entailed listening to a dramatic reading of the *Masra'*, the story of Imam Husayn's death, in a fixed location; the experience was more personal in its approach, and was hardly seen outside general religious practices involving the clerical establishment. While the 'Ashura' rituals began to change in the early twentieth century, with the introduction of a play, the major transformation took place in the aftermath of the Iranian revolution. Politically charged marches, slogans, rituals, and speeches were introduced, all involving large crowds. The media, especially the cassette industry, paved the way for mass participation. The introduction of a new form of the Shi'i *latmiyat*, revolutionary chants for the masses of mourners, changed the experience from a passive mode to an interactive one. Mourners now beat their chests according to certain rhythms while repeating the chant in unison at the prompting of the speaker. These changes, mainly inspired by the writings of Iranian intellectual Ali Shari'ati, significantly transformed the 'Ashura' service, so that it has now become a political display, flexible enough to be adapted to different contemporary occasions. Whether confronting the Israeli occupation or its internal foes, such as the 14 March coalition, Hizbullah has the capability, in the transformed Day of ʿAshuraʾ, to draw comparisons between its enemies and Yazid, the second Umayyad caliph, who ordered the killing of Imam Husayn and his family in the battle of Karbala. The basic distinction between both forms of ʿAshuraʾ, the old and the new, lies in the latter's political utility, especially in terms of mobilising the masses.

The supernatural propaganda and the new rituals and associations of ʿAshuraʾ, discussed in Chap. 6, constitute a case of reformulating religious associations for modern political purposes. These transformations of Shiʿi practices in Iran and Lebanon demonstrate the development of flexible forms of ritual dedicated to augmenting the clerical establishment's ability to deploy religion as an effective mobilising force. In spite of the (essential) claims of historical continuity, Khomeini formulated the *Wilayat al-Faqih* doctrine in order to legitimise the clerical leadership by equating it with the divine; obedience to the Supreme Leader is now placed on an equal footing with obedience to Allah, as the former has become *Naʾeb al-Imam*, Imam Mahdi's deputy.

This shift from a traditionally quietist Shiʿi Islam to the contemporary Khomeinist variety, including the transformation of ʿAshuraʾ, took place mainly in Iran, and was, in many of its phases, a result of the clerical establishment's relations with the ruling regimes and their foreign backers. The *taqlid* tradition in Shiʿi Islam, however, began developing in the fifteenth century and crystalised into its current structure in the nineteenth century. It is worth noting here that the doctrine of *Wilayat al-Faqih*, a major element of Hizbullah's contemporary identity, is based on the Shiʿi *marjaʿiya* tradition, generally perceived as 'ancient' in Hizbullah's modern claims to historical continuity. However, as discussed in Chap. 6, the Shiʿi *Marjaʿ* position did not develop until the nineteenth century, under the leadership of Ayatollah Ansari in Najaf, and it was only under his successor, Ayatollah al-Shirazi, that the *Marjaʿ* was capable of playing a mobilising role, mainly due to the advent of print in the late nineteenth century. Al-Shirazi had issued a *fatwa*, boycotting tobacco after the ruler's decision to grant a British company a monopoly of the market. The boycott's success was a result of the widespread distribution of the printed *fatwa* throughout mosques in Iran. In general, however, the level of the clerical establishment's involvement in politics remained restricted; it was the development of Iran's early twentieth-century reform movement, and the

7 CONCLUSION   231

part it played in both opposition and government, that gradually thrust the clerical establishment into the political arena. The ideological effects are evident in the changes in Khomeini's theory of government: it was transformed from the promotion of a hybrid form of clerical–shah rule in the mid-twentieth century to the idea of an absolute clerical leadership, known as the *Wilayat al-Faqih*, during his years of exile in Najaf. Political repression and the rising challenge of communism had alerted the clerical establishment to the need for political involvement. The theory of Islamic government is thus a modern one, and the account of its historical continuity with the politics of the past is necessarily an invented narrative.

Attempts at reconciling this modern identity with the different Shiʿi contexts has created tensions, raising the question of why Hizbullah's model has proven relatively successful while other similar Shiʿi groups failed to garner such success. The major issue affecting the experiences of *Wilayat al-Faqih* groups is that of Iranian *realpolitik*, especially in Iran's neighbouring countries, and local Shiʿi relations with the state. Hazara Khomeinists in Afghanistan, for example, faced a *realpolitik* Iranian foreign policy, with Tehran backing their Tajik enemies; in this case, ethnic politics overshadowed religious ideology. In countries where the Shiʿa population was ethnically dispersed and had no nativist claims vis-à-vis the state, as in Kuwait, with its sizeable Shiʿi minority, Khomeinist movements failed to take shape or gain ground. Hizbullah, on the other hand, because it is based in Lebanon, a state that does not border Iran, has managed to develop strong relations with the Iranian leadership, amounting in some cases to a form of preferential lobbying. The Lebanese organisation's leaders provide tours and talks in the Persian language, for example, to acquaint officials at different levels of the Iranian administration with the many benefits of Tehran's support for Hizbullah. This effort explains the consistency of Iranian support for the Lebanese resistance, apart from certain fluctuations. The *Wilayat al-Faqih* rhetoric mainly manifests itself in bolstering the authority of the decisions of the organisation's local hierarchy in Lebanese Shiʿi perceptions, rather than augmenting the power of a distant Iranian Supreme Leader.

A final question is the extent to which the findings of this book are applicable to other Islamic organisations, particularly those of Sunni Islam. During the final two years of research, the Islamic State has become a powerful force in Syria and Iraq, with the promotion of a sectarian identity at the very heart of its efforts, whether through the establishment of schools, magazines, welfare institutions, or religious training programmes.

The identity work of the Islamic State bears many similarities to that of Hizbullah's, and is even more revolutionary in its ambition to transform the identity of the societies under its rule by reconstructing history, claiming continuity with early Islam, and creating new religious symbols. This case study could thus be applicable to research into the Islamic State's identity project, and to gaining an understanding of the powerful drive to reshape the identities of the old states of the post-colonial era along confessional lines.

References

Books

Makdisi, U. (2000). *The Culture of Sectarianism: Community, History, and Violence in Nineteenth-Century Ottoman Lebanon*. Berkeley: University of California Press.

Ozkirimli, U. (2005). *Contemporary Debates on Nationalism: A Critical Engagement*. Basingstoke: Palgrave.

Rahnema, A. (2011). *Superstition as Ideology in Iranian Politics: From Majlesi to Ahmadinejad*. Cambridge: Cambridge University Press.

Traboulsi, F. (2007). *A History of Modern Lebanon*. London: Pluto Press.

REFERENCES

BOOKS

Abisaab, R., & Abisaab, M. (2014). *The Shiʿites of Lebanon: Modernism, Communism, and Hizbullah's Islamists.* Syracuse: Syracuse University Press.

Abu al-Rida, H. (2012). *Al-Tarʿiya al-Hizbiya: Hizbullah Namuzajan* (Party Education: Hizbullah as a Case Study). Beirut: Dar Al-Amir.

Abun-Nasr, J. M. (1987). *A History of the Maghrib in the Islamic Period.* Cambridge: Cambridge University Press.

ʿAkef, S. (2012). *Turab Kushk al-Naʿim.* Beirut: Jamʿiat Al-Maʿaref Al-Islamiya Al-Thakafia.

ʿAkef, S., & Fakour, A. (2014). *Hajar Tantather* (Hajar Waits). Beirut: Jamʿiat Al-Maʿaref Al-Islamiya Al-Thakafia.

Alagha, J. (2006). *The Shifts in Hizbullah's Ideology: Religious Ideology, Political Ideology, and Political Program.* Amsterdam: Amsterdam University Press.

Alagha, J. (2011). *Hizbullah's Documents: From the 1985 Open Letter to the 2009 Manifesto.* Amsterdam: Amsterdam University Press.

Al-Bahrani, H. (2005). *Maʿajez Al-Imam Al-Mahdi* (The Miracles of Imam Mahdi). Beirut: Muʾassasat Al-Aʿlami Lil Matbouʿat.

Alexander, E., & Bogdanor, P. (Eds.). (2006). *The Jewish Divide Over Israel Accusers and Defenders.* Piscataway: Transaction.

Al-Hajj Hassan, A. (2008). *Tareekh Lubnan Al Muqawama: Fee Miʾat ʿAm* (The History of Resistor Lebanon: A Hundred Years). Dar Al-Wala: Beirut.

Al-Hakim, A. (2015). *Ruʾyatura Al-Tanzimiya* (Our Organizational Vision). Retrieved from http://www.almejlis.org/assets/files/5843_1_1425213297.pdf

Al-Katib, A. (1997). *The Development of Shiite Political Thought: From Shura to Wilayat Al-Faqih*. London: Alshura Publishing House.

Al-Markaz Al-Istishari Lel Derasat Wal Tawthiq (The Consultative Centre for Studies and Documentation). (2007). *Al-Tanmiya Fee Mujtamaʿat Ghair Mustaqira* (Development in Unstable Communities). Beirut: The Consultative Centre for Studies and Documentation.

Al-Muhajer, J. (1992). *Al-Taʾsis Litareekh al-Shiʿa* (The Foundation of Shiʿa History). Beirut: Dar Al Malak.

Al-Nasseri, A. (2009). *Nisaʾ Taltaqi Saheb Al-Zaman* (Women Meet Imam Mahdi). Beirut: Dar Al-Mahaja Al-Baidaʾ.

Al-Wardi, A., & Aboul-Enein, Y. (2012). *Iraq in Turmoil: Historical Perspectives of Dr. Ali al-Wardi, From the Ottoman Empire to King Faisal*. Annapolis: Naval Institute Press.

Al-Zein, A. (1954). *Maʿ al-Tareekh Al-ʿAmili*. Sidon: Al Erfan Publishing.

Al-Zubaidy, M. N. (2007). *Rejal Allah Wal Nasr Al Ilahi* (The Men of God and the Divine Victory). Beirut: Muʾassasat Al-Huda Al-Islamiya.

Al-Zubaidy, M. N. (2008). *Karamat Al-Waʿd Al-Sadeq* (The Miracles of the Honest Promise). Beirut: Dar Al-Mahaja Al-Baidaʾ.

Al-Zubaidy, M. N. (2009). *Kaifa Taltaqi Bel Imam Al-Mahdi?* (How to Meet Imam Mahdi?) Beirut: Dar Al-Mahaja Al-Baidaʾ.

Amin, S. (1981). *al-Daʿwah al-Islamiyah Fariḍah Sharʿīyah Waḍarurah Bashariyah* (The Islamic Call Is a Legal Obligation and a Human Need). Port Saʿid: Dar al-Tawziʿ wa al-Nashr al-Islamiya.

Anderson, B. (1991). *Imagined Communities: Reflections on the Origin and Spread of Nationalism*. London and New York: Verso.

Antonius, G. (1939). *The Arab Awakening*. Philadelphia: J.B. Lippincott.

Baktiari, B. (1996). *Parliamentary Politics in Revolutionary Iran: The Institutionalization of Factional Politics*. Gainesville: University Press of Florida.

Behrooz, M. (1999). *Rebels with a Cause: The Failure of the Left in Iran*. London: I.B. Tauris & Co.

Berger, P., & Luckmann, T. (2011). *The Social Construction of Reality: A Treatise in the Sociology of Knowledge*. New York: Open Road Media.

Berger, S., Donovan, M., & Passmore, K. (Eds.). (1999). *Writing National Histories: Western Europe Since 1800*. London and New York: Routledge.

Boroujerdi, M. (1996). *Iranian Intellectuals and the West: The Tormented Triumph of Nativism*. Syracuse: Syracuse University Press.

Bradsher, H. (1999). *Afghan Communism and Soviet Intervention*. Oxford: Oxford University Press.

Breuilly, J. (1993). *Nationalism and the State*. Manchester: Manchester University Press.

Breuilly, J. (2007). Nationalism and Historians: Some Reflections. The Formations on Nationalist Historiographical Discourse. In C. Norton (Ed.), *Nationalism,*

Historiography and the (Re)Construction of the Past (pp. 1–28). Washington, DC: New Academia Publishing.

Cambanis, T. (2011). *A Privilege to Die: Inside Hizbullah's Legions and Their Endless War against Israel.* New York: Free Press.

Campo, J. (2009). *Encyclopedia of Islam.* New York: Infobase Publishing.

Chalabi, T. (2006). *The Shi'is of Jabal 'Amil and the New Lebanon.* New York: Palgrave.

Chalcraft, J. (2009). *The Invisible Cage: Syrian Migrant Workers in Lebanon.* Stanford, CA: Stanford University Press.

Cockburn, A., & Cockburn, P. (2000). *Saddam Hussein, an American Obsession.* London: Verso.

Daftary, F. (2013). *A History of Shi'i Islam.* London: I.B. Tauris.

De Tollenaere, H. (1996). *The Politics of Divine Wisdom: Theosophy and Labour, National, and Women's Movements in Indonesia and South Asia 1875–1947.* Nijmegen, The Netherlands: Katholieke Universiteit Nijmegen.

Deeb, L. (2006). *An Enchanted Modern: Gender and Public Piety in Shi'i Lebanon.* Princeton, NJ: Princeton University Press.

Delanty, G., & Kumar, K. (2006). *The SAGE Handbook of Nations and Nationalism.* London and Chicago: SAGE.

Drieskens, B. (2008). *Living with Djinns: Understanding and Dealing with the Invisible in Cairo.* London: Saqi Books.

Duhainy, I. (1991). *Aljadid Fi Tadriss Al-Fiqh* (The New in Teaching Jurisprudence). Beirut: Madrasat Al-Imam Al-Mahdi (Imam Mahdi School).

Ehteshami, A. (1995). *After Khomeini: The Iranian Second Republic.* New York: Routledge.

Eickelman, D. (2002). *The Middle East and Central Asia: An Anthropological Approach.* New Jersey: Prentice Hall.

El-Khazen, F. (2000). *Breakdown of the State in Lebanon: 1967–1976.* Cambridge: Harvard University Press.

Faqih, F. (2002). *Karamat Al-Imam Al-Mahdi* (The Miracles of Imam Mahdi). Beirut: Dar al-Mahaja al-Bayda.

Fromm, E. (1950). *Psychoanalysis and Religion.* New Haven, Connecticut: Yale University Press.

Gellner, E. (1994). *Conditions of Liberty: Civil Society and Its Rivals.* London: Hamish Hamilton.

Gilsenan, M. (1973). *Saint and Sufi in Modern Egypt: An Essay in the Sociology of Religion.* Oxford: Clarendon Press.

Goffman, E. (1974). *Frame Analysis: An Essay on the Organization of the Experience.* New York: Harper Colophon.

Hamzeh, A. N. (2004). *In the Path of Hizbullah.* Syracuse: Syracuse University Press.

Harik, J. P. (2004). *Hezbollah: The Changing Face of Terrorism.* London: I.B. Tauris.

Haufler, V. (1993). Crossing the Boundary between Public and Private: International Regimes and Non-State Actors. In V. Rittberger (Ed.), *Regime Theory and International Relations* (pp. 94–111). Oxford, UK: Oxford University Press.

Hijazi, H. (2006). *Istaʿidu fa In Al-Zuhor Qarib* (Be Ready, the Appearance Is Soon). Beirut: Dar Al-Mahaja Al-Baidaʾ.

Hodgson, M. G. S. (1974). *The Venture of Islam: The Gunpowder Empires and Modern Times*. Chicago: University of Chicago Press.

Holt, P. M. (1970). *The Mahdist State in the Sudan, 1881–1898: A Study of Its Origins, Development and Overthrow*. Oxford: Clarendon Press.

Hourani, A. (1947). *Minorities in the Arab World*. Oxford: Oxford University Press.

Hourani, A. (1962). *Arabic Thought in the Liberal Age 1789–1939*. London and New York: Oxford University Press.

Hourani, A. (1991). *History of the Arab Peoples*. London: Faber and Faber.

Hudson, M. (1968). *The Precarious Republic: Political Mobilization in Lebanon*. New York: Random House.

Hutchinson, J. (1994). *Modern Nationalism*. London: Fontana Press.

International Business Publications, USA. (2012, September 1). *Iran Country Study Guide, Vol. 1. Strategic Information and Daaaevelopments*. Washington, DC: International Business Publications, USA.

Jaber Al Safa, M. (1981). *Jabal ʿAmel Fi alTareekh*. Beirut: Dar Al-Nahar.

Jamil, R. (1948). *Beirut and the Republic of Lebanon*. Beirut: Librairie Universelle.

Jamʿiyat al-Taʿlim al-Dini al-Islami. (2010a). *Al-Islam Risalatuna al-Jizʾ al-Taseʿ* (Islam Is Our Message) (9th ed.). Beirut: Dar Ajial Al-Mustafa.

Jamʿiyat al-Taʿlim al-Dini al-Islami. (2010b). *Al-Islam Risalatuna al-Jizʾ al-Hadi ʿAshar* (Islam Is Our Message) (12th ed.). Beirut: Dar Ajial Al-Mustafa.

Jamʿiyat al-Taʿlim al-Dini al-Islami. (2010c). *Al-Islam Risalatuna al-Jizʾ al-Intha ʿAshar* (Islam Is Our Message) (12th ed.). Beirut: Dar Ajial Al-Mustafa.

Janin, H., & Kahlmeyer, A. (2007). *Islamic Law: The Sharia from Muhammad's Time to the Present*. Jefferson, NC: McFarland & Co.

Juergensmeyer, M. (1993). *The New Cold War? Religious Nationalism Confronts the Secular State*. Berkeley: University of California Press.

Juneau, T., & Razavi, S. (Eds.). (2013). *Iranian Foreign Policy Since 2001: Alone in the World*. London: Routledge.

Kadhim, A. (2012). *Reclaiming Iraq: The 1920 Revolution and the Founding of the Modern State*. Austin, TX: University of Texas Press.

Keddie, N. (Ed.). (1983). *Religion and Politics in Iran. Shiʿism from Quietism to Revolution*. New Haven, CT: Yale University Press.

Kedourie, E. (1970). *Nationalism in Asia and Africa*. New York: New American Library.

Keshavarzian, A. (2007). *Bazaar and State in Iran: The Politics of the Tehran Marketplace*. Cambridge: Cambridge University Press.
Khalidi, R. (1991). *The Origins of Arab Nationalism*. New York: Columbia University Press.
Khomeini, R. (1995). *Islamic Government*. Tehran: The Institute for Compilation and Publication of Imam Khomeini's Works. Retrieved from http://www.iran-chamber.com/history/rkhomeni/books/velayat_faqeeh.pdf
Khomeini, R. (2011). *Al-Kalimat al-Qisar Lil Imam Al-Khomeini* (Imam Khomeini's Short Sayings). Beirut: Markaz Noon.
Kourani, M. (1993). *Al Jozoor Al Tarikheya Lel Moqawama Al Islamiya* (The Historical Roots of the Islamic Resistance). Beirut: Dar Al Waseela.
Kourani, H., & Al-Mahdi, M. M. (2000). *Al-Karamat Al-Ghaibiya Lil Imam Al-Khomeini* (The Unseen Miracles of Imam Khomeini). Beirut: Dar Al-Mahaja Al-Baida'.
Koya, A. (2009). *Imam Khomeini: Life, Thought and Legacy*. Selangor, Malaysia: Islamic Book Trust.
Lammens, H. (1800). *Sur La Frontier Nord de la Terre Promise*. Paris: Imprimerie de D. Dumoulin.
Lapidus, I. M. (1988). *A History of Islamic Societies*. Cambridge: Cambridge University Press.
Lenin, V. I. (1953). *Works* (Vol. 5). Moscow: Foreign Languages Publishing House.
Louër, L. (2008). *Transnational Shia Politics: Religious and Political Networks in the Gulf*. New York: Columbia University Press.
Louër, L. (2012). *Shi'ism and Politics in the Middle East*. London: C. Hurst & Co. (Publishers) Ltd.
Makdisi, U. (2000). *The Culture of Sectarianism: Community, History, and Violence in Nineteenth-Century Ottoman Lebanon*. Berkeley: University of California Press.
Maley, W. (Ed.). (1998). *Fundamentalism Reborn? Afghanistan and the Taliban*. New York: New York University Press.
Marx, K., & Engels, F. (1975). *On Religion*. Moscow: Progress Publishers.
McGrath, A. (2011). *Christian Theology: An Introduction*. United Kingdom: John Wiley & Sons.
McLellan, D. (1987). *Marxism and Religion*. London: Macmillan Press.
Mervin, S. (Ed.). (2009). *The Shi'a Worlds and Iran*. London: Saqi Books.
Moazzam, A. (1984). *Jamal ad-Din al-Afghani: A Muslim Intellectual*. New Delhi: Concept Publishing Company.
Mockaitis, T. (Ed.). (2013). *The Iraq War Encyclopedia*. Santa Barbara: ABC-Clio.
Mousavi, S. A. (1998). *The Hazaras of Afghanistan: An Historical, Cultural, Economic and Political Study*. Richmond, Surry: Curzon Press.

Nader, A., et al. (2014). *Iran's Influence in Afghanistan: Implications for the U.S. Drawdown.* Santa Monica: Rand.

Nasrallah, H. (2000). *Khitab ʿAshuraʾ.* Beirut: Dar Al-Safwa.

Nejad, A. R., et al. (2014). *Kaʿdi.* Beirut: Jamʿiyat Al-Maʿaref Al-Islamiya Al-Thakafia.

Noe, N. (Ed.). (2007). *Voice of Hezbollah: The Statements of Sayed Hassan Nasrallah.* London: Verso.

Norton, A. R. (1987). *Amal and the Shi'a: Struggle for the Soul of Lebanon.* Austin: University of Texas Press.

Norton, A. R. (2007). *Hezbollah: A Short History.* Princeton, NJ: Princeton University Press.

Noun Centre for Writing and Translating. (2014). *Wadaʿ Al-Shuhadaʾ.* Beirut: Jamʿiat Al-Maʿaref Al-Islamiya Al-Thakafia.

Ozkirimli, U. (2005). *Contemporary Debates on Nationalism: A Critical Engagement.* Basingstoke: Palgrave.

Parish, H., & Naphy, W. (Eds.). (2002). *Religion and Superstition in Reformation Europe.* Manchester and New York: Manchester University Press.

Pelletiere, S. (1992). *The Iran-Iraq War: Chaos in a Vacuum.* New York: Praeger.

Phares, W. (1995). *Lebanese Christian Nationalism: The Rise and Fall of an Ethnic Resistance.* Boulder, CO: L. Rienner.

Phillips, D. (2009). *From Bullets to Ballots: Violent Muslim Movements in Transition.* New Brunswick, New Jersey: Transaction Publishers.

Qassem, N. (2005). *Hizbullah: The Story from Within.* London: Saqi.

Rahnema, A. (2011). *Superstition as Ideology in Iranian Politics: From Majlesi to Ahmadinejad.* Cambridge: Cambridge University Press.

Raines, J. (Ed.). (1998). *Marx on Religion.* Philadelphia: Temple University Press.

Rosiny, S. (2000). *Shi'a Publishing in Lebanon: With Special Reference to Islamic and Islamist Publications.* Berlin: Verlag Das Arabische Buch.

Roy, O. (2010). The Impact of the Iranian Revolution on the Middle East. In S. Mervin (Ed.), *The Shi'a Worlds and Iran* (pp. 29–44). London: Saqi Books.

Rubin, B. (1995). *The Fragmentation of Afghanistan: State Formation and Collapse in the International System.* New Haven, CT: Yale University Press.

Saad-Ghorayeb, A. (2002). *Hizbu'llah: Politics and Religion.* London: Pluto Press.

Sadouki, H., & ʿAkef, S. (2012). *Kawa, Muʿjizat Al Thawra.* Beirut: Jamʿiyat Al-Maʿaref Al-Islamiya Al-Thakafia.

Safwan, M. (2010a). *Fatima Tuwali Awliyaʾ Allah* (Fatima Pledges Allegiance to Allah's Custodians). Beirut: Dar al-Walaʾ.

Safwan, M. (2010b). *Fatima Taʾmor Bel Maʿruf Wa Tanha ʿAn Almunkar* (Fatima Orders Virtue and Forbids Vice). Beirut: Dar al-Walaʾ.

Safwan, M. (2010c). *Fatima Tataʿalam Al-Salat* (Fatima Learns Prayers). Beirut: Dar al-Walaʾ.

Safwan, M. (2010d). *Fatima Tatabara' Min A'da' Allah* (Fatima Disown Allah's Enemies). Beirut: Dar al-Wala'.
Safwan, M. (2010e). *Fatima Tuhibo al-Jihad* (Fatima Loves Jihad). Beirut: Dar al-Wala'.
Salibi, K. (1976). *Cross Roads to Civil War: Lebanon, 1958–1976*. Delmar, NY: Caravan Books.
Salibi, K. (1977). *The Modern History of Lebanon*. Delmar, NY: Caravan Books.
Salibi, K. (1979). *Muntalaq Tarikh Lubnan* (The Basis of Lebanon's History). Beirut: Mu'assasat Nawfal.
Salibi, K. (1988). *A House of Many Mansions: The History of Lebanon Reconsidered*. London: I.B. Tauris.
Savory, R. (2007). *Iran Under the Safavids*. Cambridge: Cambridge University Press.
Sayigh, R. (1994). *Too Many Enemies*. London: Zed Books.
Sayigh, R. (2015). *Too Many Enemies*. Beirut: Dar Al Mashriq.
Seliktar, O. (2012). *Navigating Iran: From Carter to Obama*. New York: Palgrave Macmillan.
Selznik, P. I. (1952). *The Organizational Weapon: A Study of Bolshevik Strategy and Tactics*. New York: McGraw-Hill Company.
Semple, M. (2012). *The Rise of the Hazaras and the Challenge of Pluralism in Afghanistan 1978–2011*. Cambridge, MA: Harvard Center for Islamic Studies.
Sha'lan, R. (2007). *Al-Wa'd al-Sadeq: I'sar Wa Intisar* (Al-Wa'd al-Sadeq—July War: A Hurricane and a Victory). Lebanon: Dar al-Janub.
Shanahan, R. (2005). *The Shi'a of Lebanon: Clans, Parties and Clerics*. London, UK and New York: I.B. Tauris.
Sharara, W. (1996). *Al-Umma al-Qaliqa, Al-'Amiliyun wal-'Asabiyya Al Amiliya 'Ala 'Atabat Al Dawla Al-Lubnaniya* (The Concerned Nation, The 'Amilis and the 'Amili Solidarity in the Doorstep of the Lebanese State). Beirut: Dar Annahar.
Sharara, W. (1998). *Dawlat Hezbollah, Lubnan mujtami'an Islamiyyan*. Beirut: Dar Annahar.
Shatzmiller, M. (Ed.). (2005). *Nationalism and Minority Identities in Islamic Societies*. Montreal and Kingston: McGill-Queen's University Press.
Shoufani, S. (1996). *Tareekh Rumeish* (The History of Rumeish). Beirut: Deir Sayyidat Al-Bishara.
Smith, A. (2009). *Ethno-symbolism and Nationalism: A Cultural Approach*. London: Routledge.
Smith, A. D. (1993). The Nation: Invented, Imagined, Reconstructed? In M. Ringrose & A. J. Lerner (Eds.), *Reimagining the Nation* (pp. 159–175). Philadelphia: Open University Press.
Smith, A. D. (1999). *Myths and Memories of the Nation*. Oxford: Oxford University Press.

Smith, A. D. (2001). *Nationalism: Theory, Ideology, History Key Concepts.* Cambridge: Polity Press.
Smith, A. D. (2003). *Chosen Peoples: Sacred Sources of National Identity.* Oxford: Oxford University Press.
Spellman, K. (2004). *Religion and Nation: Iranian Local and Transnational Networks in Britain.* New York: Berghahn Books.
St. Maria, J., & Naghshpour, S. (2011). *Revolutionary Iran and the United States: Low-Intensity Conflict in the Persian Gulf.* Farnham, Surrey, England: Ashgate.
Stalin, J. (1932). *Foundations of Leninism.* New York: International Publishers.
Takeyh, R. (2009). *Guardians of the Revolution: Iran and the World in the Age of the Ayatollahs.* New York: Oxford University Press.
Thomas, K. (1971). *Religion and the Decline of Magic.* London: Penguin Books.
Traboulsi, F. (2007). *A History of Modern Lebanon.* London: Pluto Press.
Walbridge, L. S. (Ed.). (2001). *The Most Learned of the Shi'a: The Institution of the Marja' Taqlid.* Oxford: Oxford University Press.
Weiss, M. (2010). *In the Shadow of Sectarianism.* Cambridge, MA and London, UK: Harvard University Press.
Williams, B. G. (2011). Afghanistan, Hazaras. In A. Moghadam (Ed.), *Militancy and Political Violence in Shi'ism: Trends and Patterns* (pp. 181–200). New York: Routledge.

Journal Articles

Akhavi, S. (1987, Spring). Elite Factionalism in the Islamic Republic of Iran. *Middle East Journal, 41*(2), 181–201.
Balaghi, S. (2001). Print Culture in Late Qajar Iran: The Cartoons of "Kashkūl". *Iranian Studies, 34*(1/4) [Special Issue: Qajar Art and Society], 165–181.
Benford, R. D., & Snow, D. A. (2000). Framing Processes and Social Movements: An Overview and Assessment. *Annual Review of Sociology, 26*, 611–639.
Canfield, R. L. (2004). New Trends Among the Hazaras: From "the Amity of Wolves" to "The Practice of Brotherhood". *Iranian Studies, 37*(2), 241–262.
Chakrabarty, D. (2008). The Power of Superstition in Public Life in India. *Economic and Political Weekly, 43*, 16–19.
Edgar, I. (2006). The 'True Dream' in Contemporary Islamic/Jihadist Dreamwork: A Case Study of the Dreams of Taliban Leader Mullah Omar. *Contemporary South Asia, 15*(3), 263–272.
El-Khazen, F. (2003, Autumn). Political Parties in Post-War Lebanon: Parties in Search of Partisans. *Middle East Journal, 57*(4), 605–624.
Emadi, H. (1995). Exporting Iran's Revolution: The Radicalization of the Shi'i Movement in Afghanistan. *Middle Eastern Studies, 31*(1), 1–12.
Frankel, S. (1999). Politics and Rhetoric: The Intended Audience of Spinoza's "Tractatus Theologico-Politicus". *Review of Metaphysics, 52*(4), 897–924.

Hamzeh, N. (2000). Lebanon's Islamists and Local Politics: A New Reality. *Third World Quarterly, 21*(5), 739–759.

Hanson, B. (1983). The 'Westoxication' of Iran: Depictions and Reactions of Behrangi, al-e Ahmad, and Shariʿati. *International Journal of Middle East Studies, 15*(1), 1–23.

Harb, M., & Leenders, R. (2005). Know Thy Enemy: Hizbullah, 'Terrorism' and the Politics of Perception. *Third World Quarterly, 26*(1) [Special Issue: The Politics of Naming: Rebels, Terrorists, Criminals, Bandits and Subversives], 173–197.

Harik, I. F. (1972). The Ethnic Revolution and Political Integration in the Middle East. *International Journal of Middle East Studies, 3*, 303–323.

Harpviken, K. B. (1997). Transcending Traditionalism: The Emergence of Non-State Military Formations in Afghanistan. *Journal of Peace Research, 34*(3), 271–287.

Hassan, R., & Azadmarki, T. (2003, Spring). Institutional Configurations and Trust in Religious Institutions in Muslim Societies. *Islamic Studies, 42*(1), 97–106.

Hodgson, G. (2006). What Are Institutions? *Journal of Economic Issues, 40,* 1–25.

Hudson, M. C. (1997). Trying Again: Power-Sharing in Post-Civil War Lebanon. *International Negotiation, 2*(1), 103–122.

Hosseini, K. (2003). *The Kite Runner.* New York: Riverhead Books.

Hung, C.-t. (2008, April). The Cult of the Red Martyr: Politics of Commemoration in China. *Journal of Contemporary History, 43*(2), 279–304.

Loebenstein, J. (2003, April). Miracles in Šīʿī Thought: A Case-Study of the Miracles Attributed to Imām Ǧaʿfar al-Ṣādiq. *Arabica,* T. 50, Fasc. 2, 199–244.

Nir, O. (2004, November). The Shi'ites During the 1958 Lebanese Crisis. *Middle Eastern Studies, 40*(6), 109–129.

Ramazani, R. K. (1989). Iran's Foreign Policy: Contending Orientations. *Middle East Journal, 43*(2), 202–217.

Smith, A. (1996, December). The Resurgence of Nationalism? Myth and Memory in the Renewal of Nations. *The British Journal of Sociology, 47*(4), 575–598.

St John, R. B. (1980, August). Marxist-Leninist Theory and Organization in South Vietnam. *Asian Survey, 20*(8), 812–828.

Stern, P. (1995). Why Do People Sacrifice for Their Nations? *Political Psychology, 16,* 217–235.

Terzić, F. (2009, Spring). *The Problematic of Prophethood and Miracles: Muṣṭafā Ṣabrī's Response. Islamic Studies, 48*(1), 5–33.

Thesiger, W. (1955). The Hazaras of Central Afghanistan. *Geographic Journal, 121*(3), 312–319.

Tomass, M. (2012). Religious Identity, Informal Institutions, and the Nation-States of the Near East. *Journal of Economic Issues, 46*(3), 705–728.

Yazicioglu, I. (2011). Redefining the Miraculous: Al-Ghazālī, Ibn Rushd and Said Nursi on Qur'anic Miracle Stories. *Journal of Qur'anic Studies.*, *13*(2), 86–108.

MAGAZINES[1]

Baqiatullah Magazine, December 1998, 87
Baqiatullah Magazine, September 1999, 96
Baqiatullah Magazine, October 1999, 97
Baqiatullah Magazine, November 1999, 98
Baqiatullah Magazine, December 1999, 99
Baqiatullah Magazine, February 2000, 101
Baqiatullah Magazine, April 2000, 103
Sada Al-Jirah Magazine, May 2012, 35

REPORTS

Abrahamian, E. (2009, Spring). *Why the Islamic Republic Has Survived?* Middle East Report No. 250, The Islamic Revolution at 30, pp. 10–16.
Ibrahimi, N. (2006). *The Failure of a Clerical Proto-State: Hazarajat, 1979–1984* [Online]. London: Crisis States Research Centre, LSE. Retrieved May 8, 2015, from http://r4d.dfid.gov.uk/PDF/Outputs/CrisisStates/wp6.2.pdf
Ibrahimi, N. (2009). *The Dissipation of Political Capital Among Afghanistan's Hazaras: 2001–2009* [Online]. London: Crisis States Research Centre, LSE. Retrieved May 8, 2015, from http://eprints.lse.ac.uk/28493/1/WP51.2.pdf
Makdisi, U. (1993). *Reconstructing the Nation-State: The Modernity of Sectarianism in Lebanon.* Middle East Report No. 200, Minorities in the Middle East: Power and the Politics of Difference (Jul.–Sep.), pp. 23–26, 30.

NEWS ARTICLES

Afrasiabi, K., & Entessar, N. (2014, August 12). *Iran Uses Hamas for Leverage in Nuclear Negotiations.* Retrieved from http://america.aljazeera.com/opinions/2014/8/iran-hamas-palestinenuclearnegotiations.html
Al-Hakim, B. (2011, August 9). Hamla ʿala alghalibun: Kafa Tazwiran lil Tarikh (A Campaign Against Alghalibun: Enough with this Forgery of History). *Al-Akhbar*, p. 14.

---

[1] Hizbullah magazines feature articles without a biline, especially in the sections discussed in this book.

Assafir. (2001, December 15). *Ihtifalat Wa Massirat Wa Oroodat Fi al-Dahiya Wa Bʿalbak Wa Sour*. *Assafir*, p. 2.

Badrpress. (2014, August 18). *Badr, Al-Janah Alʾaskari Li Monazamat Badr: Lasna Militia Wa Lan Nusharek Behelf Maʾ Amrika* (The Badr Organization's Military Branch: We Are Not a Militia and Will Not Participate in an Alliance with the U.S.). Retrieved from http://badrpress.com/badr/feeds.php?lang=ar&page_name=politic&id=26461

Boonen J. (2010, October 25). *Hamid Karzai Admits Office Gets 'Bags of Money' from Iran*. Retrieved from http://www.theguardian.com/world/2010/oct/25/hamid-karzai-office-cash-iran

Chalhoub, E. (2012, February 14). *Imad Mughniyeh in Iran: The Stuff of Legends*. Retrieved from http://english.al-akhbar.com/node/4198

Filkins, D. (2013, September 30). *The Shadow Commander*. Retrieved from http://www.newyorker.com/magazine/2013/09/30/the-shadow-commander

Habib, S., & Mohammadi, I. (2012). *Role of Iran in Assassination of Baba Mazari*. Retrieved July 20, 2014, from www.hazarapeople.com/2012/04/24/iran-and-hizbe-wahdat-e-islami/

Hage Ali, M. (2012, July 3). *Iraqi Intrigue in Lebanon*. Retrieved from http://www.executive-magazine.com/business-finance/finance/iraqi-intrigue-in-lebanon

Harrison, E. (2013, June 3). *Afghan Taliban Send Delegation to Iran*. Retrieved from http://www.theguardian.com/world/2013/jun/03/afghan-taliban-send-delegation-iran

Howenstien, N., & Ganguli, S. (2010, March 24). *India-Pakistan Rivalry in Afghanistan*. Retrieved from http://jia.sipa.columbia.edu/india-pakistan-rivalry-afghanistan/

Luts, M. (2010, July 6). *Shiite Muslim Cleric Mourned in Lebanon*. Retrieved from http://articles.latimes.com/2010/jul/06/world/la-fg-fadlallah-funeral-20100707

Mohsen, A. (2014, August 15). *'Harb Tamuz ... Noqtat Tahawol'* (July War ... Transformation Point). *Al-Akhbar*, p. 8.

Mustapha, G. (2013, February 12). *'Moqawama fi Jabal 'Amil'* (Resistance in Jabal ʿAmil). *Assafir*, p. 9.

Obeid, H. (2015, August 15). *'Nasrallah: Noreed al-Dawla al-ʿadila ... al-Mabniya ʿala al-Sharaka al-Haqiqiya'* (Nasralla: We Want the Just State Based on True Partnership). *Assafir*, p. 3.

Shari'ati, A. (2015, May 4). *"Red Shiʿism: The Religion of Martyrdom; Black Shiʿism: The Religion of Mourning"*. Retrieved from http://www.Shariati.com/english/redblack.html

Links

Al-ʿAhd. (2013). Shaykh Qassem: Shuhada al-Wajeb al-Jihadi Hum Shuhada Almuqawama Dod Israel Wa Mashruʿaha (The Martyrs of the Jihadi Duty are Martyrs against Israel and its Project). *Al-ʿAhd News*, 21 May. Retrieved July 6, 2014, from https://goo.gl/PLAzsU

Al-Musawi, N. (2015, February 15). *Limowasalat al-Hiwar Wal Wosol Ila Tafahomat L'injaz al-Istihqaqat Wabel'akhas al-Reʾasa* (To Continue Dialogue and Reach Understandings to Accomplish the Requirements, Especially the Presidential Elections). Retrieved June 23, 2015, from http://goo.gl/kDh0WY

Al-Shaykh, Q. (2013, May 21). *Shuhadaʾ al-Wajeb al-Jihadi Hom Shuhadaʾ al-Muqawama Dod Israel Wa Mashruʿaha* (The Martyrs of the Jihadi Duty Are the Martyrs of Resistance Against Israel and Its Project). Retrieved December 20, 2014, from http://goo.gl/1XZifN

Baghdadi, S. (2014, September 29). *Mawqef Samahat al-Sayed Wada alneqat ala al Horoof Fee Malaf Al Makhtofeen* (The Position of Sayyid Nasrallah on the Dossier of the Kidnapped Has Clarified Things). Retrieved November 27, 2014, from http://www.Al-Manar.com.lb/wapadetails.php?eid=982661

Derasat Shakhsiat al Muhaqiq al-Shaikh Ali Ben Aʿbd al-Aʿl al-Mais fee Muʾtamar Khas (The Study of al Muhaqiq al-Shaikh Ali Ben Aʿbd al-Aʿl al-Mais in a Special Conference), June 9, 2014. Retrieved October 15, 2014, from http://www.Al-Manar.com.lb/adetails.php?fromval=0&cid=0&frid=0&seccatid=0&eid=864763

Engels, F. (1894). *On the History of Early Christianity*. Retrieved December 21, 2014, from https://www.marxists.org/archive/marx/works/1894/early-christianity/

Jabal ʿAmil yahtafel bel faizin wal mubdein fee mosabaqat Midad al Jabal al Sheriya (Jabal ʿAmil Celebrates the Winners and Innovators in the Midad al Jabal al Sheriya Contest), June 30, 2014. Retrieved October 30, 2014, from http://www.Al-Manar.com.lb/wapadetails.php?eid=885377

Jaber, K. (2008). ʿAshuraʾ al-Nabatieh Hadath Sanawy Yastaqteb al-Alaf (ʿAshuraʾ in Nabatieh, an Annual Event that attracts Thousands). Al-Akhbar, 15 January. Retrieved June 5, 2011, from http://www.al-akhbar.com/node/126136

Kourani, M. (2010, May 19). *ʾIntilaq al-Moqawama al-Islamiya ʿabr al-Tareekh Mina al-Mabdaʾ al-ʿaqaʾidi Wal Tashreeʿ Daleel Aʿla Nasaʿatiha Wa Istimrariyatihaʾ* (The Launch of the Islamic Resistance Throughout History from the Islamic Ideology and Laws Is a Proof of Its Purity and Continuity). Retrieved November 21, 2013, from http://www.moqawama.org/essaydetails.php?eid=16901&cid=199

Nasrallah, S. (2014, March 29). *Al-Moqawama Alyawm Aqwa Wa Aqdar Wa Hiya Najahat Haithu Fashala alʾalam Kullah* (The Resistance Is Stronger and More Capable Today, and Has Succeeded Where the Whole World Failed).

Retrieved July 23, 2015, from http://www.almanar.com.lb/wapadetails. php?eid=796057

Omsiya She'riya fee Tebnin Bere'ayat Layon (A Layon-Sponsored Poetic Evening in Tebnin), July 14, 2012. Retrieved November 23, 2013, from http://www.Al-Manar.com.lb/wapadetails.php?eid=268069

Qassem, Q. (2010). Man Yasna' al-'Aql al-Shi'i Fee al-Dahiya Al-Janubiya (Who Creates the Shi'i mind in the Southern Suburbs?). Islam Times, 29 October. Retrieved June 5, 2012, from https://goo.gl/yhhTVB

Shari'ati, A. (1972). *Red Shi'ism. The Religion of Martyrdom. Black Shi'ism: The Religion of Mourning*. Retrieved May 4, 2015, from http://www.Shariati.com/english/redblack.html

Shia Translation: *Dr. Ali Shari'ati on the Guardianship of the Jurist* [Eng Subs]. Retrieved April 22, 2015., from https://www.youtube.com/watch?v=Vf4RWPx7ogA

Ta'hil Qala'at al-Shaqif Yakshif Atharan Tarikhiya Masture (The Renovation of Beaufort Castle Exposes Hidden Historical Sites), June 19, 2014. Retrieved October 15, 2014, from http://www.Al-Manar.com.lb/adetails.php?eid=875389

Videos

Al-Manar. (2013). *Qaherat al-Ghozat: Tareekh al-Madina al-Moqawem* [Online]. Retrieved May 8, 2014, from http://www.almanar.com.lb/programs/pdetails.php?pid=5531&eid=77174&wid=2660

MEDLEBANON2. (2013). *Qeyamat AL-Banadeq Episode 02* [Online]. Retrieved May 10, 2014, from https://www.youtube.com/watch?v=9Q5NE9yox0E&index=2&list=PLxu8Ui2VLloMVBjbiBqybUj6FAseCpAq6

Interviews

Kheshman, I. (2012). Interview by Mohanad Hage Ali. Al-Jareeh Foundation's Central Office, Bir El-'Abed, Southern Suburbs of Beirut, 15 January 2012.

Mahdi (member of Hizbullah's executive branch), interview by Mohanad Hage Ali, Bir el-'Abed, Beirut, November 6, 2014.

Mohamad Qassem, interview by Mohanad Hage Ali, The Consultative Center for Study and Documentation, Haret Hreik, Southern Suburbs of Beirut, August 21, 2012.

Qasem Qasir, interview by Mohanad Hage Ali, Southern Suburbs of Beirut, July 28, 2014.

Rahmat Foulad, interview by Mohanad Hage Ali, London, May 5, 2015.

Sayyid Ali al-Musawi, interview by Mohanad Hage Ali, Central Cultural Unit, al-Ma'moura, Southern Suburbs of Beirut, November 20, 2010.

Index[1]

A
Abu Dharr al-Ghaffari, 75
Abul Fadl Al'Abas, 162
Al 'Irfan Shi'i newspaper, 119
Al-Jarha Foundation, 51–5
al-Karama, karamat, 150, 151, 153, 155–8, 168, 171n32, 171n34
al-Ma'aref, 150
Al-Mahdi schools, 40, 54, 63n60
al-Mahdi Scouts, 40
Al-Manar TV, 40
al-marja'iyya, 210
almoqawama, resistance, 112
al-ta'bi'a, 41–2
Al-Ameri, Hadi, 209
Amili Trio, 70–2, 80, 82, 83, 85, 88, 90n13, 91n32
Ashura, 17
al-Ass'ad, Kamel Bey, 80, 82, 86
'Ayn Ibil, 111, 115, 129

B
Banu 'Ammar, 77–9
Baqiatullah, 36, 37, 42, 45–50, 52, 61n41, 62n44, 62n51
Bazzi, Mahmoud, 104, 115, 129n24

C
Central Cultural Unit (CCU), 40, 42–4, 48, 52, 57, 61n35
Cham'oun, Camille, 120
construction of identity, 1–22

D
al-Dahir, Suleiman, 70, 72, 83
"Divine Victory,", 126

E
ethnosymbolism, 18–20

---

[1] Note: Page number followed by 'n' refers to notes.

F

Fatima (The Prophet Muhammad's daughter), 193
feudal rule, 71, 80, 81
French Mandate, 112, 118, 119

G

Gellner, Ernest, 2, 14, 16, 17, 20, 21

H

al-Hakim, Ammar, 209
al-Hakim, Mohammad Baqer, 205
al-Hakim, Mohsin, 186, 196
al-Hakim, Muhammad Baqir, 196
Al-Hamza, Sadeq, 226
Hariri, Rafiq, 13, 23n1
Hazara, Hazaras, Hazarajat, 175, 187, 188, 198, 201–4, 207–9, 211, 212n22, 212–13n23, 213n25, 213n26, 214n36, 214n38, 215n48, 216n50, 216n53, 216–17n55, 216n59, 217n69

I

Ibn Khaldun, 139, 141, 142
ijtihād, 178, 184, 210, 211n4, 211n5
Imam 'Ali (Ben Abi Taleb), 144, 159, 170n23
Imam Husayn, 135, 145, 153, 162
institutionalization, 2–4, 6, 10–14
Islamic ''Amili resistance,' 108, 115, 118
Islamic Da'wa Party, 186, 196
Islamic Revolution in Iran (1979), 133, 143, 150, 155, 157, 159, 161
Israeli invasion, 122–5

J

Jabal 'Amil, 48–50, 88
Jabal 'Amil newspaper, 73

K

Khamenei, Ali, 11
Khanjar, Adham, 19, 111, 113, 115–19, 130n28, 226
al-Khoei, Abo Al-Qassem, 198
Khomeini, Ruhollah, 10–11

L

Lebanonisation, 14, 22

M

Mahdi (The Twelfth Imam), 29, 46
Majlesi, Mohamad Baqer, 133, 135, 139, 143–51, 153, 168, 170n16, 171n24
Mamluks, 65, 77–9
martyrdom, 27, 30, 34, 42, 45–50, 52, 53
Mazari, Abdul Ali (aka Baba Mazari), 202–4
mobilisation, 1–3, 7, 9, 11, 12, 13, 16, 21, 23n1

N

Najaf, Iraq, 10, 11
Nasrallah, Hassan, 9–11, 13, 14, 22, 23n8
nationalism, 1–11, 14–22, 23n13

O

Ottoman rule, 67, 71, 79–83, 85, 86

P
Palestinian resistance, 121

Q
Qassem, Naim, 11, 38, 62n53

R
Reda, Ahmad, 70, 85, 86
Revolutionary Guards, 9, 10

S
Sada Al Jirah, 52, 53
Sadr, Musa, 7, 8, 9, 23n7
Al Safa, Mohamad Jaber, 65
Safavid Empire, 133, 135, 138, 143–7, 153, 168
Shari'ati, Ali, 133, 139, 143–6, 170n13, 170n16, 170n20
Sistani, Grand Ayatollah Ali, 205, 209, 217n64
Smith, Anthony, 44, 48, 49
Suleimani, Qassem, 209

supernatural sightings, 151, 152, 165
Supreme Council of the Islamic Revolution in Iraq (SCIRI), 209, 211

T
Thaher al-Omar, 82, 91n28

W
Wadi al-Hujair, 112–14
Wahdat-e Islami Afghanistan, 202
Walī al-Faqih, 28, 29, 32, 37–9, 41, 45–7, 54, 56, 58n5, 62n44
Wilayat al-Faqih, 2, 3, 5, 10–13, 23n4

Z
Zaynab (Daughter of Imam Husayn), 32, 59n14
Zionism, Zionist, 99, 117–19, 121, 122, 124

The manufacturer's authorised representative in the EU is Springer Nature Customer Service Centre GmbH, Europaplatz 3, 69115 Heidelberg, Germany. If you have any concerns regarding our products, please contact ProductSafety@springernature.com

Printed and bound by CPI Group (UK) Ltd, Croydon, CR0 4YY

23/03/2026

02076666-0010